Sweden

WORLD BIBLIOGRAPHICAL SERIES

Robert L. Collison (Editor-in-chief)

John J. Horton   Ian Wallace

Hans H. Wellisch   Ralph Lee Woodward, Jr.

Robert L. Collison (Editor-in-chief) is Professor emeritus, Library and Information Studies, University of California, Los Angeles, and was a President of the Society of Indexers. Following the war, he served as Reference Librarian for the City of Westminster and later became Librarian to the BBC. During his fifty years as a professional librarian in England and the USA, he has written more than twenty works on bibliography, librarianship, indexing and related subjects.

John H. Horton is Deputy Librarian of the University of Bradford and currently Chairman of its Academic Board of Studies in Social Sciences. He has maintained a longstanding interest in the discipline of area studies and its associated bibliographical problems, with special reference to European Studies. In particular he has published in the field of Icelandic and of Yugoslav studies, including the two relevant volumes in the World Bibliographical Series.

Ian Wallace is Professor of Modern Languages at Loughborough University of Technology. A graduate of Oxford in French and German, he also studied in Tübingen, Heidelberg and Lausanne before taking teaching posts at universities in the USA, Scotland and England. He specializes in East German affairs, especially literature and culture, on which he has published numerous articles and books. In 1979 he founded the journal *GDR Monitor*, which he continues to edit.

Hans H. Wellisch is Professor emeritus at the College of Library and Information Services, University of Maryland. He was President of the American Society of Indexers and was a member of the International Federation for Documentation. He is the author of numerous articles and several books on indexing and abstracting, and has published *The conversion of scripts* and *Indexing and abstracting: an international bibliography*. He also contributes frequently to *Journal of the American Society for Information Science, The Indexer* and other professional journals.

Ralph Lee Woodward, Jr. is Chairman of the Department of History at Tulane University, New Orleans, where he has been Professor of History since 1970. He is the author of *Central America, a nation divided*, 2nd ed. (1985), as well as several monographs and more than sixty scholarly articles on modern Latin America. He has also compiled volumes in the World Bibliographical Series on *Belize* (1980), *Nicaragua* (1983) and *El Salvador* (forthcoming). Dr. Woodward edited the Central American section of the *Research guide to Central America and the Caribbean* (1985) and is currently editor of the Central American history section of the *Handbook of Latin American studies*.

VOLUME 80

Sweden

Leland B. Sather
Alan Swanson
Compilers
Edited by Hans H. Wellisch

CLIO PRESS
OXFORD, ENGLAND · SANTA BARBARA, CALIFORNIA
DENVER, COLORADO

British Library Cataloguing in Publication Data

Sather, Leland B.
Sweden. – (World bibliographical series; 80)
1. Sweden – Bibliography
I. Title   II. Swanson, Alan   III. Series
016.9485   Z2640.3

ISBN 1–85109–035–5

Clio Press Ltd.,
55 St. Thomas' Street,
Oxford OX1 1JG, England.

ABC-Clio Information Services,
Riviera Campus, 2040 Alameda Padre Serra,
Santa Barbara, Ca. 93103, USA.

Designed by Bernard Crossland
Typeset by Columns Design and Production Services, Reading, England
Printed and bound in Great Britain by
Billing and Sons Ltd., Worcester

THE WORLD BIBLIOGRAPHICAL SERIES

This series will eventually cover every country in the world, each in a separate volume comprising annotated entries on works dealing with its history geography, economy and politics: and with its people, their culture, customs, religion and social organization. Attention will also be paid to current living conditions – housing, education, newspapers, clothing, etc. – that are all too often ignored in standard bibliographies; and to those particular aspects relevant to individual countries. Each volume seeks to achieve, by use of careful selectivity and critical assessment of the literature, an expression of the country and an appreciation of its nature and national aspirations, to guide the reader towards an understanding of its importance. The keynote of the series is to provide, in a uniform format, an interpretation of each country that will express its culture, its place in the world, and the qualities and background that make it unique.

VOLUMES IN THE SERIES

Contents

Contents

Contents

Contents

Contents

xi

Introduction

Sweden is a long, quite narrow land in Scandinavia bordered by Norway, Finland and the Baltic Sea. At present (1987) it has a population of approximately 8.3 million people, most of whom live in urban, industrial centres. Given the relatively large size of the country, over 170,000 square miles (fourth largest in Europe), the population density is quite low (48 inhabitants per square mile), particularly in the Arctic Circle region of Norrland. Long regarded an industrial people, Sweden exports significant quantities of machinery, cars, metal products, iron ore and wood products. Swedish raw materials have made up a vital part of Sweden's exports for centuries but agriculture also formed the basis for the livelihood of most Swedes until the relatively recent advent of the Industrial Revolution in the late 19th century.

Central to Sweden's development over the centuries have been the geographical regions that are easily identifiable. Skåne is Sweden's southernmost province, a low flatland tied easily to the Danish islands and mainland with the same topographical features conducive to a prosperous agriculture. This fact helps explain Danish possession of this region until the mid-17th century. To the north of Skåne, in Småland, the land becomes rockier, less fertile, and more heavily dotted with forests before broadening out to the 'heartland' of early Sweden, Västergötland and Östergötland, surrounding Lake Vätter, and Svealand, on Lake Mälar. Thereafter the land again becomes rockier and more sparsely populated in the mining district of Dalarna and in the harsher landscape and climate of Norrbotten and Lappland. To the east, the islands of Gotland and Öland guard the approaches to the mainland, and the *skärgård* (archipelago), which begins with Lake Mälar and consists of over 20,000 islands and skerries, stretches eastwards invitingly towards the Åland islands, and eventually Finland. To the west, Kölen (the Keel mountain range) serves as the border between Sweden and Norway for most of the Scandinavian peninsula they share.

The Ice Age, which ended about 12000 BC, did much to provide Sweden with these geographical features, although it was not until about 2000 BC that the country took its present shape. Man is known to have existed there by 7000 BC, having migrated from Denmark, with a Bronze Age civilization prevailing from 1500 to 500 BC. The advent of the Iron Age in the first century BC encouraged the development of Sweden's resources of this mineral and, when coupled with the ambitious extension of Rome northwards, brought Sweden and all of Scandinavia within a wider circle of culture and civilization than before. These contacts are clear from both literary and archaeological sources. Less certain are the possible origins during this period of the Gothic tribes on Gotland or in Västergötland, making them the subject of long discussions, endless theories and popular fantasies.

The early, pre-Viking (500-800 AD) organization of Sweden developed around two centres. In the central part of Sweden, the Svear established a loose kingdom including the Uppland region around Uppsala, Lake Mälar, and the island of Gotland. They ultimately prevailed over the Goths of Östergötland and Västergötland and gave their name *Sverige* (the kingdom of the Svear) to the entire country.

While this political consolidation was taking place, the Swedes participated as fully as the Danes and Norwegians in the Viking advance on Europe during the 9th, 10th and 11th centuries. Swedish Vikings are normally presumed to have led the Scandinavian attacks through Russia to Constantinople. Indeed, it is generally thought that the word *Rus* derives from contemporary reference to Swedes or Vikings in Russia. Despite the warlike character usually associated with the Vikings, modern historical research, including that by the Swedish historian Sture Bolin, has emphasized the commercial character of the Viking experience. Swedish archaeological evidence, particularly at such early centres as Birka on Lake Mälar, has contributed much to this study.

The long-term benefits to Sweden of this extensive contact with Western Europe far outweighed even the immediate advantages of loot and trading profits. The slow development of Christianity was certainly one of the most important results. King Olof Skötkonung was baptized in 1000 AD and the elimination of Old Norse religious forms, including its most illustrious place of worship at Old Uppsala, continued through the century.

Olof Skötkonung is also regarded as the first Swedish king to unite, at least temporarily, the Svear and the Goths in a single kingdom, thereby providing the basis for the political consolidation of central Sweden during the Middle Ages. Maintaining peace and slowly establishing the foundations of a monarchy was a time-consuming and often tumultuous process. The power which Sweden's developing nobility could exert was shown by the regency of Birger Jarl during the mid-13th century. He placed his son on the throne and established Stockholm on the shores of Lake Mälar as Sweden's capital.

This period also saw the progressive development of Christianity, including the establishment of a separate archbishopric of Uppsala in 1164. Swedish influence in the Baltic region also increased: Gotland became closely attached to Sweden commercially by the mid-9th century; and Finland was influenced by the migration of Swedes from the Åland Islands. Sweden conquered Finland later through the crusade of St. Erik in 1157, the missionary work of Bishop Henry, and the military campaigns of Birger Jarl in the mid-13th century and Torgil Knutsson in the 1290s. Finland thereafter was organized as a separate duchy and ruled by a Swedish-speaking, land-owning noble élite.

Several serious problems weakened Sweden in the period after 1300. A rebellious and unruly nobility was a constant source of political ferment. The spread of the Black Death to Sweden in 1349 led not only to a dramatic loss of life at that time and for every generation for 300 years thereafter but also caused a breakdown of the country's old social and economic institutions and generated a greater concentration of power and influence among Sweden's landowning nobles than before. Further chaos enveloped Sweden and the other Scandinavian countries during the middle of the 14th century as a free-for-all struggle developed for control of the Swedish-Danish border in southern Sweden.

From this state of disorganization, the Union of Kalmar seemed to offer some relief. The Swedish and Norwegian crowns had been united by marriage in the early 1300s. The marriage of King Haakon VI to the Danish princess Margareta in 1363 then presented the prospect of an even greater union. Although Haakon died in 1380, followed by his son Olav in 1389, Margareta was able to establish herself firmly as Sweden's 'sovereign lady and rightful master' as well as ruling all of the other kingdoms and dependencies.

The union was less real than the term 'Union of Kalmar' implies. Swedes became dissatisfied with an absentee monarch in

Copenhagen, the presumed proliferation of Danish and German officials in Sweden and the increase in privileges showered on the Hansa, a strong confederation of German merchant city-states. The latter controlled Visby (the commercial centre of Gotland), the Baltic trade, Stockholm commerce, and iron and copper mining operations in Dalarna, an increasingly important economic resource from Sweden.

Not surprisingly, perhaps, the 15th century was one of conflict. The crisis consisted of a popular rising against a 'foreign' monarchy. It was also, however, a civil war directed by those opposing the Union against its Swedish sympathizers, principally among the upper clergy and the nobility. Engelbrekt Engelbrektsson, Sten Sture, and Sten Sture the Younger all failed to end the Union of Kalmar. Indeed, Kristian II apparently dealt the opponents of Union monarchy a devastating blow in 1520 when he annihilated the forces of Sten Sture the Younger, was crowned King of Sweden in Stockholm, and celebrated the occasion by executing more members of the opposition in the 'Stockholm Bloodbath'.

This proved a Pyrrhic victory, however, for Gustav Vasa rallied a broad coalition of supporters both within and without Sweden which secured the country's independence from the Union of Kalmar and in 1523 his recognition as Sweden's king. His rule is rightfully regarded as a major turning point in Swedish history because of the reforms he introduced to strengthen the royal government and to establish Lutheranism as the State Church.

The permanence of these changes was shaken by the political strife of the late 16th century as Gustav Vasa's sons fought among themselves over the succession. This not only weakened the government but also re-established the nobility as a potent political force and threatened the solidification of the Reformation in Sweden. It also emphasized the conflict developing with Poland because of the two countries' common avarice over the Baltic lands of Estonia, Latvia and Lithuania and as a result of the dynastic rivalry between Duke Karl (later King Karl IX) and his nephew, Sigismund III, who was also the King of Poland.

Although generally recognized as a great military leader by foreigners, King Gustav II Adolf's (1611-32) chief accomplishments were to provide stability at home and to strengthen the state apparatus through reforms of government, education and the economy. Assisted by his Chancellor, Axel Oxenstierna, one of the great royal ministers of Europe in the 17th century, the king was also able to use the talents of Sweden's nobility and developing middle class to create an effective governmental system. Gustav II Adolf's reign, however, was one primarily of war and the beginning of Sweden's Age of Greatness. Utilizing a highly-disciplined, technically-advanced army, Sweden soon dominated the Baltic lands and their rich resources of timber and agricultural products.

In 1629, the king became involved in the Thirty Years' War (1618-48), combining his forces with those of German Protestant princes and the Catholic French monarchy, all foes of the Holy Roman Emperor. Gustav II Adolf died in the Battle of Lützen in 1632 but his daughter, Kristina (1632-54), and Oxenstierna secured territory in northern Germany and recognition of Sweden as a major European power at the end of the war.

Kristina's rule of Sweden was erratic and ill-advised. Her abdication in 1654 and conversion to Catholicism was one of the most sensational events of the century. Her cousin and successor, Karl X (1654-60), however, continued the process of expansion by seizing both Norwegian and Danish territory to give Sweden its present Scandinavian borders.

Sweden's empire abroad was much more difficult to retain. Karl XII (1697-1718) at first successfully defended the Swedish empire against its old enemies, Poland and Denmark, but later, his reckless military adventures against Russia under Peter the Great ended in defeat and permanently changed the power balance of Northern Europe.

The main thrust of Swedish activity during the 18th century, or the Age of Liberty, centred on domestic politics. The collapse of Sweden's empire under Karl XII led to a rejection of the absolutist government which had developed in the 17th century. It was replaced by a form of government enhancing the role of the *Riksdag*, Sweden's four-estate legislature, and, particularly, its Secret Committee, comprised chiefly of nobles. This system has often been regarded as corrupt and unduly susceptible to the influence of the nobles and foreign powers but it also gave growth and experience to a parliamentary form of government which was unique to continental Europe.

King Gustav III (1771-92), however, was able to capitalize on its weaknesses and through a show of force he re-asserted royal prerogatives. Deeply influenced by the Enlightenment, he enacted economic and legal reforms which rank him as one of the most successful 'enlightened despots' of the century. He aroused, however, the hostility of the nobility, who were deprived of the power which they had exercised through the *Riksdag*. The king was assassinated in 1792 by three nobles acting on their own initiative but the deposition of his son, Gustav IV Adolf, by a bloodless coup in 1809, was the nearly unanimous expression of displeasure by influential Swedes with the king's rule. Gustav IV Adolf's foreign policy led to war in 1808 with France, Russia, and Denmark-Norway. Sweden soon lost Finland to Russia and waged an unsuccessful campaign to secure Norway. These losses and the high taxes to pay for them led to the successful coup against him.

Although seemingly on the verge of dissolution, Sweden made significant adjustments to resolve this crisis. The constitution written in 1809 provided a more stable relationship between the king and the *Riksdag* than the experiments of the previous century and remained the basis for Swedish government until 1970.

Jean Jules Bernadotte, a general of the French Revolution and marshal of Napoleon, was selected as Crown Prince in 1810 and, as Karl XIV Johan, provided able leadership from 1818 to 1844. He is the founder of Sweden's reigning royal house. He skilfully engineered Sweden's participation in the Grand Coalition against Napoleon from 1812 to 1814, receiving the compensation he desired in the acquisition of Norway from Denmark. Norwegian resistance to this action, however, led to a much looser tie between the two countries than the Swedes wished, and to the end of the union entirely in 1905.

In view of modern stereotypes of Sweden emphasizing its progressive, modern character, it is remarkable how long it took for the forces of change to manifest themselves in 19th-century Sweden. The *Riksdag* did not evolve from a four-house body of nobles, clergy, merchants and commons to a more traditional two-house model until 1866. It was not until 1917 that ministerial responsibility was clearly etablished, ending decisive royal influence on government, and not until 1922 that the last restrictions on universal suffrage for both men and women were eliminated.

Industrialization also occurred relatively later in Sweden than in other parts of Europe. From the beginning there was an emphasis on the development of the country's natural resources, such as mining and timber, and products involving technical or engineering skill. This led particularly to the development of the labour movement and its political ally, the Social Democratic Party, led by Hjalmar Branting during the first decades of this century.

Another major phenomenon associated with these developments was the process of mass emigration by well over one million Swedes, impatient to wait for these reforms. Most of the emigrants settled in the United States but sizeable groups also went to Canada and Australia. The long-term result has been the establishment of unique bonds of kinship among millions of people around the globe. During recent decades this phenomenon has also generated a significant amount of serious and productive research into migration theory and history.

Adjustments and changes came more rapidly in society and the economy after the First World War. Post-war recession, the Depression, and the shocking financial gimmickry of financier Ivar Kreuger created great economic difficulties for all Swedes. In the wake of these crises, Sweden's Social Democrats came to power in 1932, with the cooperation of the Agrarian Party, and initiated extensive social welfare programmes in housing, workers' pensions, and family assistance. These were supplemented by an effective policy of negotiation with both labour and business to control wage and price increases. The programmes attracted attention and rave reviews throughout Western Europe and led to a more productive, stable society and economy at home. Building on this base, the Social Democrats, who remained in power from 1932 to 1976, added to these programmes after the Second World War and initiated others, providing additional pension benefits in 1956 and programmes providing minimal-cost health and dental care.

During this period Sweden also attracted attention because of its foreign policy. Sweden managed to avoid the few military conflicts of the 19th century and withstood, as did other Scandinavian states, both German and Allied pressure to renounce their neutrality during the First World War.

Sweden's position during the Second World War was more delicate and subject to criticism. Although sympathizing with the Finns during their Winter War (1939-40) with Russia, the Swedish government refused to enter the hostilities. The German invasion of Norway and Denmark on 9 April 1940 presented even greater difficulties. Sweden reluctantly permitted German troops to pass through the country during the first years of the war and allowed the continued export of iron ore and ball bearings to Germany throughout the conflict. Although this policy still provokes considerable debate, what must also be considered is the futility of a declaration of war against Germany, the ability of Sweden to reduce and eventually eliminate the demands made on her by Germany, and the service Sweden provided during the war as a haven for Danish Jews, members of the Norwegian Resistance and other refugees from Nazi Europe.

Sweden has maintained this policy of neutrality in the decades following the Second World War. It is built, first, on the principle of non-alignment. This led Sweden to support a neutral Scandinavian defence alliance in the mid-1940s, reject membership of the North Atlantic Treaty Organization (NATO), support a Nordic customs union (Nordek), participate in the European Free Trade Association (EFTA), and later secure associate membership of the EEC. Swedish neutrality is also based on the need for a strong defence as a deterrent against aggression. The country, therefore, although non-aligned, relies on universal military conscription and armed forces with advanced weaponry, much of it produced at home. A sizeable portion of the national budget is devoted to defence purposes. Finally, this policy is based on moral principles by which Swedes judge both themselves and others. The result has been a very active support of the United Nations and other forums addressing issues such as disarmament. It has led to firm stands against perceived injustices, such as Olof Palme's condemnation of the United States' involvement in Vietnam, Sweden's less publicized criticism of the Russian invasion of Afghanistan, and protests against apartheid in South Africa.

Often regarded as a model by countries large and small, Sweden has continued to display the innovative spirit admired by many but it has also been forced to face serious problems familiar to the modern world. In politics, the constitutional reforms of 1970 and 1975 created a unicameral legislature and eliminated the last formal vestiges of royal influence on government. The Social Democrats were forced out of office in 1976 for the first time in forty years, only to return in 1982 when the country rejected the non-socialist coalition government which had ruled the country during the intervening years. Some of the most difficult problems for the government and the country to resolve during this period concerned Sweden's energy alternatives, including nuclear power, as the price of imported oil soared.

Differing assessments have developed of Sweden's social welfare programmes. They have been widely admired from their inception in the 1930s and continue to be so. They have, however, also been the subject of an increasing amount of criticism from many quarters: the New Right has emphasized the authoritarian character they perceive in these programmes; the

New Left has criticized the compromise with capitalism existent in these policies and an economy still ninety percent in private hands.

Since returning to power in 1982, the Social Democrats have injected new fury into this debate by the enactment in 1983 of the 'Meidner Plan', or wage-earner investment funds, whereby portions of a company's profits are allocated to investment funds controlled by Swedish trade unions. The country has been rocked as well during the 1980s by evidence of the violation of Swedish territorial waters by foreign, presumably Soviet, submarines. The result has been a considerably more intense public debate of the usually sacrosanct issues of defence and foreign policy. The migration of foreign workers to Sweden in recent decades has also produced a more heterogeneous society than before and first-hand experiences in prejudice and discrimination.

The most shocking blow, however, has been the still-unsolved assassination of prime minister Olof Palme on 28 February 1986. It has evoked comparisons with past cases in Swedish history and illustrates the fact that even Sweden is not immune to tragedy and modern political madness.

Over many centuries Sweden has produced individuals who have had a constructive impact beyond its own borders. Nathan Söderblom was an acknowledged leader of the Christian ecumenical movement earlier in this century, and Anders Nygren and Gustaf Aulén are respected Protestant theologians. Raoul Wallenberg has gained increasing fame in recent years for his efforts from 1944 to 1945 to save Hungary's Jewish population from destruction during the Second World War. His subsequent capture and imprisonment by the Russian government has only added mystery to the respect already existing for his accomplishments. Count Folke Bernadotte engaged in similarly successful efforts to rescue Jews from the Germans as an official of the International Red Cross and was assassinated in 1948, one of the first victims of the effort to resolve the problems of the Middle East in a peaceful fashion. Not long thereafter, Dag Hammerskjöld served with distinction as the Secretary-General of the United Nations from 1953 to 1961. Swedes have done well in other fields, too, ranging from ABBA in the world of popular music, to Björn Borg and Mats Wilander in professional tennis, and Ingemar Stenmark in skiing.

The cultural heritage of Sweden is as rich and varied as its people and history. Though one can trace this heritage at least as far back as the Bronze Age, through grave finds and the like, the earliest modern records come mostly from the Viking Period. We know something of pre-Christian religion, we have decorative and ritual artefacts, and we have descriptions of aspects of their daily lives, lives spent chiefly as Eastward-trading merchants. Carving in stone and wood, intricate and delicate work in gold and other metals, shipbuilding and textiles, and a complex legal system in some ways more equitable than that which followed it, all attest to a high level of cultural sophistication. Sweden's more than 3,500 runic inscriptions tell us of their makers' literacy. This is confirmed in the hundreds of mediaeval ballads and songs which, combined with later tales and stories, remind us of a rich imaginative life in an age before parchment and ink.

Among the earliest written documents in a language clearly Swedish, as opposed to the common Nordic tongue, are law codes from the 13th century. It was probably important for such things to be transmitted in the language of the people. Learned and religious discourse, however, took place in Latin for a considerable time thereafter. We see its foremost example in the *Revelationes* of St. Birgitta (1303-73), though it is an interesting question whether or not these mystical experiences were dictated in Latin or Swedish. The first author writing in Swedish whose name we know is Bishop Tomas Simonsson of Strängnäs [d. 1443], whose *Frihetsvisan* (The song of liberty – 1439) may also be the first secular Swedish poem.

Once challenged, the cultural hegemony of Latin as a literary language was broken fairly quickly. The process was hastened with the Reformation, a political as well as a religious movement. Olaus Petri's (1493-1552) translations and other writings, all in Swedish, make him one of the founding fathers of modern Swedish, a language brought to literary perfection in the 17th and 18th centuries, through writers such as Georg Stiernhielm (1598-1672), Olof von Dalin (1708-63), Johan Henric Kellgren (1751-95) and Carl Michael Bellman (1740-95).

The 17th and 18th centuries also saw the rise of Swedish music, led, ironically enough, by a German family, the Dübens, who for almost a hundred years shaped the musical life of the capital by both importing music and musicians from elsewhere and by writing and performing music to Swedish texts. The first international Swedish star was Johan Helmich Roman (1694-1758), who studied in England on a royal grant and brought the new international style to Sweden. When Gustav III (1746-92) founded opera in Swedish, later in the century, he brought to Sweden a number of foreign composers, chief among them Joseph Martin Kraus (1756-92). Kraus's operas are not numerous but they are full of a musical power also seen in his symphonies.

In all the arts, neo-Classicism was quickly replaced with a national Romanticism, not through a yearning for the past but by searching the Nordic past for values useable in modern times. These values were articulated best in poems and songs by Erik Gustaf Geijer (1783-1847), the novels and songs of Carl Jonas Love Almqvist (1793-1866), and the poetry of Esaias Tegnér (1782-1846). Towards the middle and end of the century, they were echoed in a new form in the symphonies of Frans Berwald (1796-1868), Wilhelm Stenhammar (1871-1927) and Wilhelm Peterson-Berger (1867-1942).

The end of that same century, however, saw the disturbing rise of a new sort of modernism, whose most complex expression can be seen in the prolific work of August Strindberg (1849-1912), an artist ahead of his time in every way. Strindberg wrote not only plays of world stature but he was also a novelist, short-story writer, historian, polemicist, poet and correspondent. As if that were not enough for one lifetime, he was also a painter with a radical vision (some of whose canvases are a dozen years ahead of the abstract expressionists), an enthusiastic photographer and an amateur chemist.

The 20th century has brought with it a new internationalization of Swedish culture. This is probably the greatest challenge to her artists today. In literature, the writing of lyric poetry continues unabated, so much so that one is tempted to call it the national literary form (in the sense in which the novel is the dominant Anglo-American literary form). Poets such as Harry Martinson (1904-78), Gunnar Ekelöf (1907-68) and Tomas Tranströmer (1931-) have taken up the modernist point of view put forward by the Finnish-Swedish poet, Edith Södergran (1892-1923). However, the century has also seen the coming of age of the novel as never before, in the work of Vilhelm Moberg (1898-1973), Eyvind Johnson (1900-76), Sven Delblanc (1931-), Per Olov Enquist (1934-) and P. C. Jersild (1935-). In music, the operas of Karl-Birger Blomdahl (1916-68) and the symphonies of Allan Pettersson (1911-80) have gained world-wide recognition, as have the manic visual proposals of Claes Oldenburg (1929-) and in cinema the works of Ingmar Bergman (1918-).

The bibliography

Although coverage of the Viking Age is extensive, we have nevertheless limited the number of entries to the most important general works, those pertaining most directly to Sweden, and significant works by Swedish scholars. Readers ought also to note that the Swedish alphabet includes three extra letters, å, ä, ö that are usually placed in this order after z. To facilitate the use of this bibliography by the English-speaking public, we have, however, ordered entries with words containing these vowels as if they were ordinary letters in the English alphabet. We hope this will prove helpful to most readers and neither confuse nor offend those who know better. We have generally referred to places by their Swedish name with the exception of Göteborg which is generally known outside of Scandinavia as Gothenburg. With reference to Swedish rulers, we have attempted to create some uniformity by using forms such as Karl instead of Charles and Gustav instead of the highly artificial Gustavus even though Sweden's present monarch, Carl Gustaf, is an obvious exception to these rules.

Acknowledgements

Although we accept sole responsibility for any errors or omissions in this book, there are many individuals whose assistance we greatly appreciated during the course of this project. These people include: Lena Daun, Director of the Reference Section of the Swedish Institute, Stockholm; Brita Holm and Gunvor Flodell of the Education Section of the same organization; Marna Feldt and her staff of the Swedish Information Service in New York City; Dr. Richard Cracroft, Dean of the College of Humanities, Brigham Young University for travel money for research in Sweden; Dr. Marvin Folsom, Chairman of the Department of Germanic and Slavic Languages, and Ann Marie Hamar, secretary of the department, Brigham Young University; Dr. Paul Mogren, Head of the Reference Department, Marriot Library, University of Utah; Craige Hall and the staff of the Stewart Library, Weber State College, particularly Mrs. Peggy Pierce; Weber State students Karen Burton Gholamzadeh and Douglas Haymore II; Mrs. Marilee Sackolwitz, secretary to the History Department, Weber State College; John, Katie and Brittanie Sather; and especially Wendy Sather, whose indispensable support and assistance in the preparation of this manuscript makes her a full partner in this project.

Leland B. Sather
Alan Swanson
July 1987

The Country and Its People

General

1 On being Swedish: reflections towards a better understanding of the Swedish character.
Paul Britten Austin. Stockholm: Bokförlaget Fabel, 1968. 182p.
An essay on Swedish character by a translator and writer who has lived in Sweden for a considerable time. Divided into sections on 'Society' and 'Nature,' the work is perceptive, critical, amusing and sympathetic. The volume was first published in 1967 (London: Secker & Warburg) and it was published in the United States in 1969 (Coral Gables, Florida: University of Miami Press).

2 The Swedes: how they live and work.
Paul Britten Austin. New York; Washington, DC: Praeger, 1970. 167p. map. (How They Live and Work).
Surveys the country and its people and includes sections on Swedish government, daily life, the economy, educational system, transport, leisure and attitudes on topics of current interest. The statistics used by the author now need to be revised but the work is still useful for gaining an understanding of Sweden today.

3 Round the Swedish year: daily life and festivals through four seasons.
Lorna Downman, Paul Britten Austin, Anthony Baird. Stockholm: Bokförlaget Fabel, 1972. 112p.
Provides brief, impressionistic essays on a wide range of subjects including sun-worship, May Day, crayfish, St. Martin's Day and Christmas. The work is both informative and entertaining.

4 **The new Sweden: the challenge of a disciplined democracy.**
Frederic Fleisher. New York: David McKay, 1967. 365p. bibliog.
A thoughtful survey of modern Sweden by an author who has lived there for many years. Includes consideration of government, the economy, society, culture, and of the Swedish character. A clear picture of Sweden in the 1960s and an excellent background to publications dealing with the last two decades.

5 **Sweden.**
Walter Imber, Wolf Teitze, translated by Ewald Osers, revised by Astrid Witschi-Bernz. Washington, DC; New York: Joseph J. Binns, 1979. 224p. maps.
Discusses Sweden's geography, flora and fauna, history, peoples, rural and urban life, customs, culture, and economy. A useful introduction for the general reader that is well illustrated with maps and colour photographs.

6 **Sweden in brief.**
Edited by Victor J. Kayfetz. Stockholm: Swedish Institute, 1982. 80p. maps.
A broad survey of contemporary Sweden, with contributions on subjects such as geography, government, foreign policy, social welfare policy, and economics. One of the best introductions available.

7 **Sweden.**
Steven Koblik, M. Donald Hancock, Steven Kelman.
Wilson Quarterly (autumn 1977), p. 102–35. map. bibliog.
Koblik's 'Symbolism and reality' (p. 103–10) questions some of the most common stereotypes attributed to Sweden. Hancock's contribution, 'The Swedish welfare state: prospects and contradictions' (p. 111–26) discusses the development of the social welfare state, its basic characteristics, the costs involved, and the shortcomings that persist in Swedish society. In 'The uncertain future' (p. 127–30), Kelman discusses some aspects of modern Swedish economic policy, including Gösta Rehn's model for economic growth. A concise, knowledgeable survey of modern Sweden.

8 **Of Swedish ways.**
Lilly Lorénzen. Minneapolis, Minnesota: Dillon Press, 1981. 276p. map. bibliog.
Discusses many aspects of Swedish life, including customs, myths and legends, and holiday traditions. The volume was first printed in 1964.

9 **Swedes as others see them: facts, myths or a communications complex?**
Jean Phillips-Martinsson. Lund, Sweden: Utbildningshuset Studentlitteratur, 1981. 123p. bibliog.
A cross-cultural examination of Sweden and Swedes, intended to suggest means by which Swedish businessmen in particular might communicate more effectively with their foreign counterparts, and to refute common stereotypes of Sweden.

10 **The second new nation: the mythology of modern Sweden.**
Arne Ruth. *Daedalus*, vol. 113, no. 2 (1984), p. 53–96.

A contribution to the special issue of *Daedalus* entitled 'Nordic voices', this is also a provocative and sweeping assessment of 20th-century Sweden until the early 1980s, which discusses modern politics, foreign policy, the 'Swedish model' for the economy and society, and foreign perceptions of all these subjects, although it cannot be neatly categorized into any of them. Required reading for everyone interested in Sweden.

11 **Sweden.**
Barry Turner. London: B.T. Batsford, 1976. 158p. map.

A perceptive and amusing examination of Swedish life, character, and food, with brief descriptions of Gothenburg, the Göta Canal, and Stockholm. A light but informative introduction for both the traveller and the general reader.

12 **Meet Sweden.**
Gösta Wadersjö, translated from the Swedish by Alan Harkness.
Malmö, Sweden: Liber Hermods, 1979. 238p. maps. bibliog.

Written at the request of the Swedish Ministry of Foreign Affairs, it was originally published in Sweden as *Sverige kunskap* and has also been published in English as *Sweden*. It provides a broad description of contemporary Swedish economic life, government, trade, defence, religion, education, law, culture, and social welfare programmes.

13 **Sweden in the Sixties: a symposium of facts and views in 17 chapters.**
Edited by Ingemar Wizelius, translated from the Swedish by Rudy
Feichtner. Stockholm: Almqvist & Wiksell, 1967. 295p.

A survey of Sweden by leading experts, considering Swedish history, politics, government, law, foreign relations, the economy, science and technology, education, social welfare system, and the arts. A perceptive, highly regarded study for all readers.

Sweden as part of Scandinavia

14 **Nordic democracy: ideas, issues, and institutions in politics,
economy, education, social and cultural affairs of Denmark, Finland,
Iceland, Norway, and Sweden.**
Edited by Erik Allardt, Nils Andrén, Erik J. Friis, Gylfi T.
Gislason, Sten Sparre Nilson, Henry Valen, Frantz Wendt, Folmer
Wisti, translated by Erik J. Friis, introduction by K. B.
Andersen. Copenhagen: Det Danske Selskab, 1981. 780p.
bibliog.

A collection of thirty-one essays by leading Scandinavian scholars covering subjects such as history, government, politics, law, economics, society, foreign relations, education, culture, and the mass media. The essays not only attempt to discuss particular topics but also to relate them to the central theme of the book, namely, democracy in the very broad sense of economic and social as well as political democracy. This is also the latest of several works to handle this subject. Earlier works with a similar purpose include *Scandinavian Democracy* (q.v.) and *Scandinavia between East and West* (q.v.). Articles in this work may therefore be read not only for their intrinsic value but also as a continuation of and an interesting comparison with earlier treatments of this theme.

15 **Scandinavia past and present.**
    Edited by Jørgen Bukdahl, Aage Heinberg.   Odense, Denmark:
    Arnkrone, 1959. 3 vols. maps.

The first volume covers many aspects of modern life and culture while the others present a detailed survey of Scandinavian history by some of its most distinguished scholars. Organization of the work is by topic but is generally subdivided into sections by country. The work contains a number of articles dealing specifically with Swedish history, and is therefore particularly valuable for providing information which is not available in other English-language studies.

16 **The Scandinavians.**
    Donald S. Connery.   New York: Simon & Schuster, 1966. 590p.
    map. bibliog.

The author begins with a general introduction to the region, refuting the three stereotypes of sex, suicide, and socialism attached during the 1960s by people unfamiliar with Scandinavia. Five subsequent units deal with each of the Nordic nations in turn. In the section on Sweden (p. 281–439), Connery outlines the country's geography and history, and discusses topics such as Sweden's neutrality, labour-management relations, and the welfare state.

17 **Nordic views and voices.**
    Edited by Patrik Engellau, Ulf Henning.   Gothenburg, Sweden:
    Nordic Council, 1984. 117p.

Twenty-three brief essays, many selected from previously published works, are grouped around the themes of the Nordic soul, the Nordic model, and Nordic futures. Although similar to other works dealing primarily with the welfare state, foreign policy, and politics, this study also places some emphasis on the cultural setting.

18 **Scandinavia between East and West.**
    Edited by Henning Friis.   Ithaca, New York; New York: Cornell
    University Press, 1950. 388p. bibliog. (A Publication of the New
    School of Social Research).

A collection of eleven essays describing the development and nature of Norway, Sweden, and Denmark until the mid-20th century. General subjects include politics and government, economic and social policies, and foreign relations.

Many of the articles are by now somewhat dated but continue to provide an interesting picture of the region, its past, its dreams, and the basic concepts that continue to affect the area.

19   **Scandinavian democracy: development of democratic thought and institutions in Denmark, Norway, and Sweden.**
Edited by Joseph Lauwerys.   Copenhagen: Danish Institute, Norwegian Office of Cultural Relations, Swedish Institute, in cooperation with the American–Scandinavian Foundation, 1958. 437p. bibliog.

A collection of twenty-two articles by prominent Scandinavians discussing various aspects of culture and politics, generally with the goal of showing how these subjects represent or have influenced the development of democracy in the Scandinavian countries. Although superseded by works such as *Nordic Democracy* (q.v.), these essays are interesting studies in Scandinavia's aims and outlook in the mid-20th century.

20   **Scandinavia.**
William R. Mead, Wendy Hall.   London: Thames & Hudson, 1972. 208p. maps. bibliog.

An attempt to provide a sense of the spirit and attitudes of Scandinavia, the book contains a brief historical sketch and separate chapters on each country, followed by a discussion of the states as social laboratories, the art of design, Nordic integration, and the different forms of contact that have developed between Scandinavia and the rest of the world over several centuries. A brief 'Who's who' section at the end provides short biographical sketches of prominent Scandinavians mentioned in the text.

21   **The Nordic enigma.**
Daedalus, vol. 113, no. 1 (1984), 214p.

Two issues of the journal were devoted to a discussion of contemporary Scandinavia (see also the following entry). They were published to commemorate the observance of 'Scandinavia Today' in the United States during 1982–1984 by the American–Scandinavian Foundation and several participating organizations and firms. The first issue contains nine articles by respected scholars on a variety of economic, social, cultural, and political issues. Some previous background knowledge of present-day Scandinavia is perhaps desirable but by no means necessary. The issue cited above and that of spring 1984 have been used in classes on Scandinavian literature and culture as an introduction to the region.

22   **Nordic voices.**
Daedalus, vol. 113, no. 2 (1984), 279p. bibliog.

This is the second consecutive issue of the journal devoted to Scandinavia, and consists of eight articles by leading Scandinavian scholars. The essays in this number differ from the first by being more analytical than descriptive, more critical, and reflecting a greater sense of uncertainty about Scandinavia's future.

23 **Scandinavia.**
Franklin D. Scott.   Cambridge, Massachusetts: Harvard University Press, 1975. 330p. maps. bibliog. (The American Foreign Policy Library).

Originally published in 1950 as *The United States and Scandinavia*, this work was revised and enlarged in 1975 by the doyen of American social scientists specializing in Scandinavia. An excellent introduction to late 20th-century Scandinavia, it covers its governments, economic structures, social welfare programmes, and foreign policies until the early 1970s, with a final chapter on past and present connections between Scandinavia and America.

24 **Scandinavia.**
John H. Wuorinen.   Englewood Cliffs, New Jersey: Prentice-Hall, 1965. 146p. maps. bibliog. (Modern Nations in Historical Perspective).

A basic introduction to Scandinavia which briefly describes the region's climate, resources, people, and history. There is a more detailed discussion of the region during the First and Second World Wars. About half of the book deals with the position of Scandinavia in the mid-20th century, covering its political parties, governments, post-Second World War economic patterns, foreign policy developments, and efforts at co-operation, especially the Nordic Council. Although now in need of some revision, this is still a useful sketch of the region, giving Sweden adequate consideration.

Picture books

25 **Sweden today.**
Göran Algård, Roland Romell, translated from the Swedish by W. G. Simpson.   Stockholm: Almqvist & Wiksell, 1970. rev. ed. 112p.

Richly illustrated with colour photographs, the work emphasizes Sweden's scenery, churches, castles, historical monuments, and culture, and was first published in 1965 in English and in Swedish as *Sverige av idag*.

26 **Stockholm.**
Per Anders Fogelström, Åke Mokvist, translated from the Swedish by Paul Britten Austin.   Stockholm: Svensk bokhandlareförening, 1983. 96p.

A photo-essay tribute to Stockholm with text by the city's most famous novelist.

27 **Sweden from the air.**
Karl Werner Gullers, Gustaf Munthe.   Stockholm: Kooperativa
förbundets bokförlag, 1948. [150p.]
Remarkable for its black-and-white photographs of Sweden taken exclusively
from the air, this book offers a tour of Sweden showing its scenery, palaces, and
cities from a unique perspective.

28 **Linnaeus.**
Karl Werner Gullers, Birger Strandell.   Chicago, Illinois: Gullers
International, 1977. [96p.]
A collection of colour photographs illustrating Carl Linnaeus's life and work,
including scenery described in his various travels, plants which he classified, and
buildings in which he lived or worked. An excellent visual companion to other
works by or about him.

29 **A touch of Sweden.**
Karl Werner Gullers, Gunnart Arvidson, Björn Enström, Peter
Gullers, Jan Bohman.   Stockholm: Gullers International, 1980.
104p.
Illustrated with both black-and-white and colour photographs of Sweden's cities,
workplaces, cultural contributions, forms of recreation, and most famous
contemporary citizens from many walks of life.

30 **Swedish know-how in the 80s.**
Karl Werner Gullers.   Stockholm: Gullers International, 1980.
2nd ed. 136p.
It provides visual examples of Swedish technical and industrial development at
home and abroad. For a similar work by Gullers, see *Sweden around the world*
(Stockholm: Gullersproduktion/Almqvist & Wiksell, 1968).

31 **Scandinavia.**
Ralph Hammond-Innes and the editors of *Life*.   New York: Time,
1963. 160p. maps. bibliog. (Life World Library).
Provides a brief illustrated introduction to the history of the Scandinavian
countries and modern developments. The chapter on 'The industrious Swedes'
(p. 87–99) discusses many facets of contemporary life. Other chapters describe
the work of Dag Hammarskjöld and other prominent Swedes of this century.

32 **The Royal Palace of Stockholm.**
Ralph Herrmanns, Hans Hammarskiöld, translated from the
Swedish by Ray Bradfield.   Stockholm: Bonniers, 1978. 136p.
A work richly illustrated with colour photographs, giving a descriptive narrative
of the palace's history, its artistic decoration, and its use by King Carl XVI Gustaf
and Queen Silvia.

The Country and Its People. Picture books

33 **Scandinavia.**
Edited by Martin Hürlimann, text by Erik Oxenstierna.
New York: Viking Press, 1963. 64p. maps. (A Studio Book).
Sixty-four of the 225 photographic plates (nos. 70–133) depict everyday life, scenery, and places of historical interest in Sweden. Count Oxenstierna provides a thoughtful introductory essay on Scandinavia and detailed notes to accompany each of the plates.

34 **People of eight seasons: the story of the Lapps.**
Ernst Manker, translated from the Swedish by Kathleen McFarlane. New York: Viking Press, 1964. 214p. maps. bibliog.
Describes the origins of the Lapps (*samer*) and their way of life throughout the eight seasons of the year for the Reindeer Lapps, most of whom live in Sweden and Finland. First published in 1963 (Gothenburg, Sweden: Tre Tryckare Cagner), it is richly illustrated with photographs and drawings. The author was a highly regarded expert on the subject.

35 **Lapland: the world's wild places.**
Walter Marsden and the editors of Time-Life Books. Amsterdam, The Netherlands: Time-Life Books, 1976. 184p. map. bibliog.
A picture book covering the North Cape region of Finland, Sweden, and Norway which provides an informed description of nature by means of the narrative and many colour photographs.

36 **Sweden: the land of today.**
William R. Mead. Guildford, England: Colour Library Books, 1985. 143p.
A brightly illustrated picture book with brief but pithy comments by a leading geographer specializing in Scandinavia.

37 **Stockholm, city of islands.**
Edited by Reijo Rüster, translated from the Swedish by Keith Bradfield. Stockholm: Tjernquist, 1983. 135p.
Superb photographs illustrate a narrative that does not take itself so seriously as to make heavy reading.

38 **Sverige/Sweden/Schweden.**
Bo Setterlind, Giovanni Trimboli, Göran Algård, translated from the Swedish by Paul Britten Austin, Gerta Weber-Strumföhl. Stockholm: Grako, 1977. [134p.]
A trilingual work containing 150 excellent colour photographs illustrating Sweden's countryside, nature, palaces, churches, and the daily life of the people.

39 **Scandinavia: Denmark–Sweden–Norway.**
Otto Siegner, with an introduction by Hans Obergethmann.
New York: Charles Scribner's Sons, 1971. Tri-lingual edition. 227p.
maps.
Brief introductory comments on each of the three countries are followed by
sections containing pictures of each country. Pictures of Sweden (p.
100–67) are taken from all over the country to represent everyday life, scenery, and sites of
historic interest. The complete text is provided in German, English, and French.

40 **Manor houses and royal castles in Sweden/Herrensitze und
königliche Schlösser in Schweden/Manoirs et châteaux en Suède.**
Bengt G. Söderberg. Malmö, Sweden: Allhems Förlag, 1975.
346p.
The work contains 250 photographs of Sweden's manor houses and royal castles
and their furnishings. All captions and the brief introductory remarks to each
section, based on style, are given in English, French and German.

The wonderful adventures of Nils and the further adventures of Nils.
See item no. 46.

The land of the Lapps.
See item no. 325.

Sweden.
See item no. 1003.

Sweden.
See item no. 1010.

Travellers' Accounts

41 **The land of the midnight sun: summer and winter journeys through Sweden, Norway, Lapland, and Northern Finland with descriptions of the inner life of the people, their manners, customs, the primitive antiquities, etc.**

Paul du Chaillu.   London: John Murray, 1881. 2 vols.

Two large volumes recounting the author's trips to Scandinavia from 1871 to 1878. Extensive accounts are provided in both volumes of all parts of Sweden as well as more general discussions of Scandinavian geology and archaeology. This detailed description is perhaps the most comprehensive of the many 19th-century travel accounts of Scandinavia in general and Sweden in particular.

42 **Travels in various countries of Scandinavia, including Denmark, Sweden, Norway, Lapland, and Finland.**

Edward Daniel Clarke.   London: T. Cadell & W. Davis, 1838.

3 vols. maps.

Originally published in two volumes in 1819 as part of his *Travels in various countries of Europe, Asia, and Africa: Part the third: Scandinavia* by the same publisher. Clarke began his journey with the well-known demographer Robert Malthus and other Englishmen in 1799 but the party split up when they arrived in Scandinavia. In this edition Clarke discusses his visit to Sweden in all three volumes but particularly in Volume One. The work is frequently cited for its observations on both the people and nature in Scandinavia. For a discussion of Clarke's visit to Scandinavia and that of Giuseppe Acerbi at the same time, see Henrik Sandblad's 'Edward D. Clarke och Giuseppe Acerbi, upptäcktsresande i Norden 1798–1800' (Edward D. Clarke and Giuseppe Acerbi, explorers in Scandinavia 1798–1800), *Lychnos* (1979–80), p. 155–205, including an extensive summary in English (p. 202–05).

43 **Studien zur skandinavischen Reisebeschreibung von Linné bis
Andersen** (Studies of Scandinavian travel descriptions from
Linnaeus to Andersen.)
Uwe Ebel. Frankfurt-am-Main, FRG: Haag & Herchen, 1981.
494p. bibliog.

A study of Swedish and Danish travel literature during the 18th and 19th
centuries. Among the authors considered are the Swedes Carl Linnaeus, Carl
August Ehrensvärd, Jacob Wallenberg, P.D.A. Atterbom, and K.A. Nicander.
Emphasis is given chiefly to the literary character of their works but the book is
also a significant discussion of this form of literature as it developed in these two
countries.

44 **The reindeer people.**
Marie Herbert. London: Hodder & Stoughton, 1976. 187p. maps.
bibliog.

Relates her family's visit to the Lapps of Norway, Sweden, and Finland in 1975. It
is anecdotal and a description of everyday life rather than a discussion of the
Lapps' status in Scandinavian society.

45 **Swedish life and landscape.**
Edric A. Hille. London: Paul Elek, 1947. 149p.

Originally intended as a general introduction to the country, this book might now
be more appropriately regarded as a traveller's account. The author provides
chapters on Stockholm and the Swedish countryside and then discusses such
topics as forests, housing, women, education and winter sports. An interesting
look at post-war Sweden supplemented by many photographs.

46 **The wonderful adventures of Nils and the further adventures of Nils.**
Selma Lagerlöf, translated from the Swedish by Vilma Swanston
Howard. London; Melbourne, Australia: J. M. Dent & Sons,
1984. 2 vols.

First published in Sweden as *Nils Holgerssons underbara resa genom Sverige* (Nils
Holgersson's wonderful journey through Sweden) in 1906–1907 and translated
into English by Howard in 1907. Numerous English editions have been printed
since, using the same translation. The work was commissioned by the National
School Board as an introductory geography text for young children, and its lively
and positive view of Sweden was intended in part to hinder ever-increasing
emigration to America. It is still a delightful introduction to the country, its
folktales, and its genius which will appeal to people of all ages.

47 **A tour in Sweden in 1838; comprising observations of the moral,
political and economical state of the Swedish nation.**
Samuel Laing. London: Longman, Orme, Brown, Green, &
Longmans, 1839. 431p.

One of the best-known 19th-century accounts of Sweden. Laing spent much of his
time in Stockholm but also travelled to Northern Sweden and Gotland during his

11

visit to the country in the summer of 1838. He is often critical and never without an opinion as he discusses the country and its people, history, politics, society, and economy.

48 A tour in Lapland.
Carl Linnaeus, translated from the Swedish by James Edward Smith. New York: Arno Press & New York Times, 1971. 2 vols. in one. (Physician Travelers).

A reprinting of *Lachesis Lapponica or a tour in Lapland, now first published from the original manuscript of the celebrated Linnaeus* (London: White & Cochrane, 1811). The Swedish 18th-century botanist's descriptions of travels to many parts of Sweden were later published in Latin, Swedish, and several other languages. The first of these famous trips was to Lapland from 12 May–10 October 1732. In his account Linnaeus discusses the flora of the regions extensively but also describes the animal life and people. For a detailed list of the literature regarding his travels, see *Itineraria Svecana* (q.v.).

49 A journey in Lapland: the hard way to Haparanda.
Richard Lister. London: Chapman & Hall, 1965. 256p.

The author's account of a summer hiking tour of the region stretching through Northern Sweden, Finland, and Norway includes descriptions of the countryside, and the native Lapps.

50 The description of Swedland, Gotland, and Finland.
George North, with an introduction by Marshall Swan. New York: Scholar's Facsimiles and Reprints, 1946. 28 leaves.

First published in 1561 in London at a time when Sweden's King Erik XIV wished to marry England's Queen Elizabeth I, this work is one of the first books in English on Sweden. Reproduced here in its original form, it includes a brief geographical description of Sweden, the mythological founding of the country, and its political history during the Middle Ages and the reign of Gustav Vasa.

51 A clean, well-lighted place: a private view of Sweden.
Kathleen Nott. London: Heinemann, 1969. 207p.

Best known for its critical comments on Sweden's social welfare programmes but, like many such assessments, also an outsider's reflections on the country and its people. Anecdotal, critical and controversial.

52 Small boat through Sweden.
Roger Pilkington. London: Macmillan; New York: St. Martin's Press, 1961. 227p. maps.

The experiences of an English family travelling by yacht from Gothenburg to Stockholm and into the interior by means of the many lakes and canals that link Sweden's waterways. The account is spiced with personal anecdotes and references to Sweden's past.

53   **The icicle and the sun.**
William Sansom.   New York: Reynal, 1958. 159p.
A tour of Scandinavia. The section on Sweden (p. 43–77) is a brief but perceptive view of the country, people, and their way of life.

54   **The challenge of Scandinavia: Norway, Sweden, Denmark and Finland in our time.**
William L. Shirer.   Boston, Massachusetts; Toronto, Canada:
Little, Brown, 1955. 437p. map. bibliog.
The relatively extensive section on Sweden (p. 109–215) discusses Swedish foreign policy at greater length than any other subject but also deals with features of the Swedish economy and government. It can no longer be regarded as up-to-date but is a worthwhile assessment of Sweden in the mid-20th century by a well-known journalist.

55   **Recollections of a tour in the North of Europe in 1836–1837.**
Charles William Stewart, the Third Marquis of Londonderry.
London: Richard Bentley, 1838. 2 vols.
There is a brief discussion of Sweden in Chapters IV and V of the first volume, in which the author is quite critical of the country, but describes at greater length his activities with King Karl XIV Johan, whom he had also known earlier during the Napoleonic Wars. More interesting for its description of the Swedish Royal Court than that of the country and its people.

56   **Sweden: model for a world.**
Hudson Strode.   New York: Harcourt, Brace, 1949. 371p. map.
bibliog.
Describes the author's visits to Sweden in 1939 and 1946. It discusses the country, prominent Swedes of the mid-20th century, Swedish history, the welfare state, and the Swedish character.

57   **Northern travel: summer and winter pictures of Sweden, Denmark and Lapland.**
Bayard Taylor.   New York: G.P. Putnam, 1858. 436p.
Describes his journey to Scandinavia during 1856–57. Arriving in Stockholm in December 1856, Taylor spent much of the winter in the Lapland region common to Norway, Sweden, and Finland. He then journeyed through much of southern Sweden, made a brief visit to Denmark, and travelled extensively through Norway before concluding his visit to the North in central Sweden. Interesting for the author's observations and attitudes regarding the daily life and customs of the people.

Travellers' Accounts

58 **A journal of the Swedish embassy in the years 1653 and 1654.**
Bulstrode Whitelocke, edited by Charles Morton, revised by Henry
Reeve. London: Longman, Brown, Green, & Longman, 1855. 2
vols. rev. ed.
An account of Whitelocke's appointment and tenure as England's Ambassador to
Sweden while it was ruled by Queen Christina. Although it offers few new
insights into the Queen's court, it is still interesting for its observations on Anglo-
Swedish relations and on Swedes during the mid-17th century. First published by
Morton in 1772 and revised for re-publication by Reeve.

59 **A wayfarer in Sweden.**
Frederic Whyte. Boston, Massachusetts; New York: Houghton
Mifflin, 1926. 207p.
A description of the author's visit to Sweden that also contains reflections on
other subjects such as a comparison of Swedes and Englishmen, Swedish history,
Bulstrode Whitelocke's embassy to Sweden in the 17th century, and the Swedish
artist, Carl Larsson.

60 **Letters written during a short residence in Sweden, Norway, and
Denmark.**
Mary Wollstonecraft, edited and introduction by Carol H.
Poston. Lincoln, Nebraska: University of Nebraska Press, 1976.
200p.
Mary Wollstonecraft, best known for *A vindication of the rights of women*, spent
the summer of 1795 in Scandinavia and one year later published her letters from
the trip. Although most of the work deals with her experiences in Norway,
Letters I–IV (p. 7–36) describe her journey from Gothenburg to Norway at the
beginning of her visit and Letters XVI–XVII (p. 135–47) discuss her brief trip
through the same region on her way to Copenhagen afterwards. It was first
published in London in 1796 and was translated into Norwegian in 1976 by Per A.
Hartun as *Min nordiske reise: beretninger fra et opphold i Sverige, Norge og
Danmark 1795* (Oslo: Gyldendal Norsk Forlag, 1976). A valuable reference work
that should be consulted in connection with her *Letters* is Per Nyström's *Mary
Wollstonecraft's Scandinavian journey* (Gothenburg, Sweden: Kungl. Vetenskaps-
och Vitterhets-Samhället, 1980).

**Itineraria Svecana: bibliografisk förteckning över resor i Sverige fram till
1950.** (Itineraria Svecana: a bibliographical listing of travels to Sweden
until 1950.)
See item no. 965.
Travels.
See item no. 1009.

Geography

General and Sweden as part of Northern and Western Europe

61 **An advanced geography of Northern and Western Europe.**
Ronald James Harrison Church, Peter Hall, G.R.P. Lawrence,
William R. Mead, Alice F.A. Mutton. Amersham, England:
Hulton Educational Publications, 1980. 3rd ed. 480p. maps. bibliog.

Three introductory chapters discussing the physical geography, population, and economic developments of the entire region precede several chapters devoted to the individual countries. The chapter on Sweden by William R. Mead (p. 72–91) outlines the country's physical geography and its influence on economic developments.

62 **Scandinavia: an introductory geography.**
Brian Fullerton, Alan F. Williams. New York: Praeger Publishers;
London: Chatto & Windus, 1972. 374p. maps. bibliog. (Praeger
Introductory Geographies).

The first section of the book discusses the physical geography of Denmark, Sweden, Finland, and Norway. This is followed by a study of each country in turn, providing an economic introduction and a discussion of its various regions. The chapters on Sweden (p. 159–231) study these same factors as they exist in Sweden's main regions. Each chapter contains suggestions for further reading in addition to the bibliography at the end of the book.

63 **Urban development in the Alpine and Scandinavian countries.**
E. A. Gutkind. New York: The Free Press; London: Collier-Macmillan, 1965. 500p. maps. bibliog. (International History of City Development).

The extensive section on Sweden (p. 381–455) consists of a brief general discussion on Swedish urban settlements and short summaries of the historical development of twenty-six Swedish cities up to the 19th century. It is well illustrated with numerous maps and sketches of the cities mentioned in the text.

64 **Historical geography in Scandinavia.**
Staffan Helmfrid. In: *Progress in Historical Geography*. Edited by Alan R. H. Baker. Newton Abbot, England: David & Charles, 1972, p. 63–89. maps. bibliog.

A bibliographical essay discussing the research done by Scandinavian historical geographers during the 1950s and 1960s.

65 **Scandinavia: a new geography.**
Brian S. John. London; New York: Longmans, 1984. 365p. maps. bibliog.

John does not devote separate units or chapters to each of the Scandinavian states. Instead, he studies them thematically in twenty-three chapters arranged around five main subjects: the physical and cultural environment; spatial expressions of the human economy; regional inequalities between the 'heartland' and outlying regions; sample studies of local landscapes (including a chapter on Rödlöga, a community in the Stockholm archipelago); and recent examples of cooperation that stand in contrast to continued differences of opinion and national policy. The book is supplemented by an excellent and extensive bibliography.

66 **Norden: crossroads of destiny and progress.**
Vincent H. Malmström. Princeton, New Jersey: D. Van Nostrand, 1965. 128p. maps. bibliog.

A brief survey of the geography and culture of the Nordic region followed by chapters on each of the five states. The chapter entitled 'Sweden: neutral fulcrum' (p. 65–80) is a brief historical-geopolitical sketch of the country from Viking times until the post-war period.

67 **Northern Europe.**
Vincent H. Malmström. In: *A geography of Europe: problems and prospects*. Edited by George Hoffman. New York: John Wiley, 1983. 5th ed. p. 306–44. maps. bibliog.

First published in 1953, this article has been revised to provide a brief up-to-date description of the physical and economic geography of Scandinavia, ending with a concise but cogent view of contemporary problems.

68   **An economic geography of the Scandinavian states and Finland.**
William R. Mead.   London: University of London Press, 1958.
302p. maps.

Mead divides the work into three main sections: the resource variable, the human variable, and primary economic activities. The first is a discussion of physical geography, the impact of changes that have occurred, and the effects of snow and ice. The middle section studies population growth and movement with a consideration of land and resource exploitation and industrialization. The third is a description of basic economic activities such as farming, fishing, mining and energy.

69   **An historical geography of Scandinavia.**
William R. Mead.   London: Academic Press, 1981. 313p. maps.
bibliog.

A chronological study of the human and physical geography of Scandinavia. Emphasis is given to the environment, geopolitics, rural and urban settlements, communication and transport patterns, and principal economic activities. A unique and interesting feature is the discussion of the pattern of daily life during the different periods. It is profusely illustrated with maps and diagrams and extensive bibliographies follow each chapter.

70   **Problems of Norden.**
William R. Mead.   *Geographical Journal*, vol. 151, no. 1 (1985),
p. 1–10. map. bibliog.

Examines three major and interlocking problems common to all of the Scandinavian states: energy needs, regional inequalities, and conservation. Common Nordic efforts to resolve these difficulties are also considered.

71   **The Scandinavian lands.**
Ray Millward.   New York: St. Martin's Press; London: Macmillan,
1965. 488p. maps. bibliog.

A basic geographical introduction to Scandinavia. A chapter is devoted to each of the four continental Scandinavian countries in the first section, including one on Sweden (p. 44–79). It provides brief surveys of the geological, geographical, historical, and economic features of Sweden's main regions. Subsequent chapters in Part Two discuss these topics in more detail and within a general Scandinavian context.

72   **The countries of north-western Europe.**
F. J. Monkhouse.   London: Longmans, 1971. 2nd ed. 526p. maps.
bibliog. (Geographies: an Intermediate Series).

The chapter on Sweden (p. 17–58) describes its geological past, physical geography, climate, economic resources, means of communication, and brief surveys of its main regions. The work was first published in 1965.

Geography. General and Sweden as part of Northern and Western Europe

73 **The Scandinavian world.**
Andrew C. O'Dell. London: Longmans, Green, 1957. 549p. maps.
bibliog. (Geographies for Advanced Study).
The opening chapters discuss the geological structure, climate, the seas surrounding Scandinavia and the early development of man. Two specific chapters on Sweden (p. 110–80) emphasize its physical and economic features. O'Dell concludes with a thorough survey of economic geography in which several factors are treated on a comparative basis and in more analytical detail than in the other sections. There are more richly illustrated or more readable geographies of Scandinavia, but O'Dell's work is distinguished for its data and scholarship.

74 **A geography of Norden: Denmark, Finland, Iceland, Norway, Sweden.**
Edited by Axel Sømme. Stockholm: Läromedelsförlagen; Oslo:
J. W. Cappelens; New York: Wiley; London: Heinemann, 1968.
new ed. 363p. maps. bibliog.
A collaborative work first published in 1960. Seven chapters by different scholars discuss basic geographical and geological factors affecting all of the Nordic states such as climate, natural resources, the surrounding seas, and plant life. In the series of chapters dealing separately with each country, Karl Erik Bergsten writes on Sweden's economic and natural resources and gives a brief overview of her population and settlement (p. 292–349). In addition to the maps and tables in text, the volume also includes an appendix of 12 plate maps of the region, illustrating various factors discussed in the text.

75 **Sweden: official standard names approved by the United States Board on Geographic Names.**
Washington, DC: Office of Geography, Department of Interior,
1963. 1033p. map. (Gazetteer no. 72).
Contains 74,200 entries listing places and features in Sweden and the islands of Öland and Gotland. Entries are made by name, nature, such as airport, populated area, location by longitude and latitude and location by *län* (county); there is a reference code for the source of information.

Regional studies

General

76 **Economic geografical (*sic*) excursion to Middle Sweden.**
Edited by Olof Jonasson, Bo Carlsund. Gothenburg, Sweden:
Elanders, 1960. 87p. maps. (Handelshögskolan i Göteborg
Skriftserie, 1960, no. 1. Meddelande från Geografiska Institutionen,
no. 67).
A collection of essays describing the geography and economic development of
central Sweden from Gothenburg in the south-west to Dalarna in the north. The
city of Gothenburg is featured, as are the Göta River valley, and such industries
as mining, iron and steel and hydroelectricity.

77 **From the plains of Middle Sweden to the high mountains.**
P. O. Nordell, Harald Rydberg. *Geografiska Annaler*, vol. 41
(1959), p. 170–92. maps. bibliog.
Examines the geology and geography of Central Sweden or the region north of
Stockholm, through the province of Dalarna to the mining region of Bergslagen.
The topics considered include the area's geological structure, landforms, climate,
population, and the economic activities pursued there – agriculture, forestry,
mining, and manufacturing.

78 **Gotland.**
Arthur Spencer. Newton Abbot, England: David & Charles, 1974.
175p. maps. bibliog. (Island Series).
A survey of the island discussing its geological features, physical geography,
history, and economic development. Special consideration is given to its role
during the Viking Age, Danish rule in the Middle Ages, and more recent
developments. Its capital, Visby, is also featured, as are its unique medieval
churches.

Northern Sweden

79 **A geographical excursion through central Norrland.**
Edited by Carl Magnusson Mannerfelt. Stockholm:
Generalstabens Litografiska Anstalt, 1960. 128p. maps.
Prepared as an excursion for participants in the International Geographical
Congress held in Stockholm in 1960. The eleven essays view the region from the
standpoint of geography, geology, and its economic resources, particularly its
hydroelectric power and timber industries.

Geography. Regional studies

80 **The Scandinavian northlands.**
William R. Mead. Oxford: Oxford University Press, 1974. 48p.
maps. bibliog. (Problem Regions in Europe).

This study of *Nordkalotten*, the North Cape regions of Norway, Sweden, and Finland within the Arctic Circle treats the Swedish *län* (county) of Norrland. The book examines the political, economic, and social problems of the region as a product and interaction of four variables: the physical environment, population, technology and organization.

81 **From the Bothnian Gulf through southern and central Lapland to the Norwegian fiords.**
Sten Rudberg, Erik Bylund. *Geografiska Annaler*, vol. 41 (1959), p. 261–88. maps. bibliog.

A geological and geographical description, primarily of south-central Lapland through the Swedish counties of Norrland and Västerbotten. Among the topics considered include the area's geological structure, geomorphology, climate, settlement, and chief economic activities: forestry, mining, and reindeer herding.

82 **Norrbotten – land of the Arctic Circle: a book about the Far North of Sweden.**
Edited by Folke Thunborg, Bengt Andersson. Stockholm: P. A. Norstedt & Söner, 1960. 3rd ed. 193p. maps.

Twenty articles by prominent inhabitants discussing the economic resources, transport facilities, and cultural features of the large Northern county. First published in 1953.

Stockholm

83 **Geographic features of Stockholm's skärgård.**
Bertil Hedenstierna. Stockholm: [Esselte], 1960. 26p. maps.
(Congrès International de Géographie).

Discusses many facets of the large archipelago east of Stockholm including its geological features, history, population, and economic resources. A summary of an article by the same author in Swedish in *Geografiska Annaler*, vol. 30 (1948), p. 1–444.

84 **Northward but gently: an introduction to the Stockholm archipelago.**
Alan Tapsell. Stockholm: P. A. Norstedt & Söner, 1969. 151p. maps.

Describes a sailing tour of the Stockholm archipelago (*skärgård*). Reference is made in each chapter to the specific charts for the region as the author covers the area from approximately forty miles south of Stockholm to about the same distance to the north, as well as describing Stockholm itself and the Åland Islands, although the latter are outside Swedish territorial waters.

85   **Stockholm: structure and development.**
     W. William-Olsson.   Uppsala, Sweden: Almqvist & Wiksell, 1961.
     96p. maps. bibliog.
A detailed survey of Stockholm that briefly discusses its origins, climate, topography, economic character, housing, communications system, and suburbs. Although now in need of revision, it is an important work on Stockholm's character in the mid-20th century.

Specific features

86   **The present climatic fluctuation.**
     Hans Ahlmann.   *Geographical Journal*, vol. 102 (July–Dec. 1948),
     p. 165–95. maps.
Reproduces a paper read at the Royal Geographical Society in London on 3 May 1948, and the discussion that followed. The author points out the significant changes which have taken place in temperature and precipitation since regular records have been kept. Although the author provides data from several European countries, much of his evidence comes from Scandinavia, including Sweden.

87   **Blueprint for the future Swedish Weather Service system.**
     Svante Bodin.   In: *Nowcasting*. Edited by K. A. Browning.
     London; New York: Academic Press, 1982, p. 25–36. map. bibliog.
Outlines the weather service system to be established during the 1980s by the Swedish Weather Service, improving both short-range and long-range forecasting by Swedish meteorologists. The article developed from a contribution by the author to the Nowcasting Symposium held in Hamburg, West Germany, during August 1981 as part of the Third Scientific Assembly of the International Assembly of the International Association of Meteorology and Atmospheric Physics.

88   **The climate of Scandinavia.**
     T. Werner Johannessen.   In: *Climates of Northern and Western*
     Europe. Edited by C. C. Wallin.   Amsterdam; London; New
     York: Elsevier Publishing Company, 1970, p. 23–79. maps. (World
     Survey of Climatology, vol. 5).
Discusses many factors affecting Scandinavia's climate such as atmospheric circulation, air temperature and precipitation. Climatic fluctuations are considered and extensive climatic tables are provided.

89 **Bergeron Memorial Volume.**
Edited by Gösta H. Liljequist. *Pure and Applied Geophysics*,
vol. 119, no. 3 (1980–81), p. 407–691. maps. bibliog.
A tribute to the Swedish meteorologist Tor Bergeron (1891–1977). Included among the seventeen articles are a biographical sketch of Bergeron (p. 409–42); an article by Bergeron on the history of weather analysis and forecasting (p. 443–72), R. Jewell's 'Tor Bergeron's first year in the Bergen School: towards an historical appreciation' (p. 474–90): and J. Namias' 'The early influence of the Bergen School on synoptic meteorology in the United States' (p. 491–500).

90 **The Baltic Sea.**
Edited by Aarno Voipio. Amsterdam; Oxford; New York: Elsevier Scientific Publishing, 1981. 418p. maps. bibliog. (Elsevier Oceanography Series, vol. 30).
A detailed scholarly study of the Baltic, with eight chapters studying its geology, hydrology, oceanographic features, fish, pollution, and management.

Maps and atlases

91 **Agricultural atlas of Sweden.**
Compiled by Olof Jonasson, Ernst Höijer, Thure Björkman.
Stockholm: Lantbrukssällskapets Tidskriftsaktiebolag, 1938. 176p.
maps.
A collection of maps, charts, tables, and text illustrating the nature of Swedish agriculture and the factors such as temperature and rainfall that have an important effect on it. Although its value is limited by the length of time since its publication, it is the only work available on the subject.

92 **KAK Bilatlas.** (KAK automobile atlas.)
Stockholm: Generalstabens Litografiska Anstalts Förlag, 1975.
280p.
The road atlas published by *Kungliga Automobil Klubben* (the Royal Automobile Club) of Sweden, containing 47 detailed road maps of different parts of Sweden, maps of many towns and cities, and brief descriptions of their tourist facilities.

93 **Atlas över Sverige/National Atlas of Sweden.**
Edited by Magnus Lundqvist, Carl-Julius Anrick, Gerd Enequist, Ivar Högbom, Gunnar Arpi, Olof Hedbom, Gunnar Hoppe.
Stockholm: Generalstabens Litografiska Anstalts Förlag, 1953–71.
[not paginated].
Produced by Svenska Sällskapet för Antropologi och Geografi (The Swedish Society for Anthropology and Geography), the work consists of 520 maps dealing with many topics, such as geology, natural resources, population, economics,

culture and politics. The table of contents and all maps are labelled both in Swedish and English, and the Swedish text to the maps is accompanied by an extensive English summary.

94 **A map book of Scandinavia.**
A. J. B. Tussler, R. P. Buckby. Houndmills, Basingstoke, England; London: Macmillan Education, 1979. 72p. maps. (A Map Book).

Maps, charts and text describing the physical and economic geography of all of Scandinavia and more detailed studies of each country's main cities and regions. Useful for students, scholars, and the general reader.

Geology

95 **Changing water-levels and settlement in the Mälar district since A.D. 700.**
Björn Ambrosiani, translated from the Swedish by Phyllis Andersson. *Striae*, vol. 14 (1981), p. 140–43. bibliog.

Revising previous explanations for the changes in land elevation surrounding Lake Mälar, including Viking Age Birka and present-day Stockholm, the book is important for its consideration of the influence of land levels on mediaeval settlement.

96 **Shore displacement at Stockholm during the last 1000 years.**
Lars-Erik Åse. *Geografiska Annaler*, Series A, vol. 62, nos 1–2 (1980), p. 83–91. map. bibliog.

Examines the factors that have affected the water level or shore displacement on Lake Mälar at Stockholm. A discussion of the historical and archaeological material available to record this data in the past is also included.

97 **Glacial deposits in North West Europe.**
Edited by Jürgen Ehlers. Rotterdam, The Netherlands: A. A. Balkema, 1983. 470p. maps. bibliog.

The section on Sweden (p. 75–159) includes several important articles discussing geological developments in Sweden during the Quaternary Age. In particular, see Jan Lundqvist's 'The glacial history of Sweden' (p. 77–82), 'Tills and moraines in Sweden,' (p. 83–90), 'Glaciofluvial deposits in Sweden' (p. 91–96) and Hans G. Johansson's 'Tills and moraines in northern Sweden' (p. 123–30).

98 **Geology of the European countries: Denmark, Finland, Iceland, Norway, Sweden.**
Paris: Bordas, 1980. 456p. maps. bibliog. (Geology of the European Countries, [vol. 2]).

A volume prepared in conjunction with three others, for the 26th International Congress, held in Paris during July 1980. The section on Sweden (p. 211–343) was

23

written by Erik Fromm, Thomas Lundqvist, David G. Gee, Ebbe Zachrisson, Harald Agrell, and Rudyard Frietsch, and is divided into sub-chapters on the Precambrian, Caledonides, Quaternary, and the ore deposits found in Sweden.

99 **A symposium on the genesis of till.**
Hans G. Johansson. *Boreas*, vol. 6, no. 2 (1977), p. 71–227. maps.
bibliog.

A selection of papers from a symposium entitled 'Till/Sweden–76' held in Stockholm 16–18 August 1976. Till is a sediment which covers over 75 per cent of Sweden's land area. Most of the articles deal with Scandinavia and two particularly with Sweden: Jan Lundqvist's 'Till in Sweden' (p. 73–85), and Erik Lagerlund's more specialized 'Till studies and neotectonics in northwest Skåne' (p. 159–66).

100 **The deglaciation of Scandinavia earlier than 10,000 B.P.: the 1978 Uppsala symposium.**
Edited by Lars-König Königsson, Jan Lundqvist. *Boreas*, vol. 8, no. 2 (1979), p. 79–253. maps. bibliog.

Selected papers from the symposium of the same name. Six of the twenty papers concern work on Swedish topics, including Björn E. Bergland's 'The deglaciation of southern Sweden 13,500–10,000 B.P.' (p. 89–117); Åke Hillefors' 'Deglaciation models from the Swedish West Coast' (p. 153–69); and Nils-Axel Mörner's 'The deglaciation of southern Sweden: a multi-parameter consideration' (p. 189–98). For a sequel to this topic, see *Boreas*, vol. 9, no. 4 (1980), containing papers from the 1979 Uppsala Symposium discussing deglaciation in Scandinavia after 10,000 BP. For Sweden, the chief work is Jan Lundqvist, 'The deglaciation of Sweden after 10,000 B.P.' (p. 229–38).

101 **The Quaternary of Sweden.**
Jan Lundqvist. In: *The Quaternary*, vol. 1. Edited by Kalervo Rankama. New York: Wiley-Interscience Publisher, 1965, p. 139–198. maps. bibliog. (Geologic Systems Series).

A survey of the Quaternary period (the geological Present) emphasizing the characteristics, Quaternary deposits, the glaciation history of the country, and the changes that occurred with the beginning of the deglaciation process.

102 **Scandinavian Caledonides.**
T. Strand, Oskar Kulling. London; New York: Wiley-Interscience, 1972. 302p. maps. bibliog. (Regional Geology Series).

Oskar Kulling, in the second half of the book, considers these rock formations which have developed in the north-west part of Sweden. He discusses their development at different thrust levels, their geological importance, and economic value.

Sweden.
See item no. 5.

Sweden in brief.
See item no. 6.

Lapland: the world's wild places.
See item no. 35.

The land of the midnight sun: summer and winter journeys through Sweden, Norway, Lapland, and Northern Finland with descriptions of the inner life of the people, their manners, customs, the primitive antiquities, etc.
See item no. 41.

A tour in Lapland.
See item no. 48.

A journey in Lapland: the hard way to Haparanda.
See item no. 49.

Northern travel: summer and winter pictures of Sweden, Denmark and Lapland.
See item no. 57.

Social science research in Sweden.
See item no. 431.

Swedish agriculture.
See item no. 722.

Luleå and Narvik: Swedish ore ports.
See item no. 727.

The iron ores of Sweden.
See item no. 729.

Zinc and lead deposits of central Sweden.
See item no. 730.

The origin of the iron ores in central Sweden and the history of their alterations.
See item no. 731.

Boreas. An International Journal of Quaternary Geology.
See item no. 928.

Geografiska Annaler.
See item no. 931.

Scandinavia in social science literature: an English-language bibliography.
See item no. 972.

Vanishing Lapland.
See item no. 998.

Tourism and Travel Guides

103 **Stockholm: the city on the water.**
Erik Asklund, Gunnar Erkner, translated from the Swedish by
Paul Britten Austin. Stockholm: P. A. Norstedt & Söner, 1968.
135p. map.
A guide to Stockholm that covers all of its major attractions including a discussion
of *Gamla stan* (Old Town). It is sprinkled with interesting historical anecdotes
and legends about the city and the past. An excellent introduction for the general
reader and potential traveller.

104 **Stockholm town trails: from the Old Town to the new 'city'.**
Elly Berg. Stockholm: Akademilitteratur, 1979. 208p.
Organized as four tours of the city (three on foot, one by underground). An
excellent guide to the old and new historic places, leading to interesting corners
possibly unfamiliar even to natives of Stockholm.

105 **On foot through Europe, a trail guide to Scandinavia: includes
Denmark, Finland, Greenland, Iceland, Norway and Sweden:
walking, backpacking, ski touring, climbing – everything you can
do on foot.**
Craig Evans. New York: Quill, 1982. 393p. maps.
Contains detailed information, particularly for hikers but extremely useful for all
tourists wishing to participate in these sports.

106 **The Old Town: a guide to *Gamla Stan*, the Royal Palace and
Riddarholmen.**
Beatrice Glase, Gösta Glase, translated from the Swedish by D.
Simon Harper, Roger G. Tanner. Stockholm: Trevi, 1977. 160p.
A detailed, building-by-building description of the historic core of Stockholm.
The volume is out-of-date only occasionally in its description of current tenants
(who change frequently on the ground floors of buildings in some parts of the Old
Town).

107 **Travel, study, and research in Sweden.**
Compiled by Adèle Heilborn.   Stockholm: LTs Förlag, 1975. 7th
ed. 286p. map. bibliog.
Published in cooperation with the Sverige–Amerika Stiftelsen, this is the most
thorough and useful guide to Sweden. Intended primarily for the long-term visitor
but of great value to the tourist as well. Includes suggestions on pre-trip planning,
customs, specific university programmes, and general information necessary to
adapt well to a foreign country. First published in 1951 as *Study in Sweden* by an
organization devoted to educational exchange programmes between Sweden and
the United States and Canada.

108 **A guide to the industrial archaeology of Europe.**
Kenneth Hudson.   Bath, England: Adams & Dart, 1971. 186p.
Describes industrial workplaces and transport systems of historical interest. Most
are no longer operating but are still accessible to interested visitors. The section
on Sweden (p. 137–47) deals especially with iron works.

109 **The Stockholm guide.**
Ulf Kindborg, Göran Welander, translated from the Swedish by
Stanley Reitz.   Stockholm: Kindborg & Welander, 1972. 128p.
maps.
A very useful guide listing and rating lodging and eating establishments. It also
provides the addresses of leading museums, art galleries, shops, and tourist
attractions.

110 **Scandinavia today.**
Jacques Legros.   Paris: Éditions Jeune Afrique, 1975. 223p. maps.
A brief general background to Denmark, Norway, and Sweden is followed by
sections on each country that include brief surveys of its major cities. A final
chapter provides more detailed tourist information and tours of Scandinavia that
can be taken. Also published in French in the same year as *La Scandinavie
d'aujourd'hui*.

111 **Sweden: holiday guide for the disabled.**
Edited by Sonja Lindh.   Stockholm: Sveriges Turistråd, 1986.
149p.
The only guide for the disabled describing accommodation and tourist attractions
by region. It also includes in its introduction general advice on travel and
transport facilities and the difficulties they pose for the disabled.

112 **Scandinavia: Denmark, Finland, Iceland, Norway and Sweden.**
Sylvie Nickels.   New York; Chicago; San Francisco, California:
Rand McNally, 1983. 128p. maps.
Includes general travel information for all of Scandinavia and separate sections
for each country listing major tourist attractions. The book does not include
specific lists of lodgings but nonetheless it is a useful, compact travel guide.

27

113 **The Nordiska Museet and Skansen: an introduction to the history
      and activities of a famous Swedish museum.**
      Mats Rehnberg, translated from the Swedish by Alan Tapsell.
      Stockholm: Nordiska Museet, 1957. 194p.

A dated but still useful work on the development of the museum. For a more
recent 'coffee-table' work of photographs displaying the breadth of activity in the
world's first open-air ethnographical museum, see *Boken om Skansen* (Book
about Skansen), edited by Nils Erik Baehrendtz (Höganäs, Sweden: Bra Böcker,
1980).

114 **Scandinavia: Denmark, Sweden and Norway.**
      New York: Random House; Toronto, Canada: Random House of
      Canada, 1973. 128p. (*Holiday* Magazine Travel Guide).

First published in 1960, this is a pocket-sized tour guide which includes general
information on Scandinavia, tourist suggestions, and separate chapters on each of
the three countries. A brief concluding chapter provides lodging, eating, shopping
and sight-seeing suggestions.

115 **Working and living in Sweden: a guide to important measures
      applicable to foreigners assigned to Sweden.**
      Swedish Employers' Confederation, translated from the Swedish
      by David Jenkins.   Stockholm: Swedish Employers'
      Confederation, 1981. 112p.

Provides travel information which is most suitable for those anticipating
employment or a long residence in the country. Discusses the process of hiring
foreign employees, procedures to be followed before departure to Sweden,
suggestions regarding education and housing, formalities on arrival in Sweden,
and taxation and social security measures.

Of Swedish ways.
See item no. 8.

Swedes as others see them: facts, myths, or a communications complex?
See item no. 9.

The second new nation: the mythology of modern Sweden.
See item no. 10.

Sweden.
See item no. 11.

KAK Bilatlas. (KAK automobile atlas.)
See item no. 92.

Sweden: a general introduction for immigrants.
See item no. 340.

Museiboken: Sveriges länsmuseer. (Museum book: Sweden's county museums.)
See item no. 905.

Museiguiden: vägledning till svenska museer. (Museum guide: an introduction to Swedish museums.)
See item no. 906.

Flora and Fauna

General

116 **Wings and seasons.**
Gunnar Brusewitz, translated from the Swedish by Walstan
Wheeler.   Stockholm: Wahlström & Widstrand, 1980. 119p.
An anecdotal journey through Sweden which describes characteristic Swedish
flora and fauna. Well illustrated and suitable for all readers.

117 **Mountain flowers of Scandinavia.**
Olav Gjærevall, Reidar Jørgensen.   Trondheim, Norway:
Trondhjems Turist Forening, 1978. 175p. maps.
The authors introduce their subject with a brief discussion of the plant forms of
Scandinavia's mountainous regions, their origins and distribution. Contains colour
illustrations of 164 flowers of the region. A good introduction for the general
reader or traveller.

118 **Norsk og svensk flora.** (Norwegian and Swedish flora.)
Johannes Lid.   Oslo: Norske Samlaget, 1963. 800p.
Most entries in the table of contents, the main portion of the book, and index
references are by the Latin name for the plant as well as the Norwegian and
Swedish name. Entries contain information regarding size, appearance, and
places in both countries where the species is most likely to occur. Many black-
and-white illustrations are included. The book was published in two editions
beginning in 1944 as *Norsk flora* (Norwegian flora).

Carl Linnaeus

119 **The complete naturalist: the life of Linnaeus.**
Wilfrid Blunt, assisted by William T. Stearn. New York: Viking
Press, 1971. 256p. maps. bibliog.

A biography that describes Linnaeus' early life, travels, position as a professor at
the University of Uppsala, and his scientific work in general terms. Stearn has
treated his work in botany more specifically in a short appendix, 'Linnaean
classification nomenclature and method' (p. 242–49). An introduction for non-
experts interested more in Linnaeus' life than a detailed knowledge of his work, it
also discusses Linnaeus' travels abroad and within Sweden at length. For a more
detailed account of Linnaeus' scientific work, see James L. Larson, *Reason and
experience: the representation of natural order in the work of Carl von Linne*
(Berkeley; Los Angeles, California; London: University of California Press,
1971). A paperback edition has also been published (London: Collins, 1984).

120 **Linnaeus: the man and his work.**
Edited by Tore Frängsmyr, translated from the Swedish by
Michael Srigdey, Bernard Vowles. Berkeley; Los Angeles,
California; London: University of California Press, 1983. 203p.

Four essays by the editor, Sten Lindroth, Gunnar Eriksson, and Gunnar Broberg,
discussing Linnaeus' character, his work as a botanist and geologist, and his
classification system of Man. Serious studies both for the general reader and
scholars working in these fields.

121 **Carl Linnaeus.**
Knut Hagberg, translated from the Swedish by Alan Blair.
London: Jonathan Cape, 1952. 264p. maps. bibliog.

A biography quoting frequently from Linnaeus' own works and other contemporary sources to describe his life, scientific work, and travels throughout
Sweden. Well written and appropriate both for the scholar and the general
reader. For another work on Linnaeus, see Norah Gourlie, *The prince of
botanists: Carl Linnaeus* (London: H. F. & G. Witherby, 1953).

122 **Daniel Carl Solander, naturalist on the *Endeavour*.**
Roy Anthony Rauschenberg. Philadelphia: American
Philosophical Society, 1968. 66p. bibliog. (Transactions of the
American Philosophical Society, new series, vol. 58, no. 8).

A cogent, well-written discussion of the life and work of Solander (1733–82), a
student of Linnaeus, well-known 18th-century naturalist, and participant in
Captain James Cook's first voyage on the *Endeavour* to the South Pacific
(1768–71). For a shorter work on Solander, see Dudley Glass' 'The world of Dr.
Solander', *American–Scandinavian Review*, vol. 58, no. 4 (1970), p. 392–98.

123 **Linnaeus and the Linnaeans: the spreading of their ideas in systematic botany, 1735–1789.**
Frans A. Stafleu.   Utrecht, The Netherlands: A. Oosthoek's Uitgeversmaatschappij, 1971. 386p. bibliog.
Published for the International Association for Plant Taxonomy, it emphasizes Linnaeus' scientific work and its impact on other 18th-century European scientists, including a brief chapter on Linnaeus' own students, most of whom were Swedish. An excellent, readable study.

Sweden.
See item no. 5.

Linnaeus.
See item no. 28.

Lapland: the world's wild places.
See item no. 35.

A tour in Lapland.
See item no. 48.

Nordic Journal of Botany.
See item no. 934.

Travels.
See entry no. 1009.

Prehistory and Archaeology

124 **Urban archaeology in Sweden.**
Björn Ambrosiani, Hans Andersson. In: *European towns: their archaeology and early history.* Edited by M. W. Barley. London; New York: Academic Press, 1977, p. 103–26. maps. bibliog.
Studies the development and shifting location of early town sites in early Sweden. Emphasis is placed on conditions surrounding Lake Mälar and Lund, with a section by Andersson on the Gothenburg area. Published for the Council for British Archaeology as the proceedings of a conference on the theme. German and French summaries of the article are included. For a study of the origin of Scandinavian towns during the pre-Viking period, including Birka and Helgö in Sweden, see Herbert Jankuhn's 'New beginnings in Northern Europe and Scandinavia' (p. 355–71) in the same work.

125 **The testimony of the spade.**
Geoffrey Bibby. New York: Alfred A. Knopf, 1956. 414p. maps. bibliog.
A history of the development of European archaeology. Scandinavian evidence and Scandinavian archaeologists figure prominently in the work. An extensive study is made, for example, of the work of the Swedish archaeologist Oscar Montelius (p. 177–93).

126 **The Sutton Hoo ship-burial: comments on general interpretation.**
Rupert Bruce-Mitford. In: *Aspects of Anglo-Saxon archaeology: Sutton Hoo and other discoveries.* London: Victor Gollancz, 1974, p. 1–72. map.
The author, an acknowledged expert on this subject, discusses the Swedish origins and connections with the Sutton Hoo ship-burial. This account is one of a collection of essays previously published elsewhere, in this case in the *Proceedings*

33

of the Suffolk Institute of Archaeology and National History, vol. 25 (1949), p. 1–78. As indicated, many of the articles in the book also deal with other aspects of the subject. The article possesses no bibliography but the author's extensive notes fulfil the same purpose. For a thorough discussion of the actual excavation of the Sutton Hoo ship and its artefacts, see the author's *The Sutton Hoo ship burial: a handbook* (London: British Museum, 1968). new ed. (first published in 1947).

127 **Iron and man in prehistoric Sweden.**
Karin Calissendorff, Wilhelm Holmqvist, Åke Hyenstrand, Inga Serning, Lena Thålin-Bergman, edited and translated from the Swedish by Helen Clarke, foreword by Arne S. Lundberg.
Stockholm: Jernkontoret, 1979. 180p. maps. bibliog.

Six essays based on archaeological research on the Swedish island of Helgö discussing the production of iron and Sweden's trade in iron up to the end of the 11th century. Important works for both the scholar and interested general reader.

128 **The earlier Stone Age settlement of Scandinavia.**
Grahame Clark. London: Cambridge University Press, 1975. 282p. maps. bibliog.

Studies the development of continuous human settlement of Scandinavia during the late and post-glacial ages and the ways in which the natural resources of the region were used to sustain social life. Emphasis is given particularly to southern Scandinavia (Denmark and the Swedish province of Skåne) but the rest of Sweden is also considered more briefly later in the work. The settlement, subsistence, and technological forms of these early Scandinavians are discussed.

129 **The Mesolithic settlement of Northern Europe: a study of the food-gathering peoples of Northern Europe during the early post-glacial period.**
J. G. D. Clark. New York: Greenwood Press, 1970. 284p. maps. bibliog.

First published in 1935 and reprinted in 1953, the book examines the main food-gathering cultures that developed in Northern and Western Europe from ca. 8000–2500 BC. Discussion of the Scandinavian evidence of these groups figures prominently in the work.

130 **The cultural heritage in Sweden.**
Edited by Nanna Cnattingius, Jutta Waller, Birgitta Windahl-Clerborn. Stockholm: Central Board of National Antiquities and the Swedish National Committee of ICOMOS, 1981. 385p. maps. (ICOMOS, Bulletin, no. 6).

A collection of brief essays which discuss planning and legislation to preserve many forms of cultural monuments in Sweden and some of the projects which have been implemented. Each of the essays is presented in English, French and German.

131 **The Northmen.**
Thomas Froncek, introduced by Birgitta L. Wallace. New York: Time-Life, 1974. 160p. maps. bibliog. (The Emergence of Man).
A study of life in Scandinavia from ca. 2000–500 BC. Much of the research was done in Denmark but represents developments and conditions that also prevailed in Sweden. Colourful, informative, and a good introduction for the general reader.

132 **Ancient monuments and prehistoric society.**
Åke Hyenstrand, translated from the Swedish by Bert Hellberg, Phyllis Anderson. Stockholm: Central Board of National Antiquities, 1979. 165p. maps. bibliog.
A technical study that discusses the surveys undertaken of Sweden's archaeological sites during the last few decades, and the research problems that still have to be solved.

133 **Ancient hunters and settlements in the mountains of Sweden: archaeological and ethnological investigations carried out in connection with power-station projects and lake regulation schemes.**
Sverker Janson, Harald Hvarfner, translated from the Swedish by Richard Cox. Stockholm: Riksantikvarieämbetet, 1966. 128p. maps. bibliog.
Ten chapters by the two authors describing the archaeological results of work done near the rivers and lakes of Norrland prior to the construction of power stations. Emphasis is given to the hunting and fishing communities from the Stone Age and Iron Age that were found. The text is accompanied by 123 photographic plates.

134 **The runes of Sweden.**
Sven B. F. Jansson, translated from the Swedish by Peter G. Foote. New York: Bedminster Press, 1962. 168p. map. bibliog.
Describes some of the oldest runic inscriptions found in Sweden and those of the 11th century which are divided into the runes referring to Viking expeditions abroad and to various activities within Sweden itself. Later chapters deal with other characteristics of runes and those inscribed after the introduction of Christianity. Published in Swedish in the same year (Stockholm: P. A. Norstedt & Söner).

135 **A history of Scandinavian archaeology.**
Ole Klindt-Jensen. London: Thames & Hudson, 1975. 144p. maps. bibliog. (The World of Archaeology).
A survey of the nature and development of Scandinavian archaeology since the 16th century. A chronological approach is used for the most part, incorporating

Prehistory and Archaeology

work done in all of the countries together. However, the work of Oscar Montelius is discussed in 'Scandinavian dialogue: Montelius and Müller' (p. 84–96) and that of 20th-century Swedish archaeologists in a separate chapter, 'Recent Swedish archaeology' (p. 105–15).

136 **The civilisation of Sweden in heathen times.**
Oscar Montelius, translated from the Swedish by H. F. Woods.
New York: Haskell House Publications, 1969. 214p. map.

Although Montelius does not discuss the first settlement of Sweden, his work does describe human life until about the 8th century AD, based on archaeological artefacts. Over 200 illustrations of these prehistoric finds are included in this work, first published in 1888.

137 *Vasa*, **the king's ship.**
Bengt Ohrelius, translated from the Swedish by Maurice Michael.
Philadelphia; New York: Chilton Books, 1962. 124p. maps.

Describes the sinking of the *Vasa* in Stockholm harbour in 1628, early efforts to recover the ship, the successful salvage operations of 1959, and the efforts made thereafter to conserve the ship and the artefacts that were also found. A basic, non-technical work.

138 **The world of the Norsemen.**
Eric Oxenstierna, translated from the German by Janet
Sondheimer. Cleveland, Ohio; New York: World Publishing Co.;
London: Weidenfeld & Nicolson, 1967. 163p. map. bibliog.
(Ancient Civilizations).

Originally published in Stuttgart in 1957, this is a discussion of the archaeological work done in Scandinavia mainly on the pre-Viking period. It is informative, scholarly, but also anecdotal in style.

139 **Scandinavian archaeology.**
Haakon Shetelig, Hjalmar Falk, translated from the Norwegian by
E. V. Gordon. Oxford: Clarendon Press, 1937. 458p.

A discussion of the archaeological remains in Scandinavia from its earliest settlement through the Viking period. The major portion of the book is organized on a chronological basis describing the different archaeological periods and their characteristics. In the last section, however, several topics are discussed including decorative art, subsistence, dwellings, costume, seafaring, weapons, and religion. This was the standard work on the subject for decades and is still an important study.

36

140 **Sweden.**
Marten Stenberger, translated from the Swedish by Alan
Binns. New York: Frederick A. Praeger, 1962. 229p. maps.
bibliog. (Ancient Peoples and Places, vol. 30).

A survey of prehistoric Sweden from about 10,000 BC to 800 AD, when the
Viking Age began. The author briefly discusses the development of the
Scandinavian landmass and then divides the remainder of the book into an
account of the Mesolithic, Neolithic, Bronze and Iron Ages. It is accompanied by
a large number of maps and illustrations of the archaeological remains used as
evidence for the period. Useful particularly as an introduction to the subject.

**The land of the midnight sun: summer and winter journeys through
Sweden, Norway, Lapland, and Northern Finland with descriptions of
the inner life of the people, their manners, customs, the primitive
antiquities, etc.**
See item no. 41.

The Vikings.
See item no. 162.

The Vikings.
See item no. 163.

**La Suède et l'Orient: études archéologiques sur les relations de la Suède
et de l'Orient pendant l'âge des Vikings.** (Sweden and the East:
archaeological studies on the relations of Sweden and the East during
the Viking Age.)
See item no. 164.

Studies in Northern coinages of the eleventh century.
See item no. 165.

**The Vikings: an illustrated history of their voyages, battles, customs and
decorative arts.**
See item no. 169.

The Varangians in Soviet archaeology today.
See item no. 173.

The Vikings.
See item no. 174.

Archaeology of the boat: a new introductory study.
See item no. 177.

The Norsemen.
See item no. 183.

The Viking world.
See item no. 186.

Prehistory and Archaeology

The Vikings and America.
See item no. 189.

The Vikings and their origins: Scandinavia in the first millennium.
See item no. 192.

Acta Archaeologica.
See item no. 926.

Ancient Scandinavia.
See item no. 1013.

History

General

Surveys

141 **A concise history of Sweden.**
Alf Åberg, translated from the Swedish by Gordon Elliot,
introduction by Bengt Nyström, Kerstin Holmquist. Stockholm:
LTs Förlag, 1985. 104p.

Originally published in 1985 as *Sveriges historia i fickformat* (A pocket-sized
history of Sweden) in cooperation with the Swedish Museums Association and the
Board of Museum Directors in Stockholm, it is a concise survey of Swedish
history from prehistoric to modern times by a recognized historian. A useful
introduction for the general reader and traveller.

142 **Swedish history in brief.**
Ingvar Andersson, Jörgen Weibull. Stockholm: Swedish
Institute, 1985. 3rd rev. ed. 72p.

A revision by Weibull of a popular work first published by Andersson in 1965. A
concise survey that emphasizes developments during the last two centuries
including constitutional reforms and political developments since 1970. Written by
two able historians who have contributed much to Swedish historical scholarship.

143 **Sweden: a political and cultural history.**
Eric Carl Elstob. Totowa, New Jersey: Rowman & Littlefield,
1979. 209p. maps.

A survey of Swedish history that covers both Sweden's political development and
the arts. It provides relatively equal treatment of most periods, although

39

discussion of the 20th century is brief. Emphasis is particularly on architecture and art in the two chapters on Swedish culture.

144 **A history of the Swedish people.**
Vilhelm Moberg, translated from the Swedish by Paul Britten Austin. New York: Pantheon Books; London: William Heinemann, 1971–72. 2 vols. map.

A translation of Moberg's two-volume *Min svenska historia* (My Swedish history) (Stockholm: P. A. Norstedt & Söner, 1970–71). Based on the principle that 'The history of Sweden is the history of her commons', Moberg writes a social history of Sweden from Viking time to the beginning of the Kalmar Union in the first volume and discusses the Swedish peasant risings against authority from Engelbrekt Engelbrektsson in the 15th century to Nils Dacke's revolt against Gustav Vasa a century later. Although criticized by historians for its inaccuracy and lack of scholarship, it is a unique work by a gifted writer.

145 **A short history of Sweden.**
Stewart Oakley. New York; Washington, DC: Frederick A. Praeger, 1966. 292p. maps. bibliog.

Emphasizes political events but also gives cultural developments proper consideration. Does not favour any period to excess and carries its account to the end of the 1950s. Published in Great Britain as *The Story of Sweden* (London: Faber & Faber).

146 **Sweden.**
Irene Scobbie. New York; Washington, DC: Praeger, 1972. 254p. maps. bibliog. (Nations of the Modern World).

A relatively brief but able survey of Sweden's history from the Viking Age until about 1970. A final portion (p. 166–226) provides a critical view of Sweden at the beginning of the 1970s: its industries, taxes, social welfare programmes, and culture.

147 **Sweden: the nation's history.**
Franklin D. Scott. Minneapolis, Minnesota: University of Minnesota Press, 1977. 654p. maps. bibliog.

The most recent, complete, and authoritative survey in English of Sweden's history. Scott moves swiftly through the Vikings and the Middle Ages to a full treatment of Sweden since the beginning of the 16th century. Political developments are emphasized but economics and culture are also discussed at length. The equivalent of the most important survey of Sweden's history in Swedish, the two-volume *Svensk historia*, by Sten Carlsson and Jerker Rosén (Stockholm: Bonniers, 1961–62) which was later expanded by the same authors into the ten-volume *Den svenska historien* (Stockholm: Bonniers, 1966–68). Other surveys still worth consulting are Carl Jakob Herman Hallendorff and Adolf Schück's *History of Sweden* (Stockholm: C. C. Fritze, 1938), first published in 1929; Ragnar Svanström and Carl Fredrik Palmstierna's *A short history of Sweden*

(Westport, Connecticut: Greenwood Press, 1975), first published in 1934; and Ingvar Andersson's *History of Sweden* (Westport, Connecticut: Greenwood Press, 1975), first published in 1956.

Miscellaneous

148   **Swedish politics during the 20th century.**
Stig Hadenius, translated from the Swedish by Victor J. Kayfetz.
Stockholm: Swedish Institute, 1985. 173p. bibliog.
A political history of Sweden that concentrates chiefly on events since the Second World War. It and *Swedish history in brief* (q.v.) are therefore valuable supplements to works published earlier and valuable discussions in their own right. Contains clear and relatively extensive treatment of events since 1968 (p. 124–64). For a more detailed study in Swedish of the same topic, see the work by Hadenius, Bengt Owe Birgersson, Björn Molin, and Hans Wieslander, *Sverige efter 1900: en modern politisk historia* (Sweden after 1900: a modern political history) (Stockholm: Bonniers, 1984), 10th rev. ed.

149   **North-east passage: Adolf Erik Nordenskiöld, his life and times.**
George Kish.   Amsterdam: Nico Israel, 1973. 283p. maps.
A thorough study of the Arctic explorer (1832–1901), including a description of his journey through the North-east passage to Siberia on the *Vega* 1878–79. An informative account for all readers.

150   **To the heart of Asia: the life of Sven Hedin.**
George Kish.   Ann Arbor, Michigan: University of Michigan Press; Rexdale, Canada: John Wiley & Sons Canada, 1984. 153p. maps. bibliog.
Describes Hedin's (1865–1952) work as an explorer but also discusses his political activity in Sweden. A timely, excellent introduction for the general reader.

151   **Sweden's development from poverty to affluence, 1750–1970.**
Edited by Steven Koblik, translated from the Swedish by Joanne Johnson.   Minneapolis, Minnesota: University of Minnesota Press, 1975. 380p. bibliog.
First published as *Från fattigdom till överflöd: en antologi om Sverige från frihetstiden till våra dagar* (From poverty to affluence: an anthology on Sweden from the Age of Freedom to our own time) (Stockholm: Wahlström & Widstrand, 1973), it consists of thirteen essays by leading Swedish scholars and introductory comments to each by Koblik. All deal with economic, social, and political issues and developments during the period.

152 **Antarctica or two years amongst the ice of the South Pole.**
Otto Nordenskjöld, Joh. Gunnar Andersson, foreword by Sir
Vivian Fuchs. London: C. Hurst, 1977. 608p. maps.

A reprint of *Antarctic, två år bland sydpolens isar* (Stockholm: Albert Bonnier,
1904) and of the first English edition of 1905. An account of the expedition of
1901–03 to the South Pole.

153 **Grandeur et liberté de la Suède (1660–1792).** (The grandeur and
liberty of Sweden 1660–1792.)
Claude Nordmann. Paris: Béatrice-Nauwelaerts; Louvain,
Belgium: Éditions Nauwelaerts, 1971. 551p. maps.
bibliog. (Publications de la Faculté des Lettres et Sciences
Humaines de Paris-Sorbonne: Series 'Recherches', vol. 63.
Travaux du Centre de Recherches sur la civilisation de l'Europe
moderne, vol. 9).

A detailed study of an important period in Swedish history. It is divided into four
parts: the Age of Greatness under Karl XI, the height and collapse of the Swedish
empire under Karl XII, the Age of Liberty covering much of the 18th century,
and finally the Age of Enlightened Absolutism under Gustav III. Much of the
work deals with domestic politics and diplomacy but detailed consideration is also
given to cultural, economic and social developments. Contains an extensive
bibliography, valuable particularly for its French and German entries that are not
cited frequently elsewhere.

154 **Essays in Swedish history.**
Michael Roberts. Minneapolis, Minnesota: University of
Minnesota Press, 1967. 358p.

Ten essays by Roberts on various facets of Swedish history, from the 16th to 18th
century. All but one have been published separately as articles and discuss the
rulers Gustav II Adolf, Queen Christina, and Karl XI, and topics such as
aristocratic constitutionalism, the general crisis in 17th-century Sweden, the
Swedish aristocracy in the 18th century, and British policy towards Sweden at the
time of Gustav III's coup in 1772. First published in 1953.

155 **From great power to welfare state: 300 years of Swedish social
development.**
Kurt Samuelsson. London: Allen & Unwin, 1968. 304p.

Published in Sweden in the same year as *Från stormakt till välfärdsstat*, to
commemorate the 300th anniversary of *Sveriges Riksbank* (National Bank of
Sweden). The work discusses the interaction of economics, society, and
governmental policy to create modern Sweden. It is both a continuation of Eli
Heckscher's *An economic history of Sweden* (q.v.) and the presentation of a
different point of view.

Sweden in Scandinavian history

156 **A history of Scandinavia: Norway, Sweden, Denmark, Finland and Iceland.**
T. K. Derry. Minneapolis, Minnesota: University of Minnesota Press, 1979. 447p. map. bibliog.
This single-volume survey of Scandinavian history in English fills a long-felt need. About half of the work covers the period from 1814 to the mid-1970s, with Sweden receiving ample consideration. Emphasis is on politics but two chapters discuss cultural and other contributions by Scandinavians during the 19th and 20th centuries.

157 **Les pays nordiques aux XIXe et XXe siècles.** (The Nordic countries during the 19th and 20th centuries.)
Jean-Jacques Fol. Paris: Presses Universitaires de France, 1978. 327p. maps. bibliog. (Nouvelle Clio: l'histoire et ses problèmes, vol. 48).
Provides a survey of Scandinavian history from the beginning of the 19th century until the mid-1970s. Political events are discussed, as are economic conditions, cultural developments, and contemporary issues. Covers a field and period not yet considered by others.

158 **Les Scandinaves: histoire des peuples scandinaves: épanouissement de leurs civilisations des origines à la Réforme.** (The Scandinavians: history of the Scandinavian people: development of their civilization from its origins to the Reformation.)
Maurice Gravier. Paris: Éditions Lidis-Brepols, 1984. 686p. maps. bibliog.
A detailed history of Scandinavia that stresses the Viking period, the development of Christianity, the Kalmar Union period, Gustav Vasa's Sweden, and the introduction of the Reformation in the 16th century. Consideration is given to economics, society, and culture as well as politics. Richly illustrated with colour photographs and maps.

159 **The Scandinavian countries, 1720–1865: the rise of the middle classes.**
Brynjolf Jakob Hovde. Port Washington, New York; London: Kennikat Press, 1972. 2 vols.
First published in 1943, it is a most thorough and knowledgeable survey of this lengthy period. Political history is included, although Hovde emphasizes economic, social, and cultural developments. Consideration is given to agriculture, trade, religion, philosophy, literature, education, and the origins of the popular folk movements that had a considerable impact throughout the 19th century.

160 **Scandinavians: selected historical essays.**
Erik Lönnroth, edited by Åke Holmberg, Per Hultqvist, Rolf
Karlbom, Gunnar Olsson, Ole Skarin. Gothenburg, Sweden:
Gothenburg, 1977. 211p. bibliog.
Eleven articles by the distinguished Swedish historian, most of which have been
published earlier. General subjects covered include the Vikings, the Late Middle
Ages, King Gustav III, and 20th-century Scandinavian foreign affairs. Ole
Christensson contributed a detailed bibliography of Lönnroth's historical works.

161 **The Scandinavians in history.**
Stanley M. Toyne, foreword by G. M. Trevelyan.
Port Washington, New York; London: Kennikat Press, 1970. 352p.
maps.
A survey of Scandinavian history first published in 1948 which concentrates
primarily on Sweden and Denmark from the Union of Kalmar in the 14th century
until the mid-19th century.

The Vikings, 900–1066

162 **The Vikings.**
Edited by Bertil Almgren, Charlotte Blindheim, Yves de Bouard,
Torsten Capelle, Arne Emil Christensen, Jr., Kristján Eldjárn,
Richard M. Perkins, Thorkild Ramskou, Peter H. Sawyer. New
York: Crescent Books, 1984. 287p. maps. bibliog.
A richly illustrated survey of the Vikings prepared by an international team of
experts. The work covers many subjects such as early Scandinavian towns
(including Birka in Sweden), the extent of Viking expansion, daily life, customs
and religious beliefs, handicrafts, and Viking ships. Based on scholarly research
and presented in an attractive, readable form. This book was first published in
1966.

163 **The Vikings.**
Holger Arbman, translated from the Swedish and introduced by
Alan Binns. London: Praeger, 1961. 212p. maps. bibliog.
(Ancient Peoples and Places).
A survey of the Vikings including archaeological evidence as well as literary
sources. Arbman describes the Scandinavian background to the Viking pheno-
menon, their activities in the British and North Atlantic isles, Western Europe
and Russia, with a concluding chapter on Viking art. Richly illustrated with black-
and-white photographs, drawings and maps, this is a useful introduction by a
Swedish expert on the subject.

164 **La Suède et l'Orient: études archéologiques sur les relations de la Suède et de l'Orient pendant l'âge des Vikings.** (Sweden and the East: archaeological studies on the relations of Sweden and the East during the Viking Age.)
T. J. Arne. Uppsala, Sweden: K. W. Appelberg, 1914. 240p. maps. bibliog.

Despite its age, still regarded as a major work on the presence of Swedes in Russia, Eastern Europe, the Byzantine Empire, Persia, Armenia, and Syria. The author describes Scandinavian artefacts discovered in Russia and objects from the East found in Sweden.

165 **Studies in Northern coinages of the eleventh century.**
Edited by C. J. Becker. Copenhagen: Munksgaard, 1981. 173p. bibliog. (Det Kongelige Danske Videnskabernes Selskab Historisk-filosofiske Skrifter 9:4).

Five essays based on silver hoards founds in Sweden. Several discuss the Scandinavian imitation of Anglo-Saxon and Byzantine coins revealed by the finds. Particularly for students of numismatics or of the Viking Age in Scandinavia.

166 **The Varangians of Byzantium: an aspect of Byzantine military history.**
Sigfus Blöndal, translated, revised and rewritten by Benedikt S. Benedikz. Cambridge, England; London: Cambridge University Press, 1978. 242p. maps. bibliog.

A study of the Norse and Russian military forces serving in the Eastern Roman Empire from the 10th to the 13th centuries. Special consideration is given to King Harald Hardråde of Norway, but warriors from all of the Scandinavian countries and their Russian relatives figured in the enterprise. A final chapter discusses 'Some individual Norse and English Varangians and travellers to Byzantium'. Unfinished when Blöndal died in 1950, Benedikz made significant revisions before its publication.

167 **Mohammed, Charlemagne and Rurik.**
Sture Bolin. *Scandinavian Economic History Review*, vol. 1, no. 1 (1953), p. 5–39.

A major study which revised previous views on the nature of early mediaeval trade by considering Scandinavian evidence, and one of the first scholarly works arguing for consideration of the Vikings as successful merchants as well as bloodthirsty villains. Peter H. Sawyer and more recent scholars have revised many of his findings but nevertheless it remains a landmark work on the Vikings and economic history.

168   **The Viking saga.**
Peter Brent.   London: Weidenfeld & Nicolson, 1975. 264p. maps.
bibliog.
A discussion of Viking expansion with detailed chapters on Viking activity in
France, England, Russia, Iceland, and Vinland. A chapter on Scandinavian
mythology is also included in this excellent introduction for the general reader.

169   **The Vikings: an illustrated history of their voyages, battles, customs
and decorative arts.**
Johannes Brøndsted, translated from the Danish by Kalle Skov.
Baltimore, Maryland: Penguin Books, 1967, 320p. maps. bibliog.
An excellent survey of the Vikings first published in 1960. Brøndsted provides a
brief chronological and country-by-country description of Viking activity,
connecting activities abroad with developments at home. This is followed by a
description of their weapons, dress, art, religion, and a particularly interesting
examination of the Viking way of life. A well-written work by a recognized
authority.

170   **The Russian Primary Chronicle.**
Samuel Hazzard Cross.   Cambridge, Massachusetts: Harvard
University Press; London: Humphrey Milford, Oxford University
Press, 1930. 320p. map. (Harvard Studies and Notes in Philology
and Literature, vol. 12).
The chief primary source for the origins and development of the Russian state
from approximately 852 until 1110, documenting the arrival of the Scandinavian
Rus or Varangians and the contact between Russia and Scandinavia during the
period. Cross presents an extensive introduction and appendixes discussing the
history of the manuscript, its authorship, and various editions that have been
published, as well as the text itself (p. 136–297). Like the Icelandic sagas, it is an
important record of the Viking phenomenon.

171   **Yaroslav the Wise in Norse tradition.**
Samuel Hazzard Cross. *Speculum*, vol. 4, no. 2 (1929), p. 177–97.
Discusses the close ties that were maintained between Yaroslav the Wise
(c. 982–1054), ruler of Kiev, and his wife Princess Ingrid of Sweden, with the
rulers of Scandinavia and the interaction that took place among them.

172   **The Viking road to Byzantium.**
Hilda Ellis Davidson.   London: Allen & Unwin, 1976. 341p.
maps. bibliog.
The first half of the work is devoted primarily to the Scandinavian penetration of
and connections with Russia. This is followed by a study of the Scandinavian

presence in Byzantium and the impact that such contact with the East had on Old Norse literature and mythology. A major study of this aspect of the Vikings in which Sweden figured prominently.

173   **The Varangians in Soviet archaeology today.**
      N. J. Dejevsky.   *Medieval Scandinavia*, vol. 10 (1977), p. 7–34.
Examines Russian archaeological and historical research of the 1960s and early 1970s regarding the Scandinavian presence in Russia during the Viking Age.

174   **The Vikings.**
      Edited by Robert T. Farrell, preface by David M. Wilson.
      London; Chichester, England: Phillimore, 1982. 306p. maps.
      bibliog.
Sixteen contributions relating to history, art, archaeology, literature, and other studies. The most important contributions are Charlotte Blindheim's 'The emergence of urban communities in Viking Age Scandinavia: the problem of continuity' (p. 42–69); C. Patrick Wormald's 'Viking studies: whence and whither' (p. 128–53); Gwyn Jones' 'The Vikings in North America' (p. 209–30); and Louis A. Pitschman's 'Norsemen in America: a select bibliography 1950–1980' (p. 231–35). Unlike many such collections, all essays are of high quality, and it should be included in every collection on the Vikings.

175   **The Viking achievement: a survey of the society and culture of early medieval Scandinavia.**
      Peter Foote, David M. Wilson.   New York; Washington, DC:
      Praeger, 1970. 473p. maps. bibliog. (Great Civilizations).
The subtitle best describes the contents of this major work: a detailed but clearly written book on Scandinavian life both during and after the Viking Age. Major emphasis is given to the nature of society, including women and children, daily life (housing, clothing, cooking), trade, means of transport, warfare, art, literature, law, and religion.

176   **The Viking world.**
      James Graham-Campbell.   New York: Tickner & Fields; London:
      Frances Lincoln, 1980. 220p. maps. bibliog.
An excellent introduction to Viking life both in Scandinavia and abroad. It does not attempt to detail political developments or Viking expansion but it does provide a good introduction for the general reader to Viking ships and their construction, home life, art, mythology, the development of Christianity, and runes. Sean McGrail, R. I. Page, and Christine Fell have contributed to the work, which is richly supplemented by photographs, illustrations, and maps.

177 **Archaeology of the boat: a new introductory study.**
     Basil Greenhill, J. S. Morrison, Sean McGrail, Eric McKee,
     introduction by W. F. Grimes.   Middletown, Connecticut:
     Wesleyan University Press, 1976. 320p. maps. bibliog.

A study of boats and boat-building that includes a discussion of Viking ships
(p. 202–49) by Greenhill and McGrail. This section describes their general
construction and particular finds that have been discovered. An excellent study
for both the expert and the general reader. For another well-illustrated account of
Viking ships, see Björn Randström's *The ship: an illustrated history* (Garden City,
New York: Doubleday, 1961), p. 52–65.

178 **A history of the Vikings.**
     Gwyn Jones.   Oxford; New York: Oxford University Press, 1984.
     rev. ed. 520p. maps. bibliog.

A scholarly, detailed, and very readable presentation first published in 1968.
Covers the Vikings abroad, Scandinavia's early, pre-Viking history, and
Scandinavia's history during the Viking Age. Jones, Emeritus Professor of
English Language and Literature at University College, Cardiff, is a highly
regarded scholar of the Viking Age, and this is probably the most informative and
comprehensive single-volume study of the subject.

179 **A history of the Vikings.**
     Thomas D. Kendrick.   New York: Barnes & Noble, 1968. 412p.
     maps. bibliog.

An extremely detailed study emphasizing the military character of the Vikings.
Extensive chapters on pre-Viking Scandinavia and political developments there
during and immediately after the Viking Age precede an account of the Viking
attacks on different parts of Europe. The major portion of the book is organized
geographically by country with a chronological description of Viking activity. First
published in 1930, it remains a useful reference work.

180 **The Vikings.**
     Howard LaFay.   Washington, DC: National Geographic Society,
     1972. 207p. maps. bibliog.

Provides a broad survey of Viking expansion and life. Illustrated with many
photographs, drawings and maps of Viking artefacts, reconstructions of scenes
from the period, the book discusses the people of Scandinavia and other regions
which the Vikings conquered. Overemphasizes Viking violence, but otherwise a
suitable introduction for the general reader.

181 **Les invasions: le second assaut contre l'Europe chrétienne
(VIIe–XIe siècles).** (The invasions: the second assault against
Christian Europe (the 7th to 11th centuries).)
Lucien Musset. Paris: Presses Universitaires de France, 1971.
2nd ed. 304p. maps. bibliog. (Nouvelle Clio: l'histoire et ses
problèmes, vol. 12).

Primary emphasis is given to the Vikings, but within the context of the migrations
undertaken by the Magyars and Saracens towards Europe at the same time. First
published in 1965.

182 **Viking ways: on the Viking Age in Sweden.**
Maj Odelberg, Lena Thålin-Bergman, Inger Zachrisson, translated
from the Swedish by Verne Moberg, Peter Foote, Elisabeth
Hall. Stockholm: Swedish Institute, 1980. 31p. maps. bibliog.

A concise survey of Viking society, religion, art, towns such as Birka, and
Swedish contributions to Viking expansion outside Scandinavia. Helpful as an
introduction for the general reader and young adult and as a preparation for more
detailed works.

183 **The Norsemen.**
Eric Oxenstierna, edited and translated from the German by
Catherine Hutter. Greenwich, Connecticut: New York Graphic
Society Publications, 1965. 320p. maps. bibliog.

An examination of several aspects of Viking life, richly embellished with black-
and-white photographs and illustrations. In common with many recent works it
emphasizes the non-warlike aspects of the Viking character, at least towards
outsiders. It discusses the archaeological evidence of the period at length and
studies the way in which this material can tell us much about Viking society,
including the role of women, festivals, and ships. The book was originally
published as *Die Wikinger* (Stuttgart, West Germany: Kohlhammar, 1959).

184 **The age of the Vikings.**
Peter H. Sawyer. London: Camelot Press, 1962. 254p. maps.
bibliog.

This major work does not attempt, as its title might suggest, to paint a broad
picture of the period. Instead, it is an investigation of the various sources,
primarily treasure hoards, that underline the commercial aspects of the Vikings
and play down their warlike character. Recommended for all serious students of
the subject.

185 **Kings and Vikings: Scandinavia and Europe AD 700–1100.**
Peter H. Sawyer. London; New York: Methuen, 1982. 182p.
maps. bibliog.

A readable and very valuable survey of the Vikings by an acknowledged expert.
Sawyer considers the nature of pre-Viking Scandinavia, the sources used for the
study of the subject and Viking raids and settlements outside Scandinavia. An

extensive bibliography including recent literature makes it a particularly valuable reference work as well. For a more detailed article by the same author, see his 'Conquest and colonization: Scandinavians in the Danelaw and Normandy,' *Proceedings of the Eighth Viking Congress* (Odense, Denmark: University of Odense Press, 1981), p. 123–31.

186 The Viking world.
Jacqueline Simpson. New York: St. Martin's Press, 1980. 192p.

Discusses aspects of Viking life disregarded by those who see Vikings as nothing more than warlike barbarians. Basing her work primarily on archaeological material, Simpson describes many aspects of Viking life including their ships, weapons, homes, family life, and social relationships. Originally published as *Everyday life in the Viking age* (New York: G. P. Putnam, 1967), this is an informative and valuable introduction.

187 The Varangians in Russian history.
Stuart R. Tompkins. In: *Medieval and historiographical essays in honor of James Westfall Thompson.* Edited by James Lea Cate, Eugene N. Anderson. Chicago: University of Chicago Press, 1938, p. 465–90.

Discusses the etymology of the words 'Rus' and 'Varangian' and the dispute that developed regarding the Scandinavian origins of the first Russian state. An excellent introduction to these issues and the literature on them up to the late 1930s.

188 Viking Issue.
Scandinavian Review, vol. 68, no. 3 (1980).

A special issue devoted to the Vikings. Three articles of particular importance include James Graham-Campbell's 'The other side of the coin' (p. 6–19) dealing with Viking trade; Peter G. Foote and David M. Wilson's article on slavery in Viking society, 'The descendants of thrall' (p. 35–48); and Magnus Magnusson's 'End of an era' (p. 58–69) on the significance of the English succession crisis of 1066 to Scandinavian history.

189 The Vikings and America.
Eric Wahlgren. London: Thames & Hudson, 1986. 192p. maps. bibliog. (Ancient Peoples and Places, vol. 102).

Describes the Viking settlement of Greenland, the literary evidence from the sagas of the Viking discovery of America, the erroneous evidence discovered or manufactured to verify the Viking presence there, Helge Ingstad's archaeological discoveries on Newfoundland, and theories constructed by the author from literary sources to re-interpret Viking exploration along the coast of North America. It is a significant study by a recognized expert in past scholarship and nonsense on the subject, a provocative new direction in research, which possesses an excellent bibliography covering past work on the topic.

190 **Social Scandinavia in the Viking age.**
Mary W. Williams. New York: Macmillan, 1920. 451p. map.
bibliog.
Despite its age, this work is still highly recommended, as its treatment of many
topics involving society and social life have not been superseded. These include
the position of women, childhood, marriage and the home.

191 **Economic aspects of the Viking age.**
Edited by David M. Wilson, Marjorie L. Caygill. London:
British Museum, 1981. 56p. maps. bibliog. (Occasional Paper,
no. 30).
Six scholarly papers that discuss crafts, living conditions, and iron production
during the period. For an article solely on Sweden, see Björn Ambrosiani's
'Settlement structure in Viking Age Sweden' (p. 47–50).

192 **The Vikings and their origins: Scandinavia in the first millennium.**
David M. Wilson. London: Thames & Hudson; New York:
McGraw-Hill, 1970. 144p. maps. bibliog. (Library of Early
Medieval Civilizations).
An excellent introduction to pre-Viking Scandinavia and the Vikings for the
general reader. Includes numerous photographs of archaeological digs and
artefacts.

The Middle Ages, 900–1500

193 **Nordic students at foreign universities until 1660.**
Sverre Bagge. *Scandinavian Journal of History*, vol. 9, no. 1
(1984), p. 1–29.
A comparative study by country and chronological period of the universities that
Nordic students attended with explanations for the changes in pattern that
occurred.

194 **Desertion and land colonization in the Nordic countries**
c. 1300–1600: comparative report from the Scandinavian Research
Project on Deserted Farms and Villages.
Svend Gissel, Eino Jutikaala, Eva Österberg, Jørn Sandnes, Björn
Teitsson. Stockholm: Almqvist & Wiksell, 1981. 304p. maps.
bibliog.
A report by the national leaders of the research project established by the
historical associations of the respective Nordic countries. The report deals with
the planning undertaken to create the project, the methods, hypotheses, and
study areas established in each country and some of the comparisons that can be

made as a result of the research. It is a valuable addition to recent knowledge on Scandinavia in the late Middle Ages, and is indicative of the intensive research of recent years. Its extensive bibliography and list of works published as a result of participation in the project are also helpful.

195 **The peasant revolt of Engelbrekt Engelbrektsson and the birth of modern Sweden.**
John J. Murray. *Journal of Modern History*, vol. 19, no. 3 (1947), p. 193–209.
Examines Engelbrektsson's revolt against the Union of Kalmar monarch Erik of Pomerania and much of the Swedish nobility during the 1430s. A valuable English summary of this episode in Swedish history.

196 **Les peuples scandinaves au moyen âge.** (The Scandinavian people in the Middle Ages.)
Lucien Musset. Paris: Presses Universitaires de France, 1951. 342p. maps. bibliog.
The most detailed discussion of the Scandinavian states during the Middle Ages in a non-Scandinavian language. Musset begins with an account of pre-Viking Scandinavia and the activities of the Vikings abroad but most of the work studies the development of the Scandinavian states from ca. 1000 until the Kalmar Union of 1397. Although the author concentrates chiefly upon politics, attention is also given to religious, commercial, and social developments.

197 **Sweden as an aristocratic republic.**
Herman Schück, translated from the Swedish by John Toler. *Scandinavian Journal of History*, vol. 9, no. 1 (1984), p. 65–72.
Sketches administrative developments within the Swedish government during the 15th century, stressing the power of the nobility, the emergence of major institutions of the Swedish government during the period, and the connection between these developments and administrative reforms implemented later by the Vasas. A provocative and useful summary of the period and topic.

198 **The historical context of the first towns in northern and eastern Europe.**
Inge Skovgaard-Petersen. Proceedings of the Eighth Viking Congress. Odense, Denmark: Odense University Press, 1981, p. 9–18.
A brief scholarly discussion relating hypotheses on the development of towns during the Middle Ages in Scandinavia to current, more general literature on the subject.

199   **Nordic slavery in an international setting.**
Niels Skyum-Nielsen.   *Medieval Scandinavia*, vol. 11 (1978–79),
p. 126–48.
Discusses the legal aspects of Nordic slavery during the Middle Ages as defined by
Roman law. A revealing study from an unusual perspective.

The Age of Greatness, 1500–1721

200   **Rise and decline of an aristocracy; the Swedish social and political
élite in the 17th century.**
Kurt Ågren.   *Scandinavian Journal of History*, vol. 1, nos 1–2
(1976), p. 55–80.
Studies the political influence, economic position, and collective social status of
Swedish noble families to illustrate the split between the upper and lower nobility
which occurred during this century. Written by an expert on the subject.

201   **Gustav Adolf the Great.**
Nils Ahnlund, translated from the Swedish by Michael Roberts.
Princeton, New Jersey: Princeton University Press, 1940. 314p.
map.
First published in Swedish, this is regarded as one of the finest Swedish works on
Gustav II Adolf. It is not a chronological account of the king's life but a
discussion of several aspects of his life and work, including the events leading to
his accession as king in 1611, his marriage to Queen Maria Eleonora, his
character and personality, his relationship with the *Råd* (Royal Council) and the
Riksdag (Parliament), Swedish involvement in the Baltic crisis of the 17th
century, and Sweden's participation in the Thirty Years' War.

202   **The life of Charles XII, King of Sweden 1697–1718.**
Frans Gunnar Bengtsson, translated from the Swedish by Naomi
Walford, introduction by Eric Linklater.   London: Macmillan;
New York: St. Martin's Press, 1960. 495p. maps.
An abridgement of the original two-volume *Karl XIIs levnad* (Stockholm: P. A.
Norstedt & Söner, 1935–36). A thorough treatment by the well-known Swedish
novelist which presents the king in heroic proportions. Still a valuable, enjoyable,
and worthwhile work for all readers.

203   **The Livonian estates of Axel Oxenstierna.**
Edgars Dunsdorfs.   Stockholm: Almqvist & Wiksell, 1981. 248p.
maps. bibliog.
Examines the acquisition and administration of the estates in Livonia of Axel
Oxenstierna, Gustav II Adolf's distinguished Chancellor. Of interest to economic
historians and students of Sweden's administration of conquered territory during
its Age of Greatness.

History. The Age of Greatness, 1500–1721

204 Queen Christina.
J. H. Elliot. *Horizon*, vol. 9, no. 3 (1967), p. 67–79.
Sketches Christina's rule of Sweden (1632–1654) and later life in self-chosen exile (1654–1689). Well-written and accompanied by many illustrations of contemporary art and artefacts relating to Christina's life.

205 The 'Price Revolution' of the sixteenth century: some Swedish evidence.
Ingrid Hammarström. *Scandinavian Economic History Review*, vol. 5, no. 2 (1957), p. 118–54.
Offers evidence of radical price increases in Sweden during the 16th century as a contribution to the historical debate of the 1950s on the explanations for the Price Revolution. An important article still highly regarded both for the data and interpretations it offers. Also published in the Bobbs-Merrill Reprint Series in European History (Indianapolis, Indiana: Bobbs-Merrill, 1971) and in *The Price Revolution in Sixteenth Century Europe*, edited by Peter H. Ramsey (London, 1971).

206 Charles XII of Sweden.
Ragnhild M. Hatton. New York: Weybright & Talley; London: Weidenfeld & Nicolson, 1968. 656p. maps. bibliog.
The most thorough, scholarly, and recent of the major studies of Karl XII in English. Includes treatments of the king, his government of Sweden, his military campaigns, and the controversy regarding his death. The extensive notes and bibliography are particularly helpful for additional research. See also her briefer but very cogent *Charles XII* (London: Historical Association, 1974). For a solid treatment in German, see Otto Haintz, *König Karl XII von Schweden* (Berlin: Gruyter, 1958) 2nd ed. 3 vols.

207 Salt and cloth in Swedish economic history.
Karl-Gustaf Hildebrand. *Scandinavian Economic History Review*, vol. 2, no. 2 (1954), p. 74–102.
Discusses the foreign trade of Sweden in the 16th century, the uses of salt by the fishing industry, and the dietary habits of consumers. It also indicates the influence which Eli Heckscher had on contemporary economic historians who used his works as points of departure for their own.

208 Large scale farming in Scandinavia in the seventeenth century.
Eino Jutikaala. *Scandinavian Economic History Review*, vol. 23, no. 2 (1975), p. 159–66.
A concise discussion particularly of the existence and growth of *säteri*, tax-exempt demesne farms in the four Scandinavian countries.

209 **The rise of the Baltic question.**
Walter Kirchner.   Newark, Delaware: University of Delaware
Press, 1954. 283p. maps. bibliog. (University of Delaware
Monograph Series, vol. 3).
Studies the dissolution of the Order of the Brethren of the Sword in 1560 and the
attempts made as a result during the 1560s and 1570s by Russia, Denmark,
Sweden, and Poland to conquer Livonia. The interests and actions of each are
treated in detail as the author sets the scene for the larger struggle for the same
area that occurred in the 17th century.

210 **The Swedish 'military state', 1560–1720.**
Jan Lindegren.   *Scandinavian Journal of History*, vol. 10, no. 4
(1985), p. 305–36.
A sweeping synthesis of the Age of Greatness from the standpoint of historical
materialism which describes the creation of the 'military state' during this period
and its economic and social effects. This is a provocative work reflecting more
recent perspectives on the period by some Swedish historians and it forms part of
an issue concerned with 'The emergence of the modern state in the Scandinavian
countries during the sixteenth and seventeenth centuries'.

211 **The struggle for the supremacy of the Baltic 1600–1725.**
Jill Lisk.   New York: Funk & Wagnalls, 1967. 282p. maps.
bibliog.
Although it also treats developments in Prussia, Russia, and Denmark, this work
is chiefly an introduction to Sweden's Age of Greatness for the general reader.
Diplomatic and military affairs are emphasized but the domestic reforms of
Gustav II Adolf are also discussed.

212 **Council, king and estates in Sweden 1713–1714.**
Carl Lennart Lundquist.   Stockholm: Almqvist & Wiksell, 1975.
215p. bibliog. (Studies presented to the International Commission
for the History of Representative and Parliamentary Institutions).
Discusses the work of the Royal Council and the *Riksdag* (Parliament) session of
1713–14 held in the absence of, and against the wishes of, King Karl XII. A
welcome study of governmental and parliamentary institutions in contrast to the
frequent attention given to Sweden's kings during the period.

213 **Queen Christina of Sweden: documents and studies.**
Edited by Magnus von Platen.   Stockholm: P. A. Norstedt &
Söner, 1966. 389p. (Analecta Reginensia, vol. 1).
Twenty-six articles in English, French, German, and Italian relating both to
Queen Christina and 17th-century Swedish culture. See, for example, Allan
Braham's 'The tomb of Christina' (p. 48–58) and Carl Nordenfalk's 'Queen
Christina's Roman collection of tapestries' (p. 266–95).

214 **Charles XI.**
Michael Roberts. *History*, vol. 50, no, 169 (1965), p. 160–92.
A very readable, knowledgeable discussion of the rule of Sweden by one of its least-known but most important kings (1660–97).

215 **Gustavus Adolphus: a history of Sweden 1611–1632.**
Michael Roberts. London; New York: Longmans, Green, 1953–58. 2 vols. maps. bibliog.
A thorough, competent treatment of the famous Swedish king and survey of his country during the first half of the 17th century by an expert. Roberts divides his chronological treatment of Gustav II Adolf between the two volumes and includes detailed discussions of politics, religion, education, culture, economy, society, and Sweden's military system in the work. Exhaustive bibliographies at the end of both volumes provide a detailed list of published works on these subjects. The most important single work in English on Gustav II Adolf and 17th-century Sweden.

216 **Gustavus Adolphus and the rise of Sweden.**
Michael Roberts. London: English Universities Press, 1973. 207p. maps. bibliog.
A biography of Gustav II Adolf that emphasizes the king's diplomatic and military activities from his succession to the throne in 1612 until his death in 1632. An excellent introduction to the subject for the general reader.

217 **On aristocratic constitutionalism in Swedish history 1520–1720.**
Michael Roberts. London: University of London Press, 1966. 45p. (The Creighton Lecture in History, 1965).
Discusses a major political issue of the 16th and 17th centuries, and frequent source of conflict between Sweden's kings and nobles. A clear and concise work by the chief authority in English of this period. For a concise discussion of the same subject by Roberts, see 'The constitutional development of Sweden in the reign of Gustav Adolf', *History*, new series, vol. 24, no. 96 (1948), p. 328–41.

218 **Queen Christina and the General Crisis of the Seventeenth Century.**
Michael Roberts. In: *Crisis in Europe 1560–1660*. Edited by Trevor Aston, introduction by Christopher Hill. Garden City, New York: Doubleday & Company, 1967, p. 206–34.
The entire work was first published in England (London: Routledge & Kegan Paul, 1965) and Roberts's article was presented earlier in *Past and Present*, no. 22 (1962), p. 36–59. The article studies the *Riksdag* of 1650 as a protest against the Queen's economic policies, and as an aspect of widespread discontent in Europe. An important survey of politics and society in Sweden during the 17th century.

219 **Sweden as a great power 1611–1697: government; society; foreign policy.**
Edited by Michael Roberts.   London: Edward Arnold; New York: St Martin's Press, 1968. 183p. (Documents of Modern History).

A translation of forty-three documents from the period which describe the nature of Swedish government, society, social crises, and foreign affairs. The editor also provides a brief historical sketch of the century to explain the importance of the documents and connect them to each other.

220 **Sweden's Age of Greatness, 1632–1718.**
Edited by Michael Roberts.   New York: St Martin's Press, 1973. 314p. bibliog.

Eight essays by six Swedish scholars and Roberts on Swedish government, individuals, and society during the 17th century. Among the works included are Sven-Erik Åström's 'The Swedish economy and Sweden's role as a great power 1632–1697' (p. 58–101); Roberts's 'The Swedish church' (p. 132–73); and Alf Åberg's 'The Swedish army, from Lützen to Narva' (p. 265–87).

221 **The dubious hand: the history of a controversy.**
Michael Roberts.   *Karolinska Förbundets Årsbok*, (1981–82), p. 174–242.

Examines the evidence and legends which have developed attributing Karl XII's death on 30 November 1718 to an assassin instead of a shot from the Norwegian fortress of Frederikssten. It is detailed, critical, provocative and entertaining.

222 **The early Vasas: a history of Sweden, 1523–1611.**
Michael Roberts.   Cambridge, England: Cambridge University Press, 1968. 509p. maps. bibliog.

A political history of Sweden in the 16th century. Roberts begins with a discussion of the break-up of the Union of Kalmar and the revival of Swedish independence in the early 1500s, followed by five main sections that each cover the reign of successive Swedish monarchs during the 16th century and the crisis of the 1590s by which Karl IX became king. The only major work on a century of Swedish history which deserves more attention than it has received.

223 **The Swedish imperial experience 1560–1718.**
Michael Roberts.   Cambridge, England: Cambridge University Press, 1979. 156p. maps. (The Wiles Lectures, 1979).

An analytical rather than a chronological description of the Swedish empire during the 17th century. Subjects discussed include the empire's resources, nature, and disintegration. It assumes some background knowledge of the subject but is a thoughtful and scholarly presentation.

224 **Europe and Scandinavia: aspects of the process of integration in the 17th century.**
Edited by Göran Rystad. Stockholm: Esselte Studium, 1983. 330p. maps. (Lund Studies in International History; Scandinavian University Books).

Sixteen essays in German and English prepared as part of a research project on 'The Europeanization of Sweden in the 17th century' by the Institute of History at the University of Lund. Most of the articles discuss the relationship of Sweden with the rest of Europe during the century in fields such as government, law, education, and society. A major work by outstanding scholars.

225 **Christina of Sweden.**
Sven Stolpe, edited by Sir Alec Randall, translated from the Swedish by Sir Alec Randall, Ruth Mary Bethell. New York: Macmillan, 1966. 360p.

An abridgement and translation of Stolpe's two-volume *Drottning Christina* (Queen Christina) (Stockholm: Albert Bonniers, 1960–61) which has also appeared in German. A thorough biography that is both sympathetic and critical with an interesting analysis of previous biographies of the Swedish queen. Well written for both the general reader and serious student.

226 **Lion of the North: Charles XII of Sweden.**
Voltaire, translated from the French by Michael F. O. Jenkins. East Brunswick, New Jersey: Farleigh Dickenson University Press; London; Toronto, Canada: Associated Universities Presses, 1981. 270p.

A biography of Karl XII that begins with his accession to the throne in 1697. A classic that has been reproduced countless times since it was first published in both French and English in 1731. It also represents both the awe and the distaste with which Karl XII was commonly viewed.

227 **Christina of Sweden.**
Curt Weibull, translated from the Swedish by Alan Tapsell.
Stockholm: Svenska Bokförlaget-Bonniers, 1966. 186p. bibliog.

A scholarly, well-written work that emphasizes in particular her rule of Sweden, conversion to Catholicism, abdication, and first years of self-imposed exile. First published in Swedish in 1931 and 1934, it is the most thoughtful and least sensational of several biographies in English on the subject.

Eighteenth-century Sweden (1721–1814)

228 Gustavus III and his contemporaries (1742–1792): an overlooked chapter of 18th century history (from original documents).
Robert Nisbet Bain. New York: Bergman, 1970. 2 vols. bibliog.

Published originally in 1894 (London: Kegan Paul, Trench, Trubner), this work is, amazingly enough, the only full-length biography of Gustav III in English. It is literary and eloquent but now dated because it lacks access to the research done on the Swedish king during the 20th century. For a brief but able summary of this monarch for the general reader, see Oliver Warner's 'Gustavus III, King of Sweden', *History Today*, vol. 16, no. 2 (1966), p. 103–10.

229 The amazing career of Bernadotte 1763–1844.
Dunbar Plunket Barton. London: John Murray, 1930. 2nd ed.
404p. maps. bibliog.

First published in 1929, it summarizes Barton's earlier three-volume biography of the French Revolutionary general and Swedish king: *Bernadotte, the first phase (1763–99)*, (London: John Murray, 1914); *Bernadotte and Napoleon (1799–1810)* (London: John Murray, 1921); and *Bernadotte, Prince and King (1810–44)* (London: John Murray, 1925). It is a clear, thorough study.

230 Count Axel von Fersen: aristocrat in an age of Revolution.
H. Arnold Barton. Boston, Massachusetts: Twayne, 1975. 530p.
bibliog. (Library of Scandinavian Studies, vol. 3).

The major work in English on the Swedish aristocrat that describes his participation in the American Revolutionary War, involvement in the French Revolution, and role in Swedish politics during the reigns of Gustav III and Gustav IV Adolf. It contains a detailed bibliography of works relevant to both European and Scandinavian history during the late 18th century.

231 Gustav III and the Enlightenment.
H. Arnold Barton. *Eighteenth Century Studies*, vol. 6, no. 1
(1972), p. 1–34.

Discusses the early influence of Enlightenment *philosophes* on the king, his reforms in Sweden, and his gradual disenchantment with the movement during the 1780s.

232 **Late Gustavian autocracy in Sweden: Gustav IV Adolf and his opponents, 1792–1809.**
H. Arnold Barton. *Scandinavian Studies*, vol. 46, no. 3 (1974), p. 265–84.

A scholarly treatment of the enigmatic king (1792–1809), the instigators of the revolution in 1809 which unseated him, and of the period's significance in Swedish history. A concise but major treatment of the period.

233 **Russia and the problem of Sweden–Finland, 1721–1809.**
H. Arnold Barton. *East European Quarterly*, vol. 5, no. 4 (1972), p. 431–55.

Considers the conflict between the Hats and Caps in the *Riksdag* (Parliament) on foreign policy and the events that led to the cession of Finland to Russia in 1809.

234 **Scandinavia in the revolutionary era, 1760–1815.**
H. Arnold Barton. Minneapolis, Minnesota: University of Minnesota Press, 1986. 445p. maps. bibliog. (Nordic Series, vol. 12).

Emphasis is placed on economic and cultural developments as well as on internal political affairs and the involvement of the Scandinavian states in the Napoleonic Wars. Topics affecting Sweden in particular include the rule of Gustav III (1772–92), the Revolution of 1809, Sweden's participation in the final coalition against Napoleon, and the union of Sweden and Norway in 1814.

235 **The Swedish succession crises of 1809 and 1810, and the question of Scandinavian union.**
H. Arnold Barton. *Scandinavian Studies*, vol. 42, no. 3 (1970), p. 309–33.

Discusses the interest in a reunification of Denmark, Norway, and Sweden that prevailed in the late 18th century and the role this dream played in the search by Sweden for a successor to the throne in both 1809 and 1810. Useful both for its discussion of Scandinavianism and the political crisis that prevailed throughout Scandinavia during this part of the Napoleonic period.

236 **Sweden in the 1760s.**
Sten Carlsson. In: *Sweden's development from poverty to affluence, 1750–1970*. Edited by Steven Koblik. Minneapolis, Minnesota: University of Minnesota Press, 1975, p. 17–35.

Examines political developments in Sweden during the decade and their social and economic implications, using the ideas developed by Robert R. Palmer in *The age of democratic revolution* (Princeton, New Jersey: Princeton University Press, 1969–70), 2 vols., as a point of reference for his observations. An excellent introduction to mid-18th century Sweden. For a thorough study of 18th-century

History. Eighteenth-century Sweden (1721–1814)

Swedish society by the same author, see his *Ståndssamhälle och ståndspersoner 1700–1865: studier rörande det svenska ståndssamhällets upplösning* [Social class and the élite, 1700–1865: studies of the dissolution of the Swedish class-system] (Lund: Gleerup, 1973).

237 **Tyrannicide and the right of resistance, 1792–1809: a study of J. J. Anckarström.**
Stig Jägerskiöld. *Scandinavian Studies in Law*, vol. 8 (1964), p. 67–103.
A thoughtful essay on the role of tyrannicide and right of resistance as they influenced the murderers of King Gustav III in 1792 and the 'men of 1809' who deposed Gustav IV Adolf.

238 **Russia, England and Swedish party politics 1762–1766: the interplay between Great Power diplomacy and domestic politics during Sweden's Age of Liberty.**
Michael F. Metcalf. Stockholm: Almqvist & Wiksell International; Totowa, New Jersey: Rowman & Littlefield, 1977. 278p. bibliog. (Studies presented to the International Commission for the History of Representative and Parliamentary Institutions).
Examines the interests that Britain and Russia possessed in Swedish politics and foreign policy, the means they employed to influence members of Sweden's *Riksdag* (Parliament) and the results of the body's deliberations: a detailed study of an important aspect of 18th-century Swedish political life. A dissertation prepared as part of a research project in history at the University of Stockholm, 'The development of a party system: parties, parliamentary practice and parliamentary ideas in Sweden, 1680–1772'.

239 **The first 'modern' party system?: political parties, Sweden's Age of Liberty and the historians.**
Michael F. Metcalf. *Scandinavian Journal of History*, vol. 2, no. 4 (1977), p. 264–87.
Sketches a survey of political developments in Sweden from 1720 to 1772, summarizes the views of later Swedish historians on the topic, and applies 20th-century political scientists' criteria of political parties and systems to the Hats and Caps of the 18th century. A valuable introduction to these subjects.

240 **Sweden.**
Michael Roberts. In: *The European nobility in the eighteenth century: studies of the nobilities of the major European states in the pre-Reform era.* Edited by Albert Goodwin. New York; Evanston, Illinois: Harper & Row, 1967, p. 136–53.
Surveys Sweden's aristocracy from 1718 to 1772, the country's 'Age of Liberty' when they dominated politics and all other important activities. An excellent, brief introduction.

61

241 **The Age of Liberty: Sweden 1719–1772.**
Michael Roberts. Cambridge, England: Cambridge University
Press, 1986. 233p. bibliog.

A political history of the period emphasizing foreign affairs and parliamentary
development. Concise, and well written for both the scholar and general reader.

242 **Murder at the masked ball: the assassination of Gustaf III of
Sweden.**
Gardar Sahlberg, translated from the Swedish by Paul Britten
Austin. London: Macdonald, 1974. 424p. maps.

An account of the conspiracy which developed against the Swedish king, and his
assassination in 1792. Semi-fictional because of its creation of conversations and
events which cannot be substantiated but otherwise a fair reconstruction of one of
the most shocking events in Swedish history. First published as *Den aristokratiska
ligan* (The aristocratic league) (Stockholm: Bonniers, 1969). A well-written
introduction to the period for the general reader.

243 **Bernadotte and the fall of Napoleon.**
Franklin D. Scott. Cambridge, Massachusetts; London:
Humphrey Milford, Oxford University Press, 1935. 190p. bibliog.
Harvard Historical Monographs, vol. 7).

Still a masterly study of Sweden's role among the allies opposed to Napoleon,
Crown Prince Karl Johan's (Jean Jules Baptiste Bernadotte's) rivalry with
Napoleon and his ambition to become the king of France.

244 **Castlereagh, Bernadotte and Norway.**
Lars Tangeraas. *Scandinavian Journal of History*, vol. 8, no. 3
(1983), p. 193–223.

Describes: the origin during the Napoleonic Wars of the 'Norwegian question' or
the possibility of separating Norway from Denmark and uniting it with Sweden;
Crown Prince Karl Johan of Sweden's determination to achieve this goal; his
activities during 1813–14 that led to the Treaty of Kiel in January 1814; the
apparent success of this objective; and Norwegian resistance in 1814 which
complicated the British position on this matter.

245 **Bernadotte: a biography.**
Friedrich Wencker-Wildberg, translated from the German by
Kenneth Kirkness. London: Jarrolds, 1936. 317p. bibliog.

A biography for the general reader which deals mainly with Bernadotte's career
as a French Revolutionary general and as Crown Prince of Sweden through the
defeat of Napoleon in the spring of 1814. His rivalry with the French Emperor is a
major theme.

Nineteenth-century Sweden (1814–1914)

246 **The *Mittelstand* in Swedish class society, 1870–1914.**
Tom Ericsson. *Scandinavian Journal of History*, vol. 9, no. 4 (1984), p. 313–28.

Examines the values and concerns of Sweden's lower middle class of shopkeepers and artisans at the turn of the 20th century, and places this group within a European context. An excellent, often-cited work by a leading scholar of the subject.

247 **Ideology and social policy in the mid-nineteenth century.**
Ingrid Hammarström. *Scandinavian Journal of History*, vol. 4, no. 2 (1979), p. 163–85.

Examines the forms of social policy which developed during the mid-19th century in Sweden, describes the research project at Uppsala University to study them, and places these ideas within the context of similar phenomena in Western Europe. A concise survey by an expert in the field.

248 **Structural change and economic growth in nineteenth-century Sweden.**
Lennart Jörberg. In: *Sweden's development from poverty to affluence, 1750–1970*. Edited by Steven Koblik. Minneapolis, Minnesota: University of Minnesota Press, 1975, p. 92–135.

Discusses factors which affected economic development in Sweden during the 19th century such as population increase and agricultural change. It also considers other important topics that contributed to the development of the Industrial Revolution in Sweden. The article is a revised version of that in *Economics and History*, vol. 8 (1965), p. 3–46; and *Essays in European economic history 1789–1914*, edited by F. Crouziet, W. H. Chaloner, and W. M. Stern (New York: St. Martin's Press, 1969), p. 259–80.

249 **Town planning in Sweden and Finland until the middle of the nineteenth century.**
Eino Jutikaala. *Scandinavian Economic History Review*, vol. 16, no. 1 (1968), p. 19–46. maps.

Analyses the implementation of town planning by the government of Sweden-Finland from 1600 until the mid-19th century, the reasons for the changes made, and the consequences of this policy. An interesting facet of governmental policy by a distinguished Finnish scholar.

250 **British views on Norwegian–Swedish problems 1880–1895:**
selections from diplomatic correspondence.
Edited by Paul Knaplund.   Oslo: Jacob Dybwad, 1952. 269p.
(Norsk Historisk Kjeldeskrift-Institut).

Edited correspondence between British diplomatic officials in Stockholm and
Christiania (Oslo) and the Foreign Office during the period when the 19th-century
union between Norway and Sweden was subject to increasing stress. An
important collection of primary sources for the study of both countries, the union,
and its dissolution in 1905.

251 **Scandinavia in great power politics 1905–1908.**
Folke Lindberg.   Stockholm: Almqvist & Wiksell, 1958. 330p.
(Acta Universitatis Stockholmiensis: Stockholm Studies in
History).

Examines two major issues in Swedish foreign policy prior to the First World
War. The first section discusses Norway's declaration of independence from
Sweden in 1905 and its request for an Integrity Treaty that revealed British and
Swedish security interests in the Baltic and North Sea. The second part describes
Sweden's difficulties as it was caught between competing Russian and German
interests in the Baltic during the same period.

252 **Norway–Sweden: union, disunion and Scandinavian integration.**
Raymond E. Lindgren.   Westport, Connecticut: Greenwood
Press, 1979. 298p. bibliog.

The main theme is the pressure in Norway on the union with Sweden during the
19th century and its dissolution in 1905. The book, first printed in 1959
(Princeton, New Jersey: Princeton University Press), is the chief source in English
on this subject.

253 **The economic development of continental Europe 1780–1870.**
Alan S. Milward, S. B. Saul.   London: George Allen & Unwin,
1979. 2nd ed. 548p. maps. bibliog.

Three chapters discuss general trends and developments and there are also several
chapters on specific parts of Europe. The section on Scandinavia (p. 467–535)
includes a unit on Sweden (p. 481–502) describing basic economic developments
of the period. A brief bibliography of materials in English relating to Scandinavia
is included. The book was first published in 1973.

254 **Agrarian structure and peasant politics in Scandinavia: a**
comparative study of rural response to economic change.
Øyvind Østerud.   Oslo: Universitetsforlaget, 1978. 279p. bibliog.

An extended discussion of the theoretical framework of the book is followed by a
detailed description of the agrarian structure of society, landholding and the
transformations that took place in it through enclosure and other forms of
agricultural change during the 19th century. The work concludes with a discussion
of the nature of peasant participation in politics in each of the Scandinavian

countries during the 19th century and the peasant movements that arose during the same period.

255 **Years of crisis, 1906–1914.**
Berndt Schiller. In: *Sweden's development from poverty to affluence, 1750–1970.* Edited by Steven Koblik. Minneapolis, Minnesota: University of Minnesota Press, 1975, p. 197–228.

Three issues – suffrage, the General Strike of 1909, and defence – made the decade one of political crisis in Sweden. They also resulted in the beginning of the demise of Sweden's Liberty Party and the continued power and dominance of the Conservatives. For a similar study in the same work, see Sven Lundkvist's 'Popular movements and reforms, 1900–1920' (p. 180–83).

256 **Causes of poverty in Sweden in the nineteenth century.**
Johan Söderberg. *Journal of European Economic History,* vol. 11, no. 2 (1982), p. 369–402. maps.

Examines the extent of poverty and the reasons for it in mid-19th century Sweden and discusses several recent works that deal with this subject.

257 **Parliamentary reform in Sweden, 1866–1921.**
Douglas V. Verney. Oxford: Clarendon Press, 1957. 295p. bibliog.

Describes the process of political change in Sweden through the transformation of the *Riksdag* (Parliament) from a four- to a two-house legislative body and the establishment of universal suffrage in 1921. This is the most important study of these developments.

258 **The union with Norway.**
Jörgen Weibull. In: *Sweden's development from poverty to affluence, 1750–1970.* Edited by Steven Koblik. Minneapolis, Minnesota: University of Minnesota Press, 1975, p. 68–88.

A concise survey of the union between Sweden and Norway from 1814 to 1914, and a brief analysis of the effects which the union had on both countries. For the events of 1814, see his *Carl Johan och Norge 1810–1814* (Karl Johan and Norway 1810–1814) (Gothenburg, 1957).

Modern Sweden, 1914–40

259 **The building of modern Sweden: the reign of Gustav V 1907–1950.**
O. Fritiof Ander. Rock Island, Illinois: Augustana College, 1958. 271p. (Augustana Library Publications, no. 28).

Considerable emphasis is given to economic and social conditions prior to the First World War, Sweden's neutrality during this conflict, the development of social democracy during the Depression years, and the Second World War. A good introduction to Sweden during the first half of this century.

260 **The Aland Islands question: its settlement by the League of Nations.**
James Barros. New Haven, Connecticut; London: Yale University Press, 1968. 362p. maps. bibliog.

Discusses the controversy over ownership of the islands that developed during the First World War between Sweden and Finland and the resolution of the issue by the League of Nations. A thorough treatment of the subject.

261 **The incredible Ivar Kreuger.**
Allen Churchill. New York: Rinehart; Toronto, Canada: Clarke, Irwin, 1957. 301p.

A detailed study of the international financier and 'Match King'. Valuable for its account of the man and its discussion of Swedish business during the first decades of the 20th century.

262 **Sweden, Norway, Denmark and Iceland in the World War.**
Eli Heckscher, Knut Bergendal, Wilhelm Keilhau, Einar Cohn, Thorstein Thorsteinsson. New Haven, Connecticut: Yale University Press; London: Humphrey Milford, Oxford University Press, 1930. 593p. (Economic and Social History of the World War).

Published for the Carnegie Endowment for International Peace, this is an abridgement of the Scandinavian Series of nine monographs edited by Eli Heckscher and Harald Westergaard. Heckscher and Bergendal wrote the section on Sweden (p. 3–268), the former contributing a section on the country's monetary policy from 1914 to 1925 and the latter on Sweden's trade and shipping policy during the First World War.

263 **Economic policy in Scandinavia during the inter-war period.**
Karl-Gustaf Hildebrand. *Scandinavian Economic History Review*, vol. 23, no. 2 (1976), p. 99–115.

Reviews the conference report, *Kriser och krispolitik: Norden under mellankrigstiden* (Crises and crisis policy: Scandinavia during the inter-war period) (Uppsala, 1974) and summarizes its findings. An excellent review of the main economic and political developments in Scandinavia during the 1920s and 1930s.

264 **The Scandinavian states and the League of Nations.**
S. Shepard Jones. New York: Greenwood Press, 1969. 298p. bibliog.

Although first published in 1939 (Princeton, New Jersey: Princeton University Press for the American–Scandinavian Foundation), the volume remains the major study of this subject. Themes discussed include the role of the Scandinavian states in the founding of the League, their positions on questions of its structure, and their role in matters of conciliation, disarmament, and mandate and international territories.

265 **Scandinavia 1914–1970.**
Lennart Jörberg, Olle Krantz, translated by Paul Britten Austin. In: *Contemporary economics*. Edited by Carlo M. Cipolla. New York: Barnes & Noble; Sussex, England: Harvester Press, 1977, p. 377–459. bibliog. (Fontana Economic History of Europe, vol. 6, part 2).

An outline of the main trends in the economic development of Finland, Sweden, Norway, and Denmark during the period. The authors discuss economic growth, population developments, foreign trade, agricultural and industrial development, and the role of the state in economic policy. A concise summary of developments, given added value by numerous tables, diagrams and an extensive bibliography.

266 **Sweden: the neutral victor: Sweden and the Western Powers 1917–1918: a study of Anglo-American relations.**
Steven Koblik. Lund, Sweden: Läromedelsförlagen, 1972. 233p. bibliog. (Lund Studies in International History; Scandinavian University Books).

Examines Sweden's policy of neutrality during the First World War, the relationship between Sweden's international problems and domestic change, and the degree to which Great Britain and the United States were able to formulate a common policy towards Sweden. A well-written description of a critical period in Swedish history. For articles by Koblik pertaining to the same subject, see 'Wartime diplomacy and the democratization of Sweden in September–October 1917', *Journal of Modern History*, vol. 41, no. 1 (1969), p. 28–45 and 'The politics of Swedish neutrality: Sweden and the Western Powers', *Historisk Tidskrift* (Sweden), no. 1 (1972), p. 52–71.

267 **Who were the Fascists: social roots of European Fascism.**
Edited by Stein Ugelvik Larson, Bernt Hagtvet, Jan Petter Myklebust. Bergen, Norway: Universitetsforlaget, 1980. 816p. maps. bibliog.

Contains articles discussing the development of Fascism in different parts of Europe and comparative articles seeking to establish common factors in the various movements. 'On the fringe: Swedish Fascism' (p. 715–42) by Bernt Hagtvet examines the splintered, minuscule Fascist movement in Sweden and provides explanations for its failure to secure a larger following during the 1920s and 1930s in Sweden.

268 **Fascism in Scandinavia: 1920–1940.**
Ulf Lindström. Stockholm: Almqvist & Wiksell, 1985. 196p. maps. bibliog.

Explains the failure of Fascism to develop in the Scandinavian countries in terms of their political institutions and the policies followed by the governments of the region. A major scholarly work on the subject.

269 **How Sweden overcame the Depression 1930–1933.**
Arthur Montgomery. Stockholm: Alb. Bonniers, 1938. 91p.
Examines the nature of Sweden's economy prior to and following the First World War, the reasons for the development of the Depression in Sweden in 1930–31, and government policies to combat the crisis both before and after the creation of a Social Democratic government in 1932. Still a respected, useful discussion by a prominent economic historian.

270 **Nordic societies.**
Henrik Nissen. In: *Scandinavia during the Second World War.*
Edited by Henrik Nissen. Minneapolis, Minnesota: University of Minnesota Press, 1983, p. 3–52. (Nordic Series, vol. 9).
An introduction to the Scandinavian countries during the 1930s emphasizing economic organization and developments and the political structures of the different countries, and providing a brief outline of their foreign policies on the eve of the Second World War.

271 **The decline of neutrality 1914–1941, with special reference to the United States and the Northern neutrals.**
Nils Ørvik. Oslo: Johan Grundt Tanum Forlag, 1953. 294p. bibliog.
Studies the different forms of neutrality practised during the period, offering the United States and the Scandinavian countries as contrasting studies of the policies developed during this time of crisis.

272 **Gustaf V and Swedish attitudes toward Germany, 1915.**
Franklin D. Scott. *Journal of Modern History*, vol. 34, no. 2 (1967), p. 113–18.
A short introduction to opinion in Sweden regarding the First World War, the king's active role in government until 1915, and a translation of a memorandum of a conversation between Gustav V and two pro-German members of the Riksdag in December 1915. Valuable for its documentation of the king's views on foreign policy and his role as Sweden's king.

273 **Kreuger: genius and swindler.**
Robert Shaplen. New York; London: Garland Publishing, 1986.
251p. (Accounting Thought and Practice Through the Years).
A biography first printed in 1960 (New York: Knopf) that examines Kreuger's private life, personality, and the financial empire he created and lost. A well-written work for both the scholar and general reader. For other studies of Kreuger, See Torsten Kreuger's defence, *The truth about Ivar Kreuger: eyewitness documents, secret files, documents* (Stuttgart, West Germany: Seewald,

1968) and Lars Hassbring's solid *The international development of the Swedish Match Company 1917–1924* (Stockholm: Liber Förlag, 1979).

274 **The crisis agreement and the Social Democratic road to power.**
Sven Anders Söderpalm. In: *Sweden's development from poverty to affluence, 1750–1970.* Edited by Steven Koblik. Minneapolis, Minnesota: University of Minnesota Press, 1975, p. 258–78.

Traces the political background and negotiation of the Crisis Agreement of 1933, by which the Agrarian and Social Democratic parties entered into an historic majority coalition government. Brief consideration is also given to the continued cooperation between the two parties after the Second World War and its influence on the development of an economic policy possessing a broad, multi-party consensus. Discusses a crucial event in modern Swedish political history.

275 **The debate on the foreign policy of Sweden 1918–1939.**
Herbert Tingsten, translated from the Swedish by Joan Bulman. London; New York: Oxford University Press, 1949. 325p.

Examines major issues in Swedish foreign policy during the period and discussion of them by the Swedish press. An interesting, thorough study.

The Second World War, 1940–45

276 **Swedish foreign policy during the Second World War.**
W. M. Carlgren, translated from the Swedish by Arthur Spencer. London: Ernest Benn, 1977. 257p. maps. bibliog.

An abridged translation of *Svensk utrikespolitik 1939–1945* (Swedish foreign policy 1939–1945) (Stockholm: Allmänna Förlaget, 1973) written for the Royal Ministry for Foreign Affairs. The emphasis is almost totally on Swedish diplomacy with the warring powers from 1939 until the end of the Second World War with little discussion of the domestic implications of these developments. An excellent, thorough, even-handed introduction to the topic.

277 **Battles for Scandinavia.**
John R. Elting and the editors of Time-Life Books. Alexandria, Virginia: Time-Life Books, 1981. 208p. maps. bibliog. (World War II, vol. 28).

A survey of the Second World War in Scandinavia, illustrated with many drawings and photographs. Does not provide the depth found in more detailed scholarly studies but is still a useful introduction for the general reader and young student.

278 **The adaptable nation: essays in Swedish economy during the Second World War.**
Martin Fritz, Ingemar Nygren, Sven-Olof Olsson. Ulf Olsson.
Stockholm: Almqvist & Wiksell International, 1982. 109p. map.
bibliog. (Publications of the Institute of Economic History of
Gothenburg University, vol. 50).

Five essays that discuss particularly the themes of German–Swedish trade during
the war, the increased role of the state in the economy as a result of wartime
rearmament, and government borrowing for defence and its impact on the credit
market. Represents the strong interest that has developed among Swedish
scholars in the economic implications of neutrality during the Second World War.
See also his *German steel and Swedish iron ore 1939–1945*, translated from the
Swedish by Eva and Allan Greene (Gothenburg, Sweden: Institute of Economic
History, Gothenburg University, 1974).

279 **Diplomat: memoirs of a Swedish envoy in London, Paris, Berlin, Moscow, Washington.**
Gunner Hägglöf, foreword by Graham Greene.   London: Bodley
Head, 1972. 221p.

The author's memoirs of his service as a Swedish diplomat from the 1920s until
the end of the Second World War. The work is interesting, perceptive, anecdotal,
and suitable for all readers.

280 **Sweden's ambiguous neutrality.**
Erik Lönnroth.   *Scandinavian Journal of History*, vol. 2, nos 1–2
(1977), p. 89–105.

Discusses Swedish foreign policy at the beginning of the Second World War and
during Finland's Winter War with Russia and briefly describes the research
project 'Sweden during World War II' conducted by historians at the University
of Stockholm. An important, concise discussion of these subjects. Reprinted in
Scandinavians: selected historical essays (q.v.).

281 **Scandinavia between the Great Powers: attempts at mediation in the first year of the Second World War.**
Peter W. Ludlow.   *Historisk Tidskrift* (Sweden), no. 1 (1974),
p. 1–58.

Describes the efforts by Scandinavian governments and individuals to end the
Second World War, from the autumn of 1939 to the spring of 1940.

282 **Parliamentary politics during World War II.**
Karl Molin. In: *Sweden's development from poverty to affluence,
1750–1970.* Edited by Steven Koblik. Minneapolis, Minnesota:
University of Minnesota Press, 1975, p. 305–31.

Discusses the role of the *Riksdag* (Parliament) during the war, the centres of
opposition to governmental policy within the legislative bodies, and the varying
degrees of opposition on matters of foreign policy, defence, and budget issues. A
sound survey of the subject.

283 **The strategy of phoney war: Britain, Sweden and the iron ore
question 1939–1940.**
Thomas Munch-Petersen. Stockholm: Militärhistoriska Förlaget,
1981. 296p. map. bibliog. (Militärhistoriska Studier, no. 5).

Examines Anglo–Swedish relations from the beginning of the Second World War
to the end of the Norwegian campaign in June 1940. A thorough study that
touches on issues from an unusual and important perspective.

284 **Scandinavia during the Second World War.**
Edited by Henrik Nissen, translated by Thomas
Munch-Petersen. Minneapolis, Minnesota: University of
Minnesota Press; Oslo: Universitetsforlaget, 1983. 407p. maps.
bibliog. (Nordic Series, vol. 9).

An excellent work containing eight articles by Scandinavian scholars covering the
region from the 1930s until 1949. The chronological account stresses events in the
Scandinavian countries that actually became involved in the war but adequate
coverage is also given to the measures taken by Sweden's government to preserve
its neutrality. A detailed and partially annotated bibliography is particularly
useful.

285 **German coal and Swedish fuel 1939–1945.**
Sven-Olof Olsson, translated from the Swedish by Eva and Allan
Greene. Gothenburg, Sweden: Institute of Economic History,
Gothenburg University, 1975. 348p. maps. bibliog. (Publication of
the Institute of Economic History of Gothenburg University,
vol. 36).

A dissertation produced as part of the Institute's special research project 'Under
pressure from abroad: sectors of the Swedish economy 1939–1945'. Studies
Swedish dependence on German coal before and during the Second World War,
German efforts to use Swedish demand for coal in trade and diplomatic
negotiations with Sweden during the war, and Swedish efforts to reduce their
dependence on this source of fuel by developing domestic substitutes and
regulating fuel use. A thorough study which also reflects the interest of recent
Swedish historians in the economic ramifications of the war.

286 **The creation of a modern arms industry: Sweden 1939-1974.**
Ulf Olsson, translated from the Swedish by Eva and Allan
Greene. Gothenburg, Sweden: Institute of Economic History,
Gothenburg University, 1977. 207p. bibliog. (Publications of the
Institute of Economic History of Gothenburg University, vol. 37).
A dissertation produced as part of the 'Under pressure from abroad: sectors of
the Swedish economy 1939–1945' special research project. Concentrates primarily
on domestic rearmament efforts during the Second World War. See also the
author's article on the same subject 'The state and industry in Swedish
rearmament during the Second World War', *Scandinavian Journal of History*,
vol. 4, no. 3 (1979), p. 231–51.

Historiography

287 **Source-criticism and literary history: Lauritz Weibull, Henrik
Schück and Joseph Bédier: a discussion.**
Rolf Arvidsson, H. R. Loyn, Lucien Musset, Björn Þorsteinsson,
Algot Werin, K. Wührer, Hugo Yrwing, Tore Nyberg. *Medieval
Scandinavia*, vol. 5 (1972), p. 96–138.
An introductory essay by Arvidsson discusses the influence of the late 19th-
century historians on Lauritz Weibull, one of Sweden's most influential and
controversial historians of the early 20th century, and the possible links and
similarities between Weibull and Bédier, the prominent French literary historian.
This is followed by replies from the contributors. An important contribution to
the very limited number of discussions in English of Swedish historiography. See
also Arne Odd Johnsen's article in the same journal 'The Lauritz Weibull
discussion: a Norwegian contribution', vol. 10 (1977), p. 179–87.

288 **Gothic patriotism and Olof Rudbeck.**
Ernst Ekman. *Journal of Modern History*, vol. 34, no. 1 (1962),
p. 52–64.
Examines the tradition of 'Gothic patriotism' (belief in the establishment of the
early mediaeval Swedish state by the Goths) from the 15th century through the
historical works of Olof Rudbeck in the late 17th century. It also discusses
Rudbeck's activities as a professor of natural sciences and rector of the University
of Uppsala. A brief, valuable study of Swedish historiography.

289 **Scandinavian history in international research: some observations on Britain, France, West Germany and East Germany.**
Carl-Axel Gemzell. *Scandinavian Journal of History*, vol. 5, no. 4 (1980), p. 239–56.
A detailed account of the research done by historians as well as social scientists from these countries on Scandinavian topics.

290 **Some notes on Swedish historiography.**
Ragnhild Hatton. *History* (June 1952), p. 98–113.
Surveys historical research in Sweden during the late 19th century and first half of the 20th century. It describes the primary Swedish historians of the period, their main areas of interest, the education of historians, and the main Swedish historical publications. Points out the need for a similar article on Swedish historical work during the last three decades.

291 **Swedish medieval society: previous research and recent developments.**
Thomas Lindkvist. *Scandinavian Journal of History*, vol. 4, no. 4 (1979), p. 253–68.
Examines the major themes, basic conclusions, and most significant contributors since 1940 to the study of Swedish social history during the Middle Ages.

292 **A conversation with Ingrid Hammarström: urban history in Sweden.**
Bruce M. Stave. *Journal of Urban History*, vol. 9, no. 4 (1983), p. 473–500. bibliog.
Describes Hammarström's education and research as well as developments in, and the study of, urban history in Sweden at the present time. A bibliography of Hammarström's research is included.

293 **Recent developments in Swedish social history of the period since 1800.**
Bo Stråth. *Social History*, vol. 9, no. 1 (1984), p. 77–85. bibliog.
Discusses work by Swedish scholars in fields such as demography, emigration and social history during the 1960s and 1970s. A valuable survey with a bibliography of recent works on these topics.

294 **Minimum demands and optimum norms in Swedish historical research, 1920–1960: the 'Weibull school' in Swedish historiography.**
Rolf Torstendahl. *Scandinavian Journal of History*, vol. 6, no. 2 (1981), p. 117–41.
Studies the historiographical contributions of Lauritz and Curt Weibull, professors of history at the University of Lund, and their students. The brothers

adopted a positivist approach to historical evidence foreign to the Universities of
Stockholm and Uppsala. The historical work of Sture Bolin, Ingvar Andersson,
Sven A. Nilsson, and Erik Lönnroth is also considered.

295 **Sweden: secrecy and neutrality.**
     Krister Wahlbäck. *Journal of Contemporary History*, vol. 2,
     no. 1 (1967), p. 183–90.
Considers the difficulties associated with writing contemporary diplomatic history
in Sweden, legislation restricting access to government records, and the dearth of
publications on recent Swedish history. Should be read with the understanding
that many of these conditions have changed, although it is an interesting
commentary on historiographical conditions from 1945 to the late 1960s. Also
printed in *The new history: trends in historical research and writing since World
War II* edited by Walter Laqueur and George L. Mosse (New York; Evanston,
Illinois: Harper & Row, 1967), p. 176–84.

296 **Schweden als europäische Grossmacht der frühen Neuzeit.** (Sweden
     as a European great power of the early modern period.)
     Klaus Zernack. *Historische Zeitschrift*, vol. 232, no. 2 (1981),
     p. 327–57.
Provides a historiographical sketch of Sweden during the Age of Greatness that
includes explanations for the establishment of the Swedish empire and reasons for
its collapse. A major contribution to the study of the period by reason of its
scope, sources, and views.

Scandinavia past and present.
See item no. 15.

Scandinavia.
See item no. 24.

The description of Swedland, Gotland, and Finland.
See item no. 50.

A journal of the Swedish embassy in the years 1653 and 1654.
See item no. 58.

Urban development in the Alpine and Scandinavian countries.
See item no. 63.

Norden: crossroads of destiny and progress.
See item no. 66.

Urban archaeology in Sweden.
See item no. 124.

**Pre-industrial economy and population structure: the elements of
variance in early modern Sweden.**
See item no. 309.

Sweden's attempt to aid Jews, 1939–1945.
See item no. 333.

Reaktionen mot utvandringen: emigrationsfrågan i svensk debatt och politik 1901–1904. (The reaction to emigration: the emigration question in Swedish debate and politics, 1901–04.)
See item no. 355.

Emigrationsutredningen: betänkande och bilagor. (The emigration study: report and appendixes.)
See item no. 365.

Bishop Hill: a utopia on the prairie.
See item no. 369.

A history of New Sweden.
See item no. 370.

Svenska öden vid Delaware 1638–1831. (Swedish destinies on the Delaware, 1638–1831.)
See item no. 372.

Svenska kyrkans mission vid Delaware i Nord-Amerika. (The Swedish Church's mission on the Delaware in North America.)
See item no. 373.

Scandinavian language contacts.
See item no. 376.

Women of the Reformation from Spain to Scandinavia.
See item no. 406.

A critic of the fourteenth century: St. Birgitta of Sweden.
See item no. 407.

Olavus Petri and the ecclesiastical transformation in Sweden 1521–1552: a study in the Swedish Reformation.
See item no. 408.

Rome and the Counter Reformation in Scandinavia until the establishment of the S. *congregatio de propaganda fide* in 1622 based on the source material in the Kalsrud collection.
See item no. 411.

Emanuel Swedenborg.
See item no. 417.

Saint Bridget of Sweden.
See item no. 418.

A brief history of the Church of Sweden: origins and modern structure.
See item no. 420.

The English missionaries in Sweden and Finland.
See item no. 424.

The Swedenborg epic: the life and works of Emanuel Swedenborg.
See item no. 425.

The reception of the Augsburg Confession in Scandinavia.
See item no. 426.

Swedenborg: life and teaching.
See item no. 428.

An archbishop of the Reformation: Laurentius Petri Nericus Archbishop of Uppsala, 1531–73: a study of his liturgical projects.
See item no. 430.

A history of Uppsala University 1477–1977.
See item no. 442.

Réveil national et culture populaire en Scandinavie: la genèse de la højskole nordique. (National awakening and popular culture in Scandinavia: the birth of the Nordic folk high school.)
See item no. 452.

The evolution of social welfare policy in Sweden.
See item no. 500.

Modern social politics in Britain and Sweden: from relief to income maintenance.
See item no. 504.

The growth of social insurance programs in Scandinavia: outside influences and internal forces.
See item no. 509.

The debate on economic planning in Sweden.
See item no. 510.

The Swedish electorate 1887–1968.
See item no. 548.

The politics of compromise: a study of parties and cabinet government in Sweden.
See item no. 565.

The growth of Scandinavian law.
See item no. 576.

Stockholm: the politics of crime and conflict, 1750 to the 1970s.
See item no. 584.

Sweden's foreign policy.
See item no. 587.

Sweden and the Cold War: the structure of a neglected field of research.
See item no. 588.

Power-balance and non-alignment: a perspective on Swedish foreign policy.
See item no. 589.

Neutrality and defence: the Swedish experience.
See item no. 592.

The Scandinavian option: opportunities and opportunity costs in postwar Scandinavian foreign policies.
See item no. 596.

Winning the peace: vision and disappointment in Nordic security policy 1945–49.
See item no. 600.

'Scandinavianism'.
See item no. 601.

At gun point: a critical perspective on the attempts of the Nordic governments to achieve unity after the Second World War.
See item no. 602.

Foreign policies of Northern Europe.
See item no. 605.

Great Britain and the problem of bases in the Nordic areas 1945–1947.
See item no. 611.

America, Scandinavia and the Cold War 1945–1949.
See item no. 613.

Count Folke Bernadotte: his life and work.
See item no. 630.

Mediation and assassination: Count Bernadotte's mission to Palestine 1948.
See item no. 631.

Dag Hammarskjöld.
See item no. 632.

Dag Hammarskjold: custodian of the brushfire peace.
See item no. 634.

Hammarskjold.
See item no. 635.

With Raoul Wallenberg in Budapest: memories of the war years in Hungary.
See item no. 637.

Righteous Gentile: the story of Raoul Wallenberg, missing hero of the Holocaust.
See item no. 638.

Wallenberg.
See item no. 639.

Raoul Wallenberg: angel of rescue: heroism and torment in the Gulag.
See item no. 640.

Lost hero: the mystery of Raoul Wallenberg.
See item no. 641.

An economic history of Sweden.
See item no. 648.

Reformist programmes in the planning for post-war economic policy during World War II.
See item no. 664.

A long-term perspective on regional economic development in Sweden, ca. 1580–1914.
See item no. 666.

History of Stockholm's Enskilda Bank to 1914.
See item no. 677.

Banking in a growing economy: Svenska Handelsbanken since 1871.
See item no. 679.

Economic development and the response of labor in Scandinavia: a multi-level analysis.
See item no. 687.

Trade union strategies and social policy in Italy and Sweden.
See item no. 692.

Entrepreneurial activity and the development of Swedish industry, 1919–1939.
See item no. 714.

The small giant: Sweden enters the industrial era.
See item no. 716.

The rise of modern industry in Sweden.
See item no. 719.

History of science in Sweden.
See item no. 766.

The art of Scandinavia.
See item no. 824.

Hundred years of Swedish press history from general surveys to problem-oriented research.
See item no. 912.

Scandinavian Economic History Review.
See item no. 935.

Scandinavian Journal of History.
See item no. 937.

Scandinavian Studies.
See item no. 942.

Famous Swedes.
See item no. 949.

Dictionary of Scandinavian history.
See item no. 956.

Scandinavia: a chronology and fact book.
See item no. 960.

Scandinavia in social science literature: an English-language bibliography.
See item no. 972.

Scandinavian history 1520–1970: a list of books and articles in English.
See item no. 989.

Svensk historisk bibliografi. (Swedish historical bibliography.)
See item no. 995.

The Vikings.
See item no. 1001.

The Swedes and their chieftains.
See item no. 1002.

The Vikings.
See item no. 1012.

Ancient Scandinavia.
See item no. 1013.

Dag Hammarskjöld.
See item no. 1014.

The Vikings.
See item no. 1015.

Population

General

297 **Recent developments in Swedish population policy.**
H. Gille. *Population Studies*, vol. 2, nos 1–2 (1948–49), p. 3–70, 129–84. bibliog.
Examines the work of the Population Commission of 1941–46 and the social legislation which developed from its work.

298 **The biography of a people: past and future population changes in Sweden: conditions and consequences.**
Torsten Hägerstrand (et al.). Stockholm: Royal Ministry for Foreign Affairs, 1974. 204p. maps.
A report prepared for the National Preparatory Committee for the World Population Conference by a committee headed by Torsten Hägerstrand. Past demographic developments and policies are considered, the current situation evaluated, and projections made of future population trends. The social, economic, and educational ramifications of these situations are also considered.

299 **The population debate: the development of conflicting theories up to 1900.**
E. P. Hutchinson. New York: Houghton Mifflin, 1967. 466p.
Examines Swedish contributions to this debate in his chapter 'Swedish population theory in the eighteenth century' (p. 69–93), in which he discusses the demographic views of several 18th-century Swedish scholars. A valuable contribution to this subject. For another discussion of this question by the same author, see 'Swedish population thought in the eighteenth century', *Population Studies*, vol. 13 (1959), p. 81–102. For a discussion of Hutchinson's views, see Gustaf Utterström's 'Labour policy and population thought in eighteenth century Sweden', *Scandinavian Economic History Review*, vol. 10, no. 2 (1962), p. 262–79.

300 **Sweden.**
Lena Jonsson. In: *Population policy in developed countries.*
Edited by Bernard Berelson. New York: McGraw-Hill, 1974,
p. 113–48. bibliog. (Population Council Book).
A concise, informative survey of basic population factors such as: past population
patterns; family planning; birth control and abortion programmes and policy;
immigration to Sweden since the Second World War; and family and child
support programmes.

301 **More children of better quality?: aspects of Swedish population
policy in the 1930s.**
Ann-Sofie Kälvemark. Uppsala, Sweden: Almqvist & Wiksell,
1980. 160p. maps. bibliog. (Acta Universitatis Upsaliensis: Studia
Historica Upsaliensia, vol. 115).
Prepared as part of 'The family in the demographic and social transformation of
Sweden after 1800' research project. Studies the establishment of policies in
Sweden to increase the country's population, the influence of Gunnar and Alva
Myrdal on this programme, their short-term effects and their role in the
development of modern social policy in Sweden. A thorough, informative work
for the scholar and general reader.

302 **The country that kept track of its population: methodological
aspects of Swedish population records.**
Ann-Sofie Kälvemark. *Scandinavian Journal of History*, vol. 2,
no. 3 (1977), p. 211–30. maps.
Describes the nature of Swedish church records and uses marriage records in a
brief study of internal migration within Sweden to indicate their value in
demographic research.

303 **Population policy in Western Europe: responses to low fertility in
France, Sweden, and West Germany.**
C. Alison McIntosh. Armonk, New York; London: M. E.
Sharpe, 1983. 286p. bibliog.
Consideration is given to Swedish developments throughout the work, including a
summary of the origin of Sweden's population policy, but particularly in the
chapter 'Sweden: in pursuit of sexual equality' (p. 134–75) which discusses the
reasons for Sweden's low birth rate and the implications this might have for the
future. It is up-to-date, critical and an excellent survey of the contemporary
situation.

304 **Nation and family: the Swedish experiment in democratic family and population policy.**
Alva Myrdal, introduction by Daniel P. Moynihan. Cambridge, Massachusetts; London: MIT Press, 1968. 441p. bibliog.
First published in 1941 (New York: Harper & Brothers) as a result of the active role Myrdal had played in the formulation of a family policy for Sweden. The author describes the demographic concerns which led to the population policy, its features, and the values and rationale behind its inception. A major work in the study of the development of Sweden's family policy and Myrdal's own role in its development.

305 **Some population problems in pre-industrial Sweden.**
Gustaf Utterström. *Scandinavian Economic History Review*, vol. 2, no. 2 (1954), p. 103–65.
Examines population growth in Sweden during the 18th and 19th centuries. For a similar discussion of the 16th and 17th centuries by the same author, see 'Climatic fluctuations and population problems in Early Modern history', vol. 3, no. 1 (1955), p. 3–47.

Demographic studies

306 **Aristocrats, farmers, proletarians: essays in Swedish demographic history.**
Kurt Ågren, David Gaunt, Ingrid Eriksson, John Rogers, Anders Norborg, Sune Åkerman. Uppsala, Sweden: Almqvist & Wiksell, 1973. 119p. maps. bibliog. (Studia Historica Upsaliensia, vol. 47, Scandinavian University Books).
Four essays on Swedish demographic history that centre on the theme of mobility or migration within society. Ågren discusses demographic and occupational changes within the Swedish nobility during the 17th century; Gaunt examines family planning practices on Gotland during the 18th century; Eriksson and Rogers describe the degree of geographical mobility that existed within the mid-19th century agrarian society; and Norberg and Åkerman consider population changes in industrialized cities in the late 19th century.

307 **Tradition and transition: studies in microdemography and social change.**
Edited by Anders Brändström, Jan Sundin. Umeå, Sweden: University of Umeå, 1981. 255p. maps. bibliog. (Demographic Data Base, University of Umeå, no. 2).
Six demographic studies of conditions in Sweden prior to 1900. Two of the most important discuss methodological aspects of the field, Sune Åkerman's ' "How did the great decline in fertility start?": a study based on retrospective interviews'

(p. 187–240) and Christina Danell's 'The demographic data base at Umeå University' (p. 241–54). All reflect the significant contributions Swedish scholars have made to this field.

308 **Sweden.**
Gunnar Fridlizius. In: *European demography and economic growth.* Edited by W. Robert Lee. New York: St. Martin's Press, 1979, p. 340–405. map.
Studies the impact of demographic changes on economic and social developments in Sweden from 1750 to 1930. A scholarly study of interest to all social scientists and the general reader with some background and serious interest in the subject.

309 **Pre-industrial economy and population structure: the elements of variance in early modern Sweden.**
David Gaunt. *Scandinavian Journal of History*, vol. 2, no. 3 (1977), p. 183–210.
A respected study of selected sites during the 18th century connecting economic livelihood, fertility, and mobility variation. Scholarly, and well written for all interested readers.

310 **The demographic history of the Northern European countries in the eighteenth century.**
H. Gille. *Population Studies*, vol. 3, no. 1 (1950), p. 3–65. bibliog.
A study of demographic conditions in Sweden, Denmark and Norway with an emphasis on the range of population movement, death-rates, marriage, and the birth-rate. An important resource for the study of this subject and historical period.

311 **Swedish population history: main trends from 1750 to 1970.**
Erland Hofsten, Hans Lundström. Stockholm: National Central Bureau of Statistics, 1976. 186p. maps. bibliog. (Urval: Skriftserie utgiven av Statistiska Centralbyrån, no. 8).
Provides a basic survey of the Swedish population during the period, including a detailed discussion of such demographic factors as births, mortality rates, external migration, and distinctive features such as geographical, sex, and age differentiations.

312 **The fertility transition in Sweden: a preliminary look at smaller geographic units, 1855–1890.**
Kenneth A. Lockridge. Umeå, Sweden: University of Umeå, 1983. 140p. maps.
A scholarly study of the development of family limitation behaviour in parishes of central Sweden. Indicative of the themes, methods, and data sources developed and used in Sweden.

313 **Social and economic aspects of Swedish population movements 1750–1933.**
Dorothy Swaine Thomas.   New York: Macmillan, 1941. 487p. map.
An exhaustive study of demographic developments in Sweden and the social and economic changes that followed. Still often cited, and highly regarded for its detail despite its age.

Genealogical study and research

314 **Cradled in Sweden.**
Carl-Erik Johansson.   Logan, Utah: Everton Publishing Company, 1972. 205p.
This is the best genealogical handbook for those of Swedish ancestry, whatever their current nationality. It has everything one could want for making sense of the vast quantity of Swedish material for genealogy. There is even a chapter with illustrations of ideal and real 18th- and 19th-century handwriting.

315 **Tracing your Swedish ancestry.**
Nils William Olsson.   Stockholm: Almqvist & Wiksell, 1985. 26p. map.
Produced by the Swedish Institute for the Ministry for Foreign Affairs, it provides a brief summary of the most useful Swedish documents for genealogical research, difficulties often encountered, and the addresses of Swedish archives and American institutions of greatest assistance in family history. First published in 1963 with several subsequent reprints, by a leading expert in emigration research.

An economic geography of the Scandinavian states and Finland.
See item no. 68.

The Scandinavian northlands.
See item no. 80.

Atlas över Sverige/National Atlas of Sweden.
See item no. 93.

Scandinavia 1914–1970.
See item no. 265.

Recent developments in Swedish social history of the period since 1800.
See item no. 293.

Other dreams, other schools: folk colleges in social and ethnic movements.
See item no. 451.

Scandinavian Population Studies.
See item no. 940.

Minorities and
Special Groups

General

316 **Ethnic minorities.**
Erik Allardt. In: *Nordic democracy: ideas, issues, and institutions in politics, economy, education, social and cultural affairs of Denmark, Finland, Iceland, Norway, and Sweden.* Edited by Erik Allardt, Nils Andrén, Erik J. Friis, Gylfi T. Gislason, Sten Sparre Nilson, Henry Valen, Frantz Wendt, Folmer Wisti. Copenhagen: Det Danske Selskab, 1981, p. 627–49. bibliog.

A brief survey of minority groups in the Nordic countries, including Lapps, Jews, gypsies, and recent immigrants, particularly from Southern Europe.

317 **Minorities.**
Scandinavian Review, vol. 66, no. 1 (1978), 112p.

A special issue of the journal devoted to the subject of Scandinavia's different minority groups today. See, for example, Joseph B. Perry, Jr,'s 'Aliens in a beneficent land', p. 7–14, and Erik Allardt's 'Finns and Swedes as minorities in Sweden and Finland', p. 17–23.

318 **Invandrare och etniska minoriteter: många angelägna forskningsområden. Rapport nr. 1.** (Immigrants and ethnic minorities: many pressing areas of research.)
[Kjell Öberg.] Stockholm: Delegationen för invandrarforskning (DEIFO), 1985. 40p.

This brief but useful summary of the current position of immigration research should be supplemented by the symposium report sponsored by DEIFO in

February 1985, and by a similar survey by one of DEIFO's predecessor groups, Expertgruppen för invandrarforskning (EIFO), whose *Invandrarforskning i Sverige . . . 1975–1983* (Immigrant research in Sweden . . . 1975–1983) (Stockholm: Liber förlag, 1983), 74p, is a summary to that later date of what has been done and what was then in progress.

Lapps

319 **The Lapps.**
Roberto Bosi.   London: Thames & Hudson, 1960. 220p. maps.
bibliog. (Ancient Peoples and Places).

A general study of the Lapps as a people, with little reference to national borders. The book is divided into four basic parts describing their origins and historical development, life and culture, religious beliefs and legends, and their identity as a people. A solid study both for general readers and scholars in the field.

320 **The Lapps.**
Björn Collinder.   New York: Greenwood Press, 1969. 252p.
maps. bibliog.

This survey of the Lapps and Lapp life was first published by Princeton University Press for the American–Scandinavian Foundation in 1949. Collinder describes the development of the Lapps in Norway, Sweden, and Finland, their culture and livelihood. It is an excellent survey both for the scholar and general reader.

321 **Lapponica: essays presented to Israel Ruong.**
Edited by Arne Furumark, Sture Lagerantz, Asbjørn Nesheim,
Geo. Widengren.   Uppsala, Sweden: H. Ohlssons, 1964. 357p.
maps. (Studia Ethnographica Upsaliensia, vol. 21).

A collection of essays on many aspects of Lapp life by leading scholars; many pertain to all Lapps but some only to Swedish topics. All twenty-six essays are in English except for two in German. These contributions are more detailed and scholarly than many other introductory works.

322 **Circumpolar peoples: an anthropological perspective.**
Nelson H. H. Graburn, B. Stephen Strong.   Pacific Palisades,
California: Goodyear Publishing Company, 1973. 236p. maps.
bibliog. (Goodyear Regional Anthropology Series).

A chapter, 'The Samer (Lapps)', p. 11–30, briefly discusses Lapp origins, livelihoods, types, and relations with other peoples. The annotated bibliography at the end of the article is valuable for both the general and scholarly references it provides.

323 **The Sami national minority in Sweden.**
Edited by Birgitta Jahreskog, translated from the Swedish by Ann
Nordin, Linda Schenck. Stockholm: Almqvist & Wiksell;
Atlantic Highland, New Jersey: Humanities Press, 1982. 252p.
maps.

Published for Sweden's *Rättsfonden* (Legal Rights Foundation), it concerns the
'Taxed Mountain' legal dispute between the Lapps (Sami) and the Swedish
government over ownership of land use and other rights in Northern Sweden. The
first part of the book contains nine essays inspired by the conflict and the second
part includes a translation of the final decision made by the Swedish Supreme
Court and a dissenting opinion by one of the members of the Court. It is recent,
provocative, and should be read in conjunction with *Ethnicity and mobilization in
Sami politics* (q.v.).

324 **The Lappish nation: citizens of four countries.**
Karl Nickul. Bloomington, Indiana: Indiana University Press,
1977. 134p. maps. bibliog. (Indiana University Publications: Uralic
and Altaic Series).

An abridged version of *Saamelaiset kansana ja kansalaisana* published in 1970 by
the Society for Finnish Literature. A serious study of the Lapps in Norway,
Sweden, Finland and, to a lesser extent, Russia. An introduction to the Lapps
living in different regions and with different forms of livelihood is followed by a
more detailed study of the relationship that has existed in the past as well as the
present between the Lapps and the different governments that rule the region.
There is a detailed bibliography; 268 plates of photographs, drawings, and maps
are included as an appendix.

325 **The land of the Lapps.**
Gunnar Rönn, translated from the Swedish by Ingeborg Broström
and Harald Bergesen. [Stockholm]: Saxon & Lindströms, 1961.
[not paginated]. map.

A description of the life of the Reindeer Lapps of Sweden and Norway, profusely
illustrated with photographs and text. Of greatest interest to the general reader
and young adults.

326 **The Lapps in Sweden.**
Israel Ruong, translated from the Swedish by Alan Blair.
Stockholm: Swedish Institute for Cultural Relations with Foreign
Countries, 1967. 116p. maps. bibliog.

A brief but cogent survey of the Lapps in Sweden. It contains a survey of the
Lapps' role in Swedish history, and discusses reindeer breeding as an essential
part of Lapp life, distinctive features of Lapp culture, their literary and artistic
contributions, educational opportunities, and role as a minority in Swedish
society. Although now out of print, it is still the only comprehensive survey of
Lapp life in Sweden.

327 **The Lapps.**
Arthur Spencer. New York: Crane, Russak; Newton Abbot,
England: David & Charles, 1978. 160p. maps. bibliog. (This
Changing World).

An introduction to the Lapps discussing their development, the importance of the
reindeer to their livelihood in some areas, their culture and society, and elements
of change in their present life.

328 **Ethnicity and mobilization in Sami politics.**
Tom G. Svensson, translated from the Swedish by Elizabeth
Seeburg, Marian Percivall. Stockholm: Liber, 1976. 279p. maps.
bibliog. (Stockholm Studies in Social Anthropology, no. 4).

Discusses the development in 1950 of the *Svenska Samernas Riksförbund*
(Swedish Sami Union) and its work on behalf of six Swedish Reindeer Lapp
communities to defend their economic and political rights.

329 **Lapp life and customs: a survey.**
Ørnulf Vorren, Ernst Manker, translated from the Norwegian by
Kathleen McFarlane. London: Oxford University Press, 1962.
183p. map. bibliog.

First published as *Same kulturen: en oversikt* (Lapp culture: an overview) (Oslo:
Oslo University Press, 1957), this volume briefly discusses the existing evidence of
Lapp development and then in more detail the material culture forms of the
mountain, coast, forest, and Skalt Lapps. Manker describes Lapp intellectual and
cultural forms and Vorren concludes the work with a discussion of their social
organization and their relationship with other groups within the Scandinavian
states.

Gypsies

330 **Gypsies.**
Erik J. Friis. *Scandinavian Review*, vol. 66, no. 1 (1978),
p. 26–27.

A brief survey of the presence and status of gypsies in Scandinavia. The article is
part of a special issue of *Scandinavian Review* devoted entirely to Scandinavian
minorities.

331 **A group of Lovaro gypsies settle down in Sweden: an analysis of their acculturation.**
Claudia Marta. Stockholm: IMFO-Gruppen Institute of Education, University of Stockholm, 1979. 129p. bibliog.
A study of one particular group of gypsies, which deals specifically with acculturation as a difficulty to be overcome by the group. Reflects the author's bias against this process, but also a unique work for the problem it addresses.

332 **The gypsies in Sweden: a socio-medical study.**
John Takman, Lars Lindgren. Stockholm: Liber, 1976. 171p. bibliog.
A sociological study of the physical state of the gypsies by one of their foremost spokesmen. Contains a superb bibliography for the serious researcher.

Jews

333 **Sweden's attempt to aid Jews, 1939–1945.**
Steven Koblik. *Scandinavian Studies*, vol. 56, no. 2 (1984), p. 89–113.
A concise summary connecting the aid given to Jewish refugees to Sweden during the Second World War, and the support given abroad through the work of Raoul Wallenberg and Count Folke Bernadotte. An important work on Swedish policy during the war. See also his forthcoming book on the same subject *The stones cry out: Sweden's response to the persecution of the Jews, 1933–1945* (New York: Holocaust Library), which will also be available in Swedish translation.

334 **Action or assimilation: a Jewish identity crisis.**
Morton H. Narrowe. *Scandinavian Review*, vol. 66, no. 1 (1978), p. 47–52.
A first-hand sketch of the development of Jewish communities in each of the Scandinavian states. Part of an entire issue of the journal devoted to Scandinavian minorities.

Recent immigrants

335 **North to another country: the formation of a community in Sweden.**
Ulf Björnlund, translated from the Swedish by Gordon Elliot. Stockholm: Swedish Commission on Immigrant Research, 1981. 192p. (Stockholm Studies in Social Anthropology, vol. 9).
A detailed study of a group of Assyrian Christians persecuted in Turkey, their homeland, who then moved to Sweden in the mid-1970s. They were subjected to considerable harassment and consequently helped draw attention to Sweden's 'immigrant problem'.

336 **Migration and economy: Yugoslav–Swedish relations.**
Karlis Goppers. Stockholm: Commission for Immigration
Research/Liber förlag, 1983. 102p. (EIFO–English series,
Report 4).

After Finland, Yugoslavia has provided the most immigrants into Sweden since
the Second World War. There are long connections between the two countries.
This book might be read in conjunction with: Tommy Holm, *Migrationspolitikens
förändring och effekter under efterkrigstiden i Jugoslavien.* (The changes and
effects of migration policy since World War II in Yugoslavia.) (Stockholm:
Delegationen för invandrarforskning, 1984.) This is a study of migration's effect
on Yugoslavia and is useful to compare with the Swedish experience.

337 **European immigration policy: a comparative study.**
Edited by Tomas Hammar. Cambridge, England; London; New
York: Cambridge University Press, 1985. 319p. bibliog.

Describes current immigration policies in six European countries, including
Sweden, and compares their programmes of regulation and the policy-making
processes for common trends and tendencies. The work has been funded by the
Swedish Ministry of Labour and facilitated by the Swedish Commission on
Immigration Research and the Centre for Research on International Migration
and Ethnicity at the University of Stockholm to assist in an assessment of present
Swedish immigration policy. Hammar has contributed a chapter on Sweden
(p. 17–49) and the country figures prominently in the general discussion of
immigration policy that follows.

338 **Immigrants and the education system: an action programme for the
work of the National Board of Education in connection with
immigrant affairs.**
Stockholm: Skolöverstyrelsen, 1979. 116p.

The report which has prompted Sweden's extensive efforts to meet the need of
her recent immigrants. An important work for those interested in the problem of
in Sweden's important and unique response.

339 **Hem till Finland: Sverige–finländares återflyttning.** (Home to
Finland: the return of Swedish Finns.)
Jonni Korkiasaari. Stockholm: Delegationen för
invandrarforskning, 1986. 67p.

Finns form the largest group of immigrants into Sweden, almost half of the one
million who make up one-eighth of Sweden's population. Most are part of a
continual trans-Baltic flow of labour. This is a summary of a much longer Finnish
study of this persistent situation which also affects Sweden.

340 **Sweden: a general introduction for immigrants.**
Edited by Karin Levander, translated from the Swedish by Roger
G. Tanner. Stockholm: Statens invandarverk, 1986. 2nd ed.
246p.

The most helpful handbook for all immigrants with translations into many other
languages also available. Summarizes the immigrant's rights and obligations and
provides essential information about the country.

People of eight seasons: the story of the Lapps.
See item no. 34.

The reindeer people.
See item no. 44.

Sweden.
See item no. 300.

Svenska ord med uttal och förklaringar. (Swedish words with pronunciations and definitions.)
See item no. 378.

The Nordic countries and North–South relations.
See item no. 620.

Full employment and public policy: the United States and Sweden.
See item no. 682.

Invandrare i tystnadsspiralen. (Immigrants in the spiral of silence.)
See item no. 916.

Invandrare & minoriteter. . . .
See item no. 932.

**Swedish immigration research: introductory survey and annotated biblio-
graphy. Report 10.**
See item no. 974.

Litteratur om etniska minoritetsgrupper i Sverige. (Literature about
ethnic minority groups in Sweden.)
See item no. 992.

Invandrar- och minoritetsforskning: en bibliografi. (Immigrant- and
minority-research: a bibliography.)
See item no. 993.

Vanishing Lapland.
See item no. 998.

The land of the long night.
See item no. 999.

Overseas Population

General

341 **Towards an understanding of emigrational processes.**
Sune Åkerman. *Scandinavian Journal of History*, vol. 3, no. 2
(1978), p. 131–54. maps.
A contribution to an issue of the journal devoted to the subject of emigration.
Describes the model developed by the research project on emigration at the
University of Uppsala under Åkerman's direction. An important contribution to
the methodology of this form of historical research. See also in the same issue,
Ingrid Semmingsen's 'Nordic research into emigration' (p. 107–29) for a
discussion of the research done on this topic in the 1960s and early 1970s.

342 **The Scandinavians in America 986–1970: a chronology and fact
book.**
Edited and compiled by Howard B. Furer.   Dobbs Ferry, New
York: Oceana Publications, 1972. 154p. bibliog. (Ethnic
Chronology Series, no. 6).
The work is divided into two sections that provide a chronological sketch of
Scandinavian migration to America from the 17th century until the present, and
selected primary sources representing immigrant life there.

343 **Swedish–America: an introduction.**
Nils Hasselmo.   New York: Swedish Information Service, 1976.
70p.
An excellent but brief introduction to the subject, for those who have not time for
Lars Ljungmark's study, *Swedish Exodus* (q.v.). A short annotated reading list is
appended.

344 **Nordic population mobility: comparative studies of selected parishes in the Nordic countries 1850–1900.**
Edited by Bo Kronborg, Thomas Nilsson, Andres A. Svalestuen.
Oslo: Universitetsforlaget, 1977. 170p.

This is a final report of a Nordic comparative demographic project. It is heavily statistical, a common feature of much modern historical writing, but no less useful to those interested in Swedish emigration and migration, especially because of its comparative view-point. It is also published as: *American Studies in Scandinavia*, vol. 9, nos 1–2, 1977.

345 **Swedish exodus.**
Lars Ljungmark, translated from the Swedish by Kermit B. Westerberg. Carbondale, Illinois: Southern Illinois University Press, 1979. 165p. bibliog.

An excellent one-volume introduction to the subject of Swedish emigration to North America, offering the best general view.

346 **From Sweden to America: a history of the migration.**
Edited by Harald Runblom, Hans Norman. Minneapolis, Minnesota: University of Minnesota Press, 1976. 386p. bibliog.

These ten essays by seven writers in no way constitute a 'history of the migration', but they are a fair summary of the work done in the field by scholars associated with Uppsala University's history department between 1962 and 1976. These are largely methodological essays, in the new 'cliometric' style, but they are necessary for anyone wishing to know about the great emigrations of the late nineteenth century. It has two valuable bibliographies the first of which is annotated. It can be usefully read in conjunction with Nils Hasselmo's (editor), *Perspectives on Swedish Immigration* (Duluth, Minnesota: University of Minnesota Press/ Chicago: Swedish Pioneer Historical Society, 1978). 349p.

347 **Den första massutvandringen.** (The first mass emigration.)
Kjell Söderberg. Umeå, Sweden: Universitet i Umeå, 1981. 290p. bibliog. (Acta Universitatis Umensis, Umeå Studies in the Humanities, 39).

This is a brief English summary at the end of this valuable demographic study of Alfta parish, from which one-quarter of the Bishop Hill Erik-Janssonists came. Söderberg supplements his statistical information with numerous quotations from contemporary sources.

Special studies

348 **Letters from the promised land: Swedes in America 1840–1914.**
Edited and translated from the Swedish by H. Arnold Barton.
Minneapolis, Minnesota: University of Minnesota Press, 1975.
344p.

In some ways this is the liveliest introduction to Swedish America, for it consists of letters home by the emigrants themselves. Barton's introductions to his three periodic groupings are not to be overlooked. He understands the context of these letters better than most, and he writes well.

349 **Swedes in Chicago: a demographic and social study of the 1846–1880 immigration.**
Ulf Beijbom, translated from the Swedish by Donald Brown.
Stockholm: Läromedelsförlagen, 1971. 381p. bibliog.

Despite the somewhat forbidding aspect of all the tables, graphs, and charts in this dissertation, the reader should persist, for this is a model study of an emigrant group in a large city. Beijbom has many clear observations to draw from his vast material.

350 **Scandinavian migration to the Canadian prairie provinces, 1893–1914.**
Kenneth O. Bjork. *Norwegian–American Studies*, vol. 26 (1974), p. 3–30.

Describes the successful efforts of Canadian officials to recruit Scandinavian settlers to the provinces of Saskatchewan, Alberta, and Manitoba. Most of the Scandinavian settlers had migrated first to the United States and then sought a better life in Canada.

351 **From isolation to involvement: the Swedish immigrant press in America 1914–1945.**
Finis Herbert Capps. Chicago, Illinois: Swedish Pioneer Historical Society, 1966. 238p.

This is a classic study of the evolution of an immigrant press and how it moves, and is moved by, its constituents, as they are assimilated into the dominant culture.

352 **Cooperation in Scandinavian–American studies.**
John R. Christianson. *Swedish–American Historical Quarterly*, (1984), p. 374–86.

A brief summary of some of the joint ventures in the United States to promote Scandinavian–American studies. The article is particularly useful for its discussion of scholarly and popular programmes in the field during recent years.

353 **Scandinavians in America: literary life.**
Edited by John R. Christianson. Decorah, Iowa: Symra Literary
Society, 1985. 342p.

The only collection of essays devoted to literary questions, this book has, in
addition to specific studies of writers or genres, some essays which apply more
generally to all immigrant literature. Available from the publisher, Luther
College, Decorah, Iowa, 52101.

354 **The American–Scandinavian Foundation 1910–1960: a brief history.**
Erik J. Friis, introduction by Lithgow Osborne. New York:
American–Scandinavian Foundation, 1961. 135p.

Outlines the first fifty years of the organization including the development of its
programme of activities. Appendixes include the foundation's charter, lists of
those who received fellowships from it during this period, and its extensive
publications. For recent treatments, see C. Peter Strong, 'The foundation's story',
Scandinavian Review, vol. 64, no. 2 (1976), p. 38–45; and an entire issue on its
75th anniversary, vol. 75, no. 4 (1985).

355 **Reaktionen mot utvandringen: emigrationsfrågan i svensk debatt
och politik 1901–1904.** (The reaction to emigration: the emigration
question in Swedish debate and politics 1901–04.)
Ann-Sofie Kälvemark. Stockholm: Läromedelsförlagen, 1972.
252p. bibliog. (Studia Historica Upsaliensia 41).

This is a close study of the debate that led to the formation of the Commission on
Emigration, the official attempt to document the causes of mass emigration and
thereby stem the flow.

356 **Scandinavian immigration and settlements in Australia before
World War II.**
Olav Koivukangas. Turku, Finland: Kokkala, 1974. 333p. map.
bibliog. (Migration studies C2, Institute for Migration, Turku,
Finland).

This scholarly study provides a chronological examination of Scandinavian
emigration. Much of the work concentrates on the period from 1870 to 1914, and
attempts to treat the Scandinavian settlement of different parts of Australia
separately, as well as to discuss the Scandinavian press that existed then. A
separate chapter describes some of the basic demographic features of Scandinavian
migration as well. For a briefer treatment, see Dudley Glass's 'Scandinavian
builders of Australia', *Scandinavian Review*, vol. 60, no. 1 (1972), p. 28–36.

357 **A perspective on Scandinavian studies in the United States.**
Robert B. Kvavik. *Scandinavian Studies*, vol. 54, no. 1 (1982),
p. 1–20.

One of the latest analyses of undergraduate and graduate programmes in
Scandinavian studies in the United States, problems relating to academic research

in this field, and difficulties related to library and archive holdings. The notes are particularly valuable for their reference to the articles that have been published in the United States on the subject since 1911.

358 **An immigrant's American odyssey: a biography of Ernst Skarstedt.**
Emory Lindquist.   Rock Island, Illinois: Augustana Historical Society, 1974. 240p.
This is the only biography of the greatest Swedish–American journalist, a man of immense energy, ingenuity and wit. It does not analyse Skarstedt's work in any detail and relies heavily on his diary as its main source.

359 **The Scandinavians in Australia, New Zealand and the Western Pacific.**
J. Lyng.   Melbourne, Australia: Melbourne University Press, 1939. 207p.
Most of the work is devoted to a discussion of the Scandinavians in Australia with briefer studies of the other regions mentioned in the title. In all cases, an effort is made to describe the settlement in the area, and the forms of church and social life which the migrants have attempted to establish. The greater presence of Scandinavians in Australia also permits an examination of their press there and of the commercial contacts with Scandinavia that have developed.

360 **Homeward to Zion: the Mormon migration from Scandinavia.**
William Mulder, foreword by Oscar Handlin.   Minneapolis, Minnesota: University of Minnesota Press, 1957. 375p.
Describes the development of the Mormon Church in Scandinavia and the migration of Scandinavian Mormons from 1849 until 1905. Mulder discusses the missionary work of the Mormon Church in Scandinavia, migration experiences of Mormon converts to Utah, and their experiences there. The standard work on this aspect of Scandinavian emigration.

361 **The Swedes in Minnesota.**
Edited by Byron Nordstrom.   Minneapolis, Minnesota: Denison, 1976. 107p.
A study of Swedes in the most Swedish state in the Union. The brief general survey is complemented by chapters on religious and secular organizations, language, and politics.

362 **Building traditions among Swedish settlers in rural Minnesota: material culture – reflecting persistence or decline of tradition.**
Lena A:son-Palmqvist.   Stockholm: Nordiska Museet/Emigrant Institute, 1983. 123p. bibliog.
A brief but excellent survey of the topic, one not much researched. This is one of only two comparative material culture studies of Swedish America. The other is a report for the Department of Conservation of the state of Illinois by J. Hiram Wilson and Carolyn Anderson Wilson, *Material Culture in Bishop Hill* (1980).

Overseas Population. Special studies

363 **The divided heart: Scandinavian immigrant experience through literary sources.**
Dorothy Burton Skårdal. Oslo: Universitetsforlaget; Lincoln, Nebraska: University of Nebraska Press, 1974. 394p. bibliog.
This controversial book attempts to use literature as a means of examining historical experience. Skårdal has read extensively in Scandinavian–American literature and the bibliography alone is worth the price of the book.

364 **Lutheran higher education in America.**
Richard W. Solberg. Minneapolis, Minnesota: Augsburg, 1985. 399p. maps. bibliog.
Written for the Lutheran Educational Conference of North America, the book deals extensively with the impetus given by Scandinavian immigrants to the establishment of Lutheran colleges in the United States. See especially 'The Swedish experience' (p. 177–204) for the creation of colleges with Swedish ties.

365 **Emigrationsutredningen: betänkande och bilagor.** (The emigration study: report and appendixes.)
Gustav Sundbärg. Stockholm: Norstedts, 1908–1913. 20 vols.
This is *the* basic study of Swedish emigration. Sundbärg was a statistician, and this is a heavily statistical study and the basis of most subsequent ones. As befits its time, most of its analyses of the reasons for the mass emigrations are devoted to agricultural problems, but for the general reader, Appendix (*Bilaga*) VII, 'The Emigrants' Own Information', is of considerable interest, presenting brief specific accounts written by those who left Sweden of why they did so.

366 **Scandinavians and South Africa: their impact on the cultural, social and economic development of pre-1902 South Africa.**
Alan H. Winquist. Cape Town, South Africa: A. A. Balkema, 1978. 268p.
This study traces Scandinavian involvement in South Africa back to the early 17th century, a period of intense commercial contact between Sweden and Holland. One of its most interesting chapters deals with Scandinavian natural scientists (often Linnaeus' pupils) who travelled to Africa. Other chapters deal with emigration to South Africa and political and social assimilation into white South African society.

367 **Swedish emigrant ballads.**
Robert L. Wright. Lincoln, Nebraska: University of Nebraska Press, 1965. 209p.
A generous historical selection of emigrant songs, stretching from the 18th to the 20th century, this bilingual collection also has the music for many of the ballads. The songs are organized thematically (justification, warning, etc.).

The Bishop Hill colony (Illinois)

368 **Wheat flour messiah: Eric Jansson of Bishop Hill.**
Paul Elmen. Carbondale, Illinois: Southern Illinois University
Press, 1976. 222p.
This is the only biography of the founder of the Bishop Hill Colony (1846–62) in
Illinois and it therefore becomes a history of the movement up to his assassination
in 1850. Elmen attempts to trace Jansson's theological development, seeing it as
the underlying motive for the emigration.

369 **Bishop Hill: a utopia on the prairie.**
Olov Isaksson, Sören Hallgren, translated from the Swedish by
Albert Read. Stockholm: LTs Förlag, 1969. 183p.
This bilingual book (Swedish and English) is a good pictorial introduction to the
Swedish colony of Bishop Hill, with a most informative text. There are many
comparative photographs of the 'then-and-now' kind which give a sense of how
the community has changed and how it is still tied to its past.

New Sweden (Delaware)

370 **A history of New Sweden.**
Israel Acrelius, translated from the Swedish by William M.
Reynolds. Philadelphia, Pennsylvania: Historical Society of
Pennsylvania, 1874. 458p.
Written in 1759, this is the most complete early account of New Sweden. Acrelius
was pastor of the Swedish church in Wilmington, Delaware, and a tireless
investigator of local history. He may have been inspired in part by the visit in the
1740s of Linnaeus' pupil, the naturalist Pehr Kalm, who also spent time among
the Swedes in the Delaware Valley and wrote about them in his *Travels* (1751).

371 **Annals of the Swedes on the Delaware.**
Jehu Curtis Clay. Chicago, Illinois: Swedish Historical Society of
America, 1914. 3rd ed. 145p. + 25p.
This classic history of New Sweden was first published in 1835 and recounts the
story of the first Swedes to settle in North America, in what is now Philadelphia.
This history is largely a chronicle with contemporary documents inserted. (The
extra 25 pages contain a list of the members and the constitution of the now-
defunct society which published this edition.)

372 **Svenska öden vid Delaware 1638–1831.** (Swedish destinies on the Delaware, 1638–1831.)
Nils Jacobsson. Stockholm: Svenska Kyrkans diakonistyrelsens bokförlag, 1938. 320p.

Despite its somewhat overwhelming title, this is a standard Swedish survey of New Sweden, including the period after the formal end of the colony in 1655.

373 **Svenska kyrkans mission vid Delaware i Nord-Amerika.** (The Swedish Church's mission on the Delaware in North America.)
Otto Norberg. Stockholm: A. V. Carlssons bokförlag, 1893. 232p.

A history of New Sweden from the point of view of the Lutheran Church. There was a Swedish-speaking pastor in Philadelphia until 1831, when the congregation joined the Episcopal diocese of Pennsylvania.

Scandinavia.
See item no. 23.

Recent developments in Swedish social history of the period since 1800.
See item no. 293.

Swedish–American Historical Quarterly.
See item no. 947.

The cultural heritage of the Swedish immigrant.
See item no. 962.

Swedish commentators on America 1638–1865.
See item no. 985.

Guide to Swedish–American archival and manuscript sources in the United States.
See item no. 997.

Language

General

374 **A short history of the Swedish language.**
Gösta Bergmann, translated from the Swedish and adapted by
Francis P. Magown, Jr., Helge Kökeritz. Stockholm: Swedish
Institute, 1973. 136p.
The only study of this topic in English, this is a revised and shortened version of
the author's *Kortfattad svensk språkhistoria*, (Brief history of the Swedish
language) (Stockholm: Prisma, 1970, 256p.), which also has a large bibliography.

375 **Svenska språkets ställning i Finland.** (The position of the Swedish
language in Finland.)
Klaus Törnudd.   Helsinki: Holger Schildts förlag, 1978. 3rd rev.
ed. 96p. bibliog.
This is a splendid little summary of the topic which contains a categorized and
briefly annotated bibliography. Swedish-speaking Finns constitute the largest
Swedish-speaking population outside Sweden today and this book is an excellent
way to get to know about them.

376 **Scandinavian language contacts.**
Edited by P. Sture Ureland, Iain Clarkson.   Cambridge, England:
Cambridge University Press, 1984. 340p. bibliog.
This is a detailed, sometimes technical, collection of essays on the interaction of
the Scandinavian languages, both with each other and especially with languages
outside Scandinavia. The longest section (p. 67–170) deals with eastern
Scandinavia and contains a long discussion of recent research about the 'Rus' and
the 'Varangian question', which seeks to dispel some romantic myths on these
matters.

101

Dictionaries

377 **Engelsk–svensk teknisk ordbok.** (English–Swedish technical
dictionary.)
Edited by Henry G. Freeman, with Folke Walder, Ulf L.
Andersson, Lars Carlsson.   Stockholm: Läromedelsförlagen,
1972. 142p.

A handy translation guide, originally English–German, with about 14,000 words
(each variant is listed separately). American usage is indicated, but not British.
This book covers mining and metallurgy, construction, electronics, physics,
chemistry, machines and material, transport and industrial economics. It is a sign
of the times that neither *tram* nor *streetcar* appears in this book.

378 **Svenska ord med uttal och förklaringar.** (Swedish words with
pronunciations and definitions.)
Edited by Martin Gellerstam, Kerstin Norén.   Stockholm: Esselte
Studium, 1984. 649p. + 79p. maps.

This Swedish–Swedish dictionary, intended for immigrants, has usage illustrations
for each word, and has a supplement of many pages of pictures with all the parts
named. There are also maps of Sweden and pronunciation guides.

379 **Svensk–engelsk fackordbok: för näringsliv, förvaltning,
undervisning och forskning.** (Swedish–English technical dictionary:
for economics, administration, education and research.)
Ingvar E. Gullberg.   Stockholm: Norstedt, 1977. 1722p.

This is *the* technical translating dictionary. Where the American usage differs
from the British, the American term is indicated (US). This edition has 170,000
words.

380 **Engelsk–svensk ordbok i teknik.** (English–Swedish dictionary of
technology.)
Alex Militz, Lars Carlsson, Carl-Gustaf Lilje.   Stockholm: Liber,
1980. 710p.

This dictionary deals mostly with mechanical technology and has about 40,000
terms. More interesting is that it has at the end a list of all the Swedish terms used
and where they appear in the main text. It also has 5 appendixes with pictures or
drawings and terms of welding joints, screw types, alloy compounds, measures,
and conversion tables – Anglo-American to metric.

381 **Illustrerad svensk ordbok.** (Illustrated Swedish dictionary.)
Edited by Bertil Molde.   Stockholm: Natur & Kultur, 1982.
1917p.

The standard household dictionary for Swedes, with about 200,000 words: the first
recommendation for those needing a dictionary solely in Swedish.

382 **Nusvensk ordbok.** (Contemporary Swedish dictionary.)
Olaf Östergren, Margareta Zetterström, Gösta Holm.
Stockholm: Wahlstrom & Widstrand, 1981. 5 vols.

These five volumes form the only complete Swedish dictionary available at the moment. There are comparatively reasonably priced and have the advantage of quotations to illustrate usage. Most of this splendid book is the work of the first editor.

383 **Svensk–engelsk affärsordlista.** (Swedish–English business glossary.)
Stanley H. Pretorius. Stockholm: Esselte Studium, 1977. 128p.

A handy translator's guide to Swedish business terms with approximately 4,400 terms. Not all these words are technical terms; many might appear in a business letter outside a technical context: 'unpleasant', for instance.

384 **Svensk–engelsk ordbok. Engelsk–svensk ordbok.** (Swedish–English dictionary. English–Swedish dictionary.)
Edited by Rudolph Santesson. Stockholm: Esselte Läromedels-förlagen, 1968. 2 vols.

The standard, all-purpose translating dictionary that will negotiate all but the most recent, jargon-laden text. It tends to have a British bias.

385 **A comprehensive English–Swedish dictionary. Stora engelsk–svenska ordboken.**
Edited by Rudolph Santesson, Bo Svensen. Stockholm: Esselte, 1980. 1071p.

A large, bilingual dictionary with a clear bias against American English usage. About 120,000 words.

386 **Allting runt omkring.** (Everything around us.)
Richard Scarry, translated from the English by Karin Nyman.
Stockholm: Rabén & Sjögren, 1977. 63p.

This is the Swedish edition of what is probably the most popular dictionary for small children, *Best word book ever* (1963). This is probably the best book for children learning Swedish *or* English, for all the pictures have their words in both languages. Three points must be noted. There are only nouns; they are given without gender; the English forms are British. (This last makes the Wild West spread interesting.)

387 **Stora synonymordboken.** (The large book of synonyms.)
Edited by Alva Strömberg. Stockholm: Strömberg, 1982. 725p.

A thesaurus in dictionary form; one must know the meanings of the synonymous words to be able to make the best use of this book.

Courses and grammars

388 **Basic Swedish grammar.**
Ann-Mari Beite, Gertrud Englund, Siv Higelin, Nils-Gustav
Hildeman. Stockholm: Almqvist & Wiksell, 1963. 168p.
The most widely used English-language grammar of Swedish, this is still quite
serviceable, though organized in the classical way and slightly out of date
pedagogically. Nevertheless, the explanations and examples are clear.

389 **Nybörjarsvenska: nybörjarbok i svenska som främmande språk.**
(Beginning Swedish: beginner's book in Swedish as a foreign
language.)
Ulla Göransson, Hans Lindholm. Lund, Sweden:
Kursverksamhetens förlag, 1981. 230p.
This course requires a teacher, but the book, entirely in Swedish, is well arranged
in seventy-five short sections, with a useful vocabulary and a grammatical
summary at the end. There are supporting materials in the form of a separate
workbook, an English–Swedish glossary, a teacher's handbook and tapes.

390 **Svensk kurs: Swedish course.**
Karin Henriksson, Roger Nyborg. London: Linguaphone
Institute, 1978. 281p.
Probably the best 'do-it-yourself' Swedish course, for those willing to put time
into their learning. This comes with four tapes, a vocabulary list and an exercise
book.

391 **Deskriptiv svensk grammatik.** (Descriptive Swedish grammar.)
Edited by Brita Holm, Elizabeth Nylund. Stockholm: Skriptor,
1970. 211p. bibliog.
The most popular Swedish-language grammar is awkward to use for those who do
not know their way around a grammar book. This is mainly for reference.

392 **Swedish: a comprehensive book for beginners.**
R. J. McClean. London: Hodder & Stoughton; New York:
McKay, 1969. 322p. (Teach Yourself Books).
For those who believe one can actually learn a language from a book, this is the
most accessible course. It is comfortably old-fashioned; everything is organized by
grammatical category, which makes it convenient to look up a rule but not helpful
in ploughing one's way to a useful knowledge of the language. There are exercises
and answers. The vocabulary is not particularly well-chosen for modern Swedish,
and some words in the text do not appear in the glossary (and a good thing, too!)
One uses the word *löss* (= 'loess' or 'lice') so infrequently).

393 **Swedish: a practical grammar.**
Allan Lake Rice. Rock Island, Illinois: Augustana Press, 1958.
107p.
An eccentric but wisdom-filled supplement to language study, this brief grammar has much to offer by way of comfort and good advice.

394 **A lab manual for Swedish intonation: a workbook for the language lab.**
Beata Schmid. Providence, Rhode Island: private, n.d. 48p.
There is also a tape for this thorough guide for those who know Swedish but do not pronounce it properly. Order from the author ($10 in 1986) Box E, German Dept., Brown University, Providence, Rhode Island, 02912 U.S.A.

395 **A concise Swedish grammar.**
Åke Viberg, Kerstin Ballardini, Sune Stjärnlöf, translated from the Swedish by Michael Knight. Stockholm: Natur & Kultur, 1984. 154p.
A good beginners' grammar, reasonably complete, full of good sense for the learner, based on the way modern Swedish linguists now talk about their language.

396 **A Swedish mini grammar.**
Elsie Wijk-Andersson, translated from the Swedish by Alan Lake Rice. Uppsala, Sweden: Studieförlaget, 1979. 51p.
Good for those who want a quick review of some of the basic principles.

Anglo–Scandinavian law dictionary of legal terms used in professional and commercial practice.
See item no. 571.

Scandinavian Studies.
See item no. 942.

Scandinavica.
See item no. 945.

Förteckning över lexikon och ordlistor. (List of dictionaries and glossaries.)
See item no. 951.

Läromedelsförteckning för lärare i svenska som främmande språk utomlands. (List of materials for teachers of Swedish as a foreign language outside Sweden.)
See item no. 984.

Religion

Pre-Christian religion

397 Gods of the North.
Brian Branston.   London; New York: Thames & Hudson, 1955.
318p. bibliog.

A major work on Old Norse mythology, divided into sections discussing the creation of the earth, cosmography and the gods. Several chapters relate specific legends regarding the gods and other themes found in Old Norse mythology.

398 The Norse myths.
Edited by Kevin Crossley-Holland.   New York: Pantheon, 1980.
276p. bibliog.

The introduction provides a brief look at the Viking world and particularly at pre-Christian Nordic religion. The rest of the work consists of thirty-two Norse myths or legends taken from the *Elder Edda* and the *Prose Edda* of Snorri Sturluson with a short commentary upon each in an appendix. The myths themselves have been rendered into modern English by Crossley-Holland.

399 Gods and myths of Northern Europe.
Hilda R. Ellis Davidson.   Baltimore, Maryland: Penguin, [1964].
251p. bibliog.

Provides detailed description of the gods of early Scandinavia in a clear and comprehensible fashion. Special emphasis is placed on Odin and Thor, although consideration is given to all the main figures and chief mythological concepts.

400 **The road to Hel: a study of the conception of the dead in Old Norse literature.**
Hilda R. Ellis Davidson.   New York: Greenwood Press, 1968. 208p.
Discusses Scandinavian funeral practices during the Viking Age and concepts of life after death, worship of the dead, and man's spirit or soul. Based on literary and archaeological sources, this is a scholarly, informative and very reasonable account, first published by Cambridge University Press in 1943.

401 **Scandinavian mythology.**
Hilda R. Ellis Davidson.   London: Paul Hamlyn, 1975. 141p. bibliog.
An uncomplicated introduction to pre-Christian Norse religious beliefs by an acknowledged expert. First published in 1969, this profusely illustrated account is suitable for the general reader.

402 **Gods of the ancient Northmen.**
Georges Dumézil, edited by Einar I. Haugen, introduction by C. Scott Littleton, Udo Strutynski.   Berkeley, California: University of California Press, 1973. 157p. bibliog. (Publications of the UCLA Center for the Study of Comparative Folklore and Mythology, no. 3).
This scholarly analysis of Scandinavian mythology assumes some previous knowledge of the subject. The author frequently quotes saga source material and makes comparisons with ancient Greek and Hindu mythology. First published as *Les dieux des Germains* (Paris: Presses Universitaire de France, 1959).

403 **The chariot of the sun and other rites and symbols of the Northern Bronze Age.**
Peter Gelling, Hilda R. Ellis Davidson, foreword by Christopher Hawkes.   New York; Washington: Praeger, 1969. 200p. map. bibliog.
In the main portion of the work (c. 1500–400 BC) Gelling describes the nature of Bronze Age religion as it can be determined from rock engravings. Hilda Davidson has added a chapter on the same subject from the Vendel period. Much of their evidence is from Sweden, particularly the area around Gothenburg.

404 **Vikings: Hammer of the North.**
Magnus Magnusson.   New York: Galahad Books, 1980. 128p. maps. bibliog.
After brief chapters on pre-Viking Scandinavia, Viking expansion, and the coming of Christianity, Magnusson devotes most of the work to a discussion of Viking religion and mythology. The text contains quotations from the *Prose*

Edda, and is illustrated with numerous colour photographs, chiefly of archaeological finds emphasizing Magnusson's theme. Originally published in London in 1976 by Orbis.

405 **The nine worlds: a dictionary of Norse mythology.**
Douglas A. Rossman. Baton Rouge, Louisiana: Ormsgard Press, 1983. 63p.
Brief explanations of terms and names found in works of Norse mythology which will be of assistance to the general reader encountering this subject for the first time.

Christianity and church history

406 **Women of the Reformation from Spain to Scandinavia.**
Roland H. Bainton. Minneapolis, Minnesota: Augsburg Publishing House, 1977. 240p.
The chapter on Katarina Jagellonica (p. 183–204) discusses the development of the Reformation in Sweden during the 16th century and the efforts of Katarina and her husband Johan III (1568–92) to re-establish Catholicism. A brief but worthwhile study.

407 **A critic of the fourteenth century: St. Birgitta of Sweden.**
Conrad Bergendoff. In: *Medieval and historiographical essays in honor of James Westfall Thompson.* Edited by James Lea Cate, Eugene N. Anderson. Chicago, Illinois: University of Chicago Press, 1938. p. 3–18.
A critical study of Birgitta's role in the ending of the Babylonian Captivity of the Church (the establishment of the papal court of Avignon) and her involvement in Swedish politics. See also Johannes Jørgensen's *Saint Bridget of Sweden.*

408 **Olavus Petri and the ecclesiastical transformation in Sweden 1521–1552: a study in the Swedish Reformation.**
Conrad Bergendoff. Philadelphia, Pennsylvania: Fortress Press, 1965. 267p. bibliog.
First published in 1928, it examines the development of the Reformation by Gustav Vasa and Petri's liturgical, polemical, and theological contributions to its development until his death in 1552. A clear account of both subjects, accurate but in need of revision.

409 **Söderblom, ecumenical pioneer.**
Charles J. Curtis. Minneapolis, Minnesota: Augsburg Publishing House, 1967. 149p. bibliog.
Discusses Bishop Nathan Söderblom's life, chief theological views, and his influence on major religious issues of the 1960s, particularly ecumenicism. A

concise work for the informed general reader. For other studies of Söderblom by the same author, see *Nathan Söderblom: theologian of revelation* (Chicago, Illinois: Covenant Press, 1966) and 'Ecumenical theology: Söderblom', p. 1–20 in his *Contemporary Protestant thought* (New York: Bruce Publishing, 1970).

410 **Swedish contributions to modern theology with special reference to Lundensian thought.**
Nels F. S. Ferré, William A. Johnson.   New York; London; Evanston, Illinois: Harper & Row, 1967. 304p. bibliog.
Studies primarily the views and works of Anders Nygren and Gustaf Aulén. Designed mainly for scholars of the field but Ferré's first chapter (p. 1–33) also presents a cogent survey of Swedish theology during the first part of the 20th century. It was first published in 1939 but Johnson has contributed an extensive closing chapter (p. 242–95) on Swedish theology from 1939–1966.

411 **Rome and the Counter Reformation in Scandinavia until the establishment of the *S. congregatio de propaganda fide* in 1622 based on the source material in the Kalsrud collection.**
Oskar Garstein.   Olso: Universitetsforlaget, 1963–1980. 2 vols. bibliog.
Emphasis in both volumes is given chiefly to the activities of Laurentius Norvegus, a Norwegian Jesuit, in Sweden during the last half of the 16th century. The most complete study of this subject in English.

412 **Sweden.**
Berndt Gustafsson.   In: *Western religion: a country by country sociological inquiry*. Edited by Hans Mol, in collaboration with Margaret Hetherton, Margaret Henty. The Hague, The Netherlands: Mouton, 1972, p. 479–510. bibliog. (Religion and Reason: Method and Theory in the Study of and Interpretation of Religion, vol. 2).
A statistical and sociological study of the various Christian faiths in Sweden. In need of revision, but otherwise a valuable introduction to the study of contemporary religion in Sweden.

413 **Anders Nygren.**
Thor Hall, introduction by Bob E. Patterson.   Waco, Texas: Word Books, 1978. 230p. bibliog. (Makers of the Modern Theological Mind).
Provides a brief sketch of Nygren's career and a more extensive study of his methodology, central views, and place in 20th-century theological studies.

Religion. Christianity and church history

414 **Missions from the North: Nordic Missionary Council, 50 years.**
Edited by Carl F. Hallencreutz, Johannes Aagard, Nils E. Bloch-
Hoell. Oslo: Universitetsforlaget, 1974. 171p. (Studia Missionalia
Upsaliensia, vol. 20).
Describes Nordic missionary work from 1923 to 1973 by the Christian churches in
the Scandinavian countries, and discusses the formation and work of the Nordic
missionary Council to promote and co-ordinate these activities. A worthwhile
introduction to this important aspect of Scandinavian Christianity.

415 **Scandinavian churches: a picture of the development and life of the
churches of Denmark, Finland, Iceland, Norway and Sweden.**
Edited by Leslie Stannard Hunter.   London: Faber & Faber;
Minneapolis, Minnesota: Augsburg Publishing House, 1965. 200p.
bibliog.
Studies the Lutheran Church in 20th-century Scandinavia. The Swedish Church is
frequently discussed, and is considered specifically in Gunnar Hultgren's 'Church,
people and state in Sweden' (p. 54–60) and A. Gabriel Hebert's 'An English view
of some Swedish theologians' (p. 118–28). A valuable introduction, but now in
need of revision to consider contemporary developments.

416 **History of the Scandinavian mission.**
Andrew Jenson.   Salt Lake City: Deseret News Press, 1927. 570p.
A detailed account of Mormon (Church of Jesus Christ of Latter-Day Saints)
religious activity in Scandinavia from the 1850s until 1926. In addition to frequent
discussion of Sweden in the work, the country is dealt with specifically in the
section entitled 'History of the Swedish mission' (p. 444–86). The work also
includes biographical notes on Scandinavian Mormons who emigrated to
America, and statistical data relating to the Mormon Church in Scandinavia.

417 **Emanuel Swedenborg.**
Inge Jonsson, translated from the Swedish by Catherine
Djurklou.   New York: Twayne Publishers, 1971. 224p. bibliog.
(Twayne World Authors Series, vol. 127).
Discusses Swedenborg's (1688–1772) scientific and philosophical work prior to
1745, although his religious works and views after that date are also included.
More scholarly than many works on the Swedish scientist/mystic, it also attempts
to relate Swedenborg to scientific developments of his day. The work contains an
extensive and annotated bibliography of the voluminous literature on Swedenborg.

418 **Saint Bridget of Sweden.**
Johannes Jørgensen, translated from the Danish by Ingeborg
Lund. London: Longmans, Green, 1954. 2 vols. bibliog.
A detailed study of Sweden's well-known saint. Volume one deals with Saint
Birgitta's life from her birth in 1303 until the beginning of her pilgrimage to Rome
in 1349. The second volume begins with this journey and chronicles her efforts to
end the Babylonian Captivity of the Church, her pilgrimage to the Holy Land,
and the last years of her life. It is a serious, detailed, scholarly, and interesting
work. For related works, see Marguerita Tjader's *Mother Elisabeth: the
resurgence of the Order of St. Birgitte* (New York: Herder & Herder, 1972); and
Margaret Sperry, 'Birgitte: medieval saint and modern woman', *American–
Scandinavian Review*, vol. 61, no. 2 (1973), p. 117–26.

419 **The philosophy and theology of Anders Nygren.**
Edited by Charles W. Kegley. Carbondale; Edwardsville, Illinois:
Southern Illinois University Press; London; Amsterdam, The
Netherlands: Feffler & Simons, 1970. 434p. bibliog.
Seventeen articles by leading scholars on important aspects of Nygren's
theological views plus two works by Nygren, his 'Intellectual autobiography'
(p. 3–29), and a final rejoinder to the other contributors at the end of the work. A
detailed bibliography of his published works is also included. A unique and
essential work for the study of the Swedish theologian.

420 **A brief history of the Church of Sweden: origins and modern
structure.**
Robert Murray, translated from the Swedish by Nils G. Sahlin.
Stockholm: A. B. Verbum, 1969. 2nd rev. ed. 117p. map.
First published in 1961, it sketches the history of the Church of Sweden to the
mid-20th century, and briefly describes its organizational structure. A clear,
concise introduction for the general reader by an expert. It should be
supplemented by current fact-sheets from the Swedish Information Service
(Swedish Institute) for information on organizational changes and issues which
have developed since the book was published. For another brief work
emphasizing the church's activities in modern Sweden, see Berndt Gustafsson's
The Christian faith in Sweden (Stockholm: A. B. Verbum, 1968). A similar but
less up-to-date introduction, since it was first published in 1946, is H. M.
Waddam's *The Swedish Church* (Westport, Connecticut: Greenwood Press,
1981).

421 **The Church of Sweden: past and present: a book sponsored by the
Swedish Bishops' Conference.**
Edited by Robert Murray, translated from the Swedish by Nils G.
Sahlin. Malmö, Sweden: Allhem, 1960. 286p. maps.
Contains brief historical sketches of the Church of Sweden since the Reformation,
its general organization, descriptions of its thirteen dioceses, and its role in the
modern world. A good introduction to these subjects, well illustrated with
numerous photographs and pictures.

422 **Nordische und deutsche Kirchen im 20. Jahrhundert: Referate auf**
der internationalen Arbeitstagung in Sandbjerg/Dänemark 1981.
(The Nordic and German churches in the 20th century: reports
from the international workshop at Sandbjerg, Denmark, 1981.)
Edited by Carsten Nicolaisen. Göttingen, West Germany:
Vandenhoeck & Ruprecht, 1982. 361p. (Arbeiten zur kirchlichen
Zeitgeschichte, Series B, vol. 13).
Nineteen essays on the themes of 'The folk church', 'The State and the Church',
and 'The Church during the war'. Many discuss Swedish perspectives on these
themes and offer valuable insights into 20th-century Scandinavian Christianity.

423 **Swedish research in ecclesiastical history during the last decade: a**
bibliographical note.
Carl-E. Normann. *Journal of Ecclesiastical History*, vol. 3, no. 2
(1952), p. 201–17.
Briefly considers works written prior to 1940 and, more extensively, forms of
religious literature published from 1940 until the very early 1950s. Helpful but
also in need of revision.

424 **The English missionaries in Sweden and Finland.**
C. J. A. Opperman. London: Society for Promoting Christian
Knowledge, 1937. 221p. bibliog.
Concentrates chiefly on the development of Christianity in Sweden from the
conversion of Olof Skötkonung in the early 11th century to the establishment of
the Archbishopric of Uppsala in the late 12th century. A detailed but very
readable treatment of the subject.

425 **The Swedenborg epic: the life and works of Emanuel Swedenborg.**
Cyriel Odhner Sigstedt. London: Swedenborg Society, 1981.
517p. map. bibliog.
First published in 1952 (New York: Bookman Associates), it is a highly regarded
biography that provides a balanced account of both his early scientific career and
his spiritual views and activities after 1744. A clear, detailed work for both scholar
and general reader.

426 **The reception of the Augsburg Confession in Scandinavia.**
Trygve R. Skarsten. *Sixteenth Century Journal*, vol. 11, no. 3
(1980), p. 87–98.
An excellent summary not only of the impact of the Augsburg Confession but also
of the Lutheran Reformation in both Sweden and Denmark during the 16th
century. Part of an issue devoted to the 450th anniversary of the Augsburg
Confession.

427   **Nathan Söderblom: his life and work.**
Bengt Gustaf Malcom Sundklev.   Lund, Sweden: Gleerups, 1968.
438p.

A detailed, very readable biography of Söderblom (1866–1931) that treats his
time as student and professor at Uppsala, his influence on the Church of Sweden
as Archbishop, and important ecumenical work.

428   **Swedenborg: life and teaching.**
George Trobridge.   New York: Pillar Books, Harcourt Brace
Jovanovich, 1976. 299p.

Originally published in 1909 with a fourth, revised edition presented in 1939 by
the Swedenborg Society of London which was reprinted several times thereafter.
A sympathetic and detailed discussion of his scientific career and the development
and nature of his religious ideas. The literature on Swedenborg is extensive.
Other works that might be consulted include Signe Toksvig, *Emanuel Swedenborg:
scientist and mystic* (New Haven, Connecticut: Yale University Press, 1948); Sig
Synnestvedt (ed.), *The essential Swedenborg: basic teachings of Emanuel
Swedenborg: scientist, philosopher and theologian* (New York: Twayne, 1970);
Marguerite Beck Block, *The New Church in the New World: a study of
Swedenborgianism in America* (New York: Henry Holt, 1932).

429   **An Exodus theology: Einar Billing and the development of modern
      Swedish theology.**
Gustaf Wingren, translated from the Swedish by Erik Wahlstrom.
Philadelphia, Pennsylvania: Fortress Press, 1969. 181p. bibliog.

First published in Sweden as *Einar Billing: en studie i svensk teologi före 1920*
(Einar Billing: a study in Swedish theology before 1920) (Lund, Sweden:
C. W. K. Gleerup, 1968). Studies Billing's theological thought up till about 1930
and its impact on Swedish theology since then. A clear, concise discussion by one
of Sweden's most gifted theological scholars of recent times.

430   **An archbishop of the Reformation: Laurentius Petri Nericus
      Archbishop of Uppsala, 1531–73: a study of his liturgical projects.**
Eric E. Yelverton.   London: Epworth, 1958. 153p. bibliog.

Briefly sketches Petri's life, but emphasizes his liturgical contributions to the
Lutheran State Church of Sweden at the beginning of the Reformation.

Meet Sweden.
See item no. 12.

The Scandinavian countries, 1720–1865: the rise of the middle classes.
See item no. 159.

**The Viking achievement: a survey of the society and culture of early
medieval Scandinavia.**
See item no. 175.

The Viking world.
See item no. 176.

Les peuples scandinaves au moyen âge. (The Scandinavian people in the Middle Ages.)
See item no. 196.

Gustavus Adolphus: a history of Sweden 1611–1632.
See item no. 215.

Sweden's Age of Greatness 1632–1718.
See item no. 220.

Den första massutvandringen. (The first mass emigration.)
See item no. 347.

Homeward to Zion: the Mormon migration from Scandinavia.
See item no. 360.

Wheat flour messiah: Eric Jansson of Bishop Hill.
See item no. 368.

Bishop Hill: a utopia on the prairie.
See item no. 369.

Svenska kyrkans mission vid Delaware i Nord-Amerika. (The Swedish Church's mission on the Delaware in North America.)
See item no. 373.

Sweden: prototype of modern society.
See item no. 459.

Biblia dalecarlia: the life of Jesus in Dalecarlian paintings.
See item no. 877.

Education

General

431 **Social science research in Sweden.**
Edited by Artur Attman, Åke Bruhn-Möller, Henrik Hessler, Lars
Kebbon, translated from the Swedish by Richard Cox, Rudy
Feichtner, preface by Torgny Segerstedt. Stockholm: Swedish
Council for Social Science Research, 1972. 278p. bibliog.
(Scandinavian University Books).
Twenty-six essays by leading scholars on research and the study of the social
sciences, law, and education. Valuable for an understanding of these fields from
1945–70 but in need of revision or an additional volume to reflect developments
since its publication.

432 **Tradition and change in Swedish education.**
Leon Bucher. Oxford: Pergamon Press, 1982. 264p. maps.
bibliog. (International Studies in Education and Social Change).
Provides a detailed discussion of the Swedish education system and the reforms of
the 1970s, and analyses the achievements of these changes. Contains an extensive
bibliography for further study. An essential work on the subject.

433 **Trends in Swedish educational policy.**
Sixten Marklund, Gunnar Bergendal, translated from the Swedish
by Victor J. Kayfetz. Stockholm: Swedish Institute, 1979. 55p.
map.
Supplements *The Swedish school system* (q.v.) by discussing in more detail topics
such as higher education, adult education, continuing education, and educational
reform.

434 **The Swedish school system.**
Britta Stenholm, translated from the Swedish by Roger G.
Tanner. Stockholm: Swedish Institute, 1984. 136p. (Sweden
Books).

A survey of the organizational structure of primary and secondary education,
local and national government responsibilities for education, and distinguishing
characteristics of Swedish education. A valuable, concise introduction for all
readers.

Primary and secondary

435 **Early child care in Sweden.**
Ragnar Berfenstam, Inger William-Olsson, foreword by Halbert B.
Robinson, Nancy M. Robinson. London; New York; Paris:
Gordon & Breach, 1973. 155p. (International Monograph Series
on Early Child Care, vol. 2).

First published as a complete issue of the journal *Early Child Development and
Care*, vol. 1, no. 2 (1973). A basic overview that considers the family's role in
child care, the concept of planning applied to child care, and the child-care
facilities available outside the home. A basic reference work on the subject.

436 **Sweden's day nurseries: focus on programs for infants and toddlers.**
Joan L. Bergstrom, Jane R. Gold, foreword by Ilse Mattick.
Washington, DC: Day Care and Child Development Council of
America, 1974. 136p. bibliog.

Describes the development, operation, environment, and daily routine of the
Swedish day-care centre, with an assessment of its strengths and weaknesses. A
thorough introduction to the subject.

437 **Pre-school in Sweden: facts, trends and future.**
Bodil Rosengren, translated from the Swedish by Keith Bradfield.
Stockholm: Swedish Institute, 1973, 36p.

Discusses the development and debate in Sweden during the 1950s and 1960s
regarding nursery schools and programme changes made in the early 1970s, as
well as the nature of the Swedish nursery school. An excellent overview of the
subject.

438 **Primary education and secondary schools.**
Anne-Liisa Sysiharju.   In: *Nordic democracy: ideas, issues, and institutions in politics, economy, education, social and cultural affairs of Denmark, Finland, Iceland, Norway, and Sweden.* Edited by Erik Allardt, Nils Andrén, Erik J. Friis, Gylfi T. Gislason, Sten Sparre Nilson, Henry Valen, Frantz Wendt, Folmer Wisti. Copenhagen: Det Danske Selskab, 1981, p. 419–43. bibliog.
Provides a brief historical introduction to the development of popular education and then surveys current primary and secondary education in the Nordic countries. The major theme is the development of common programmes of primary education throughout the region and more diverse programmes of secondary education.

Higher education

439 **The compleat university: break from tradition in Germany, Sweden, and the U.S.A.**
Edited by Harry Hermanns, Ulrich Teichler, Henry Wasser. Cambridge, Massachusetts: Schenkman, 1983. 322p.
Published for the Center for European Studies, Graduate School City University of New York; printed in West Germany as *Integrierte Hochschulmodelle: Erfahrungen aus drei Ländern* (Models of the integrated university: experiences from three countries) (Frankfurt: Campus, 1982); and papers presented at conferences 1980–1981 in New York and Kassel, West Germany. The work contains three articles by Lillemor Kim, Rune Premfors, Jan-Erik Lane, Hans Stenlund, and Anders Westlund discussing the nature and impact of Swedish university reforms in 1977.

440 **The Swedish academic marketplace: the case of science and technology.**
Göran Jense.   Lund, Sweden: Studentlitteratur, 1979. 242p. bibliog.
Discusses the nature of Swedish higher education, particularly faculty research activity in science and technology. A detailed study of greatest interest to specialists in education and science.

441 **Variety of attitudes towards the comprehensive university.**
Jan-Erik Lane, Hans Stenlund, Anders Westlund.   *Higher Education*, vol. 11, no. 4 (1982), p. 441–74. bibliog.
Treats the impact of Swedish university reforms of the 1970s from the standpoint of the establishment of the comprehensive university and the new perspective this offers to Swedish education. Read in conjunction with other works on the same subject, such as *Academic power: patterns of authority in seven national systems of higher education* (q.v.).

117

442 **A history of Uppsala University 1477–1977.**
Sten Lindroth, translated from the Swedish by Neil Tomkinson,
Jean Gray. Stockholm: Almqvist & Wiksell, 1976. 260p.
Published in conjunction with the university's quincentenary in 1977, it traces its
history during the period. Informative and respectful, it was also published in a
Swedish version. Ten additional volumes were issued in English by the university
in 1976 on the different faculties of the university which are useful as well for their
discussion of these disciplines within the Swedish university.

443 **How much higher education is enough?: a comparison of public**
policy in France, Sweden, and the United Kingdom.
Rune Premfors. *Comparative Education Review*, vol. 24, no. 3
(1980), p. 302–22.
A critical study of public planning for higher education in the three countries from
the 1950s to late 1970s. For a more detailed discussion of the same topic by
Premfors, see his *The politics of higher education in a comparative perspective:
France, Sweden, United Kingdom* (Stockholm: Gotab, 1980).

444 **Systems of higher education: Sweden.**
Rune Premfors, Bertil Östergren, foreword by James A. Perkins,
Nell P. Eurich. New York: International Council for Educational
Development, 1978. 208p.
Describes Sweden's system of higher education after the major reform of 1977
and attempts to analyse its effectiveness after only a year of operation. A basic
introduction to the subject.

445 **Looking at learning: higher education and research in the Swedish**
society.
Edited by Eva Rosell, translated from the Swedish by Susan
Opper. Stockholm: Liber, 1984. 48p.
An excellent survey of the most interesting and productive aspects of the Swedish
university system. Particularly valuable for students wishing to pursue advanced
study in Sweden for the addresses it provides for helpful sources of information.

446 **Sweden: external control and internal participation: trends in**
Swedish higher education.
Olof Ruin: In: *Universities, politicians and bureaucrats: Europe
and the United States*. Edited by Hans Daalder, Edward Shils.
Cambridge, England: Cambridge University Press, 1982,
p. 329–64.
An excellent, well-written sketch of the administrative character of Swedish
universities prior to the reforms of 1977 and the process behind the reform
movement itself. Very useful in its own right or as an introductory work to those
describing the new university system in more detail.

447 **Academic power: patterns of authority in seven national systems of higher education.**
John H. Van de Graaff, Burton R. Clark, Doreta Furth, Dietrich Goldschmidt, Donald F. Wheeler. New York: Praeger, 1978. 217p. (Praeger Special Studies).

The section on Sweden (p. 67–82) by Goldschmidt discusses the administrative and structural character of Swedish universities prior to the mid-1970s reforms and the changes expected thereafter in these areas. For an assessment of Swedish higher education prior to these reforms, see the chapter on Sweden (p. 197–225) in Barbara B. Burn, Philip G. Altbach, Clark Kerr, James A. Perkins, *Higher education in nine countries: a comparative study of colleges and universities abroad* (New York: McGraw-Hill, 1971). The work was a general report for the Carnegie Commission on Higher Education.

Other studies

Adult education

448 **Adult education in the Nordic countries.**
Kim Morch Jacobsen. In: *Nordic democracy: ideas, issues, and institutions in politics, economy, education, social and cultural affairs of Denmark, Finland, Iceland, Norway, and Sweden.* Edited by Erik Allardt, Nils Andrén, Erik J. Friis, Gylfi T. Gislason, Sten Sparre Nilson, Henry Valen, Frantz Wendt, Folmer Wisti. Copenhagen: Det Danske Selskab, 1981, p. 465–94. bibliog.

An examination of the different forms of adult education in the Nordic countries. The author identifies the various programmes, outlines some of their forms and characteristics, and makes comparisons between them.

449 **Scandinavian adult education: Denmark, Finland, Norway, Sweden.**
Edited by Ragnar Lund. Westport, Connecticut: Greenwood Press, 1970. 303p.

First published in 1949 (Copenhagen: Danske Forlag), it contains an extensive section (p. 217–303) by the editor and Harry Ohlsson (translated by Donald Burton) describing the historical background and nature of the many adult education programmes in Sweden. A valuable background work for all readers.

Folk high schools

450   **Adult education for social change: research on the Swedish allocation policy.**
Edited by Robert Höghielm, Kjell Rubinson.   Lund, Sweden: Gleerup, 1980. 183p.

A technical but still useful critique of the folk high school. Dwells mainly on the problems caused by the changing ideology of the schools and official attitudes towards them.

451   **Other dreams, other schools: folk colleges in social and ethnic movements.**
Edited by Rolland G. Paulston.   Pittsburgh, Pennsylvania: University of Pittsburgh Press, 1980. 279p.

A collection of essays mainly by or in collaboration with Paulston which examine the folk high school movement in Scandinavia and North America as an institution for shaping the identities of ethnic groups and, at the same time, preparing them for change. Indicative as well of the ability of this facet of Scandinavian education to adapt itself to changing needs.

452   **Réveil national et culture populaire en Scandinavie: la genèse de la højskole nordique.** (National awakening and popular culture in Scandinavia: the birth of the Nordic folk high school.)
Erica Simon.   Paris: Presses Universitaires de France, 1960. 766p. maps. bibliog.

This extremely important work studies the development of the folk high school which originated in Denmark and spread throughout Scandinavia. The institution was more than a centre for popular education; it became the hotbed of nationalism and Scandinavianism during the mid-19th century, with all the conflicts that this entailed. An extensive section on Sweden (p. 267–511) discusses both of these topics in detail.

Special education

453   **Making ordinary schools special: a report on the integration of physically handicapped children in Scandinavian schools.**
Elizabeth M. Anderson, foreword by Jack Tizard.   London: College of Special Education, 1971. 55p. bibliog. (Guide Lines for Teachers, no. 10).

A comparative survey of the programmes and facilities for the integration of physically handicapped students in the state school systems of Denmark, Norway, and Sweden. A useful discussion of the subject.

454   Case studies in special education: Cuba, Japan, Kenya, Sweden.
Paris: UNESCO Press, 1974. 195p.
Contains a section (p. 117–68) sketching the educational services available in
Sweden for the physically impaired. A useful introduction to the subject.

The Swedes: how they live and work.
See item no. 2.

Meet Sweden.
See item no. 12.

Swedish life and landscape.
See item no. 45.

Travel, study, and research in Sweden.
See item no. 107.

The Scandinavian countries, 1720–1865: the rise of the middle classes.
See item no. 159.

Nordic students at foreign universities until 1660.
See item no. 193.

Gustavus Adolphus: a history of Sweden 1611–1632.
See item no. 215.

Europe and Scandinavia: aspects of the process of integration in the 17th century.
See item no. 224.

Gothic patriotism and Olof Rudbeck.
See item no. 288.

Immigrants and the education system: an action programme for the work of the National Board of Education in connection with immigrant affairs.
See item no. 338.

A perspective on Scandinavian studies in the United States.
See item no. 357.

Lutheran higher education in America.
See item no. 364.

Svensk–engelsk fackordbok: för näringsliv, förvaltning, undervisning och forskning. (Swedish–English technical dictionary for economics, administration, education and research.)
See item no. 379.

Swedish sociology: contemporary concerns.
See item no. 458.

Sweden: prototype of a modern society.
See item no. 459.

Children's theatre in Sweden.
See item no. 472.

Sweden's 'right to be human' sex-role equality: the goal and the reality.
See item no. 480.

Swedish women on the move.
See item no. 484.

Swedish research: policy, issues, organization.
See item no. 765.

History of science in Sweden.
See item no. 766.

The world of learning.
See item no. 961.

Fourteen years of educational and psychological research in Sweden: a bibliography of publications in English 1967–1980.
See item no. 964.

Scandinavian education: a bibliography of English-language materials.
See item no. 970.

Scandinavia in social science literature: an English-language bibliography.
See item no. 972.

Folk schools in social change: a partisan guide to the international literature.
See item no. 990.

Society

General

455 Sweden's power elite.
Larry Hufford. Washington, DC: University Press of America, 1977. 421p. bibliog.
Studies élites in Sweden based on the power élite theory. Groups examined include the economic and political élites. Issues used to test the theory include the Supplementary Pension debate of 1956, the EEC debate of 1961–62, and the nuclear weapons issue 1954–64. A work primarily for specialists but also one where non-experts can gain valuable information on powerful forces in Swedish society.

456 Report from a Swedish village.
Sture Källberg, introduction by Jan Myrdal, translated from the Swedish by Angela Gibbs. Baltimore, Maryland; Harmondsworth, England: Penguin, 1972. 327p. (Village Series).
First published as *Rapport från medelsvensk stad: Västerås* (1969), it describes twelve individuals living in Västerås, near Stockholm, encompassing three generations. The basic themes are those of discontent, a sense of powerlessness and lack of involvement in fundamental decision-making processes. An interesting and influential book.

457 The social structure of Sweden.
Anna-Lisa Kälvesten. Stockholm: Swedish Institute, [1965]. 91p. (Sweden Today).
Provides a brief sketch of Sweden's history emphasizing economic and social developments, and discussions of the family, social class, education as a social institution, and social problems. Now out of print, it remains an excellent background to modern Swedish society.

123

458 **Swedish sociology: contemporary concerns.**
Edited by Raj P. Mohan, Arthur S. Wilke. Auburn, Alabama;
Ghaziabad, India: Intercontinental Press, 1980. 193p. bibliog.
(Intercontinental Series on Sociology, no. 1).

Ten essays reflecting current sociological research in Sweden. For a study relating particularly to the field, see Ulla Bergryd's 'The background of Swedish sociology' (p. 1–15).

459 **Sweden: prototype of modern society.**
Richard F. Tomasson. New York: Random House, 1970. 302p.
(Studies in Modern Societies).

A study of Swedish politics, religion, education and society which explores the nature of the country's modernization, social development and structure. Extensive notes at the end of each chapter provide suggestions for further reading. Still a major survey and reference work on the subject.

Social problems

460 **Alcohol policy in Sweden: a survey by the Swedish Council for Information on Alcohol and Other Drugs.**
Stockholm: Centralförbundet för alkohol och narkotikupplysning,
1982. 2nd rev. ed. 32p.

First published in 1980, it contains information on the consumption of alcohol in Sweden, legislation regarding alcohol and other drugs, and the names of research and temperance organizations concerned with these problems. A brief but very informative introduction to many aspects of the problem.

461 **Drinking habits among Northern youth: a cross-national study of male teenage drinking in the Northern capitals.**
Kettil Bruun, Ragnar Hauge, translated from the Swedish and
Norwegian by Fred A. Fewster. [Stockholm]: Alcohol Research
in the Northern Countries, 1963. 97p.

A statistical and sociological study of the problem in Finland, Sweden, Norway, and Denmark.

462 **Deviant behavior in Sweden.**
Louis Bultena. New York: Exposition, 1971. 182p.

Examines social problems in Sweden, corrective measures for them, and their links with the social welfare state. Areas dealt with include crime and the correction system, alcoholism, drug abuse, suicide, and sexual practices. A suitable introduction to these subjects.

463 **Limits to pain.**
Nils Christie.   Oslo: Universitetsforlaget, 1981. 122p. bibliog.
(Institutt for Kriminologi og Straffrett Skrifter, no. 25).
A study of the punishment of crime from a sociological point of view, which
highlights the inadequacies of present systems. Includes frequent references to
Sweden and the rest of Scandinavia.

464 **Drinking and driving in Scandinavia.**
Edited by Ragnar Hauge.   *Scandinavian Studies in Criminology*,
vol. 6 (1978), 143p.
An issue of the journal devoted to the subject. Articles discuss existing laws in all
of the countries, their effect, deterrence programmes, and research on the
problem. An important, scholarly discussion.

465 **Suicide and Scandinavia: a psycho-analytic study of culture and
character.**
Harold Hendin.   New York: Doubleday, 1964. 177p.
An incisive study of suicide and national character. Hendin devotes a long chapter
to Sweden (p. 43–74), finding personality traits there as a cause for suicide to be
different from those in the other Scandinavian countries. For more recent studies
based on Hendin's work, see Jan Beskow's *Suicide and mental disorder in Swedish
men* (Copenhagen: Munksgaard, 1979) as a supplement to *Acta Psychiatrica
Scandinavica* (1979); and Jeanne Block and Bjørn Christiansen's 'A test of
Hendin's hypotheses relating to suicide in Scandinavia to child-rearing orienta-
tions', *Scandinavian Journal of Psychology*, vol. 7, no. 4 (1966), p. 267–88.

466 **The elderly and their environment: research in Sweden.**
Edited by Karin Lidmar Reinius.   Stockholm: Swedish Council
for Building Research, 1984. 172p. bibliog.
Nineteen essays dealing with the care of the elderly in Sweden; many discuss their
physical environment and housing.

467 **Everyday violence in contemporary Sweden: situational and
ecological aspects.**
Per-Olof H. Wikström.   Stockholm: Liber, 1985. 308p. maps.
bibliog. (National Council for Crime Prevention, Sweden, Report
no. 15).
A sociological study of violent crime in Stockholm and several smaller Swedish
cities. Clear, concise, and of greatest value to social scientists.

Women and the family

468 **Mothers at work: public policies in the United States, Sweden, and China.**
Carolyn Adams, Kathryn Winston. New York; London: Longmans, 1980. 312p.

A comparative study of mothers in connection with the labour force, social welfare benefits, political participation, national economic policy, and the relationship of the government to the family. This study does not provide as much detail about Sweden as other studies but it is worthwhile as an introduction to these topics and for the background information it provides to Swedish developments.

469 **Corporate employment policies affecting families and children: the United States and Europe.**
Halcyone H. Bohen. New York: Aspen Institute for Humanistic Studies, 1983. 174p. bibliog.

A critical examination of sex-role programmes provided by industrial concerns in several countries, including Sweden (p. 37–52).

470 **The changing roles of men and women.**
Edited by Edmund Dahlström, foreword by Alva Myrdal, translated from the Swedish and Norwegian by Gunnilla Anderman, Steven Anderman. Boston: Beacon Press, 1971. 302p.

First published in Sweden as *Kvinnors liv och arbete* (Women's lives and work) (Stockholm: Studieförbundet Näringsliv & Samhälle, 1962) and later in England (London: Gerald Duckworth, 1967). Six essays that discuss the issues of changing sex roles at the workplace and in the home. The authors are all Scandinavians and there is a Nordic, particularly Swedish, emphasis to most of the works. A valuable background to more recent publications and developments in Scandinavia.

471 **Sweden.**
Maud Edwards. In: *The politics of the second electorate: women and public participation: Britain, USA, Canada, Australia, France, Spain, West Germany, Italy, Sweden, Finland, Eastern Europe, USSR, Japan.* Edited by Joni Lovenduski, Jill Hills. London; Henley-on-Thames, England; Boston, Massachusetts: Routledge & Kegan Paul, 1981, p. 208–27.

Summarizes participation by Swedish women in political affairs and volunteer associations. An excellent introduction to the topic.

472 **Children's theatre in Sweden.**
Edited by Lena Fridell, translated from the Swedish by Clause
Stephenson. Stockholm: Svensk teaterunion, 1979. 96p.
This is a quick, but useful guide to what is happening in this field in Sweden.
Children's theatre is an important part of Swedish theatrical (and educational)
life, and is taken quite seriously. It often, even usually, has a strong dialectical
edge to it. This book can be complemented by a pamphlet, by Kent Hägglund,
Theatre for children in Sweden: a contemporary view (Stockholm: Swedish
Institute, 1986), 32p.

473 **Women in public.**
Edited by Carol Gold, Morete Ries. *Scandinavian Review*,
vol. 65, no. 3 (1977). 128p. bibliog.
This entire issue is devoted to articles concerning women in public life and public
discussion of this growing phenomenon.

474 **Not for sale: young people in society.**
Benny Henriksson, foreword by Thomas R. Forstenzer, preface by
Brian J. Ashley, translated from the Swedish by Susan Davies,
Irene Scobbie. Aberdeen, Scotland: Aberdeen University Press,
1983. 204p. bibliog.
A translation of the summary *Pengarna eller livet* (Money or life) of a much more
detailed report *Ej till salu* (Not for sale) published by the Swedish Youth Council
in 1981. It is a critical, well-written study of the exploitation of children by
consumer society. The evidence and examples are Swedish but the problems it
discusses are universal. A major work of importance to all who are interested in
children and adolescents.

475 **Scandinavia.**
Harriet Holter. In: *Women in the modern world*. Edited with a
foreword by Raphael Patai. New York: Free Press; London:
Collier-Macmillan, 1967, p. 437–62. bibliog.
The essay describes the changing role of women in Scandinavia after the Second
World War. Topics discussed include education, occupations, the home routine,
and divorce.

476 **Women in the world: a comparative study.**
Edited by Lynne B. Iglitzin, Ruth Ross. Santa Barbara,
California; Oxford: Clio Press, 1976. 427p. (Studies in
Comparative Politics, vol. 6).
Includes Ingunn Norderval Means' 'Scandinavian women' (p. 375–90), an
excellent survey of women's role in society throughout the Nordic countries and
Sondra R. German's 'Sweden: a feminist model' (p. 391–400) which discusses
Sweden's situation in the 20th century in particular.

477 **A study of abortion in Sweden.**
Ruth Liljeström. Stockholm: P. A. Norstedt & Söner, 1974.
104p. bibliog.

A study on the subject by the National Preparatory Committee for the World Population Conference. Although dealing briefly with the 18th and 19th centuries, it primarily examines abortion from the early 20th century until the 1970s from the standpoints of demography, economic and social developments, and the role of women within society. A non-polemical, concise study of a controversial issue.

478 **Sex roles in transition: a report on a pilot program in Sweden.**
Rita Liljeström, Gunnilla Fürst Mellestrom, Gillan Liljeström
Svensson, translated from the Swedish by Carol
Waldén. Stockholm: Swedish Institute, 1975. 104p.

A report by the Advisory Council to the Prime Minister on Equality between Men and Women as part of the United Nations' International Women's Year 1975. It discusses a pilot programme established by the council to broaden the range of jobs open to women and its results. An example of the programmes and views on this subject in modern Sweden.

479 **Sex and society in Sweden.**
Birgitta Linnér, in collaboration with Richard J. Litell, foreword
by Lester A. Kirkendall. New York: Harper & Row, 1972. 225p.
bibliog.

Examines many facets of the subject including sexual behaviour in Sweden, family planning, birth control, abortion, venereal disease, and sex education. The last third consists of sample sex education materials that are used in Sweden for different age groups. The book was first published by Pantheon Books in 1967.

480 **Sweden's 'right to be human' sex-role equality: the goal and the
reality.**
Hilda Scott. Armonk, New York: M. E. Sharpe, 1982. 191p.

Studies many related aspects of the subject including workplace programmes which have been developed, the economic and social implications for working mothers, and teaching sex-role equality in the schools. A clear, critical and up-to-date study.

481 **Equality between the sexes: myth and reality in Norden.**
Torild Skard, Elina Haavio-Mannila. *Daedalus*, vol. 113, no. 1
(1984), p. 141–67.

The article summarizes the stages of the Nordic feminist movement during the last century and the problems that still remain in the search not only for equality of opportunity but also for equality of results. See also Haavio-Mannila's article in *Nordic democracy* (q.v.) on the status of women in Scandinavia today.

482 **Swedish youth.**
Lars Thalén, foreword by Olof Palme, translated from the Swedish
by Roger G. Tanner. Stockholm: Swedish Institute, National
Swedish Youth Council, 1972. 32p.
Concise, informative summary of youth organizations and issues such as
consumption of alcohol and sexual practices. In need of revision but an excellent
introduction to the subject.

483 **Unmarried cohabitation.**
Jan Trost. Västerås, Sweden: International Library/Librairie
Internationale, 1979. 206p. bibliog.
A sociological study with evidence primarily from Sweden, the rest of
Scandinavia, and the United States. It is clear and non-polemical.

484 **Swedish women on the move.**
Birgitta Wistrand, edited and translated from the Swedish by
Jeanne Rosen. Stockholm: Swedish Institute, 1981. 112p.
Studies many different aspects of Swedish women in modern society: role within
the family, provision within the social welfare and educational systems, in the
labour force, health and protection, political influence, and sex roles in the mass
media. It includes a list of women's groups in Sweden and is written by a leader of
Sweden's women's rights movement. A clear statement of the issue by an
advocate, but non-polemical.

Housing

485 **Housing in Scandinavia: urban and rural.**
John Graham, Jr. Chapel Hill, North Carolina: University of
North Carolina Press, 1940. 223p.
A comparative study of housing in Denmark, Finland, Norway and Sweden which
examines land, municipal housing, housing societies and rural housing. It reflects
conditions and policy in the Scandinavian states prior to the Second World War,
provides an introduction to post-war programmes in these countries, and indicates
the glaring need for a study of the post-war period.

486 **The Swedish building sector in 1990: the need for research and
development in the eighties.**
Translated from the Swedish by L. J. Gruber. Stockholm:
Swedish Council for Building Research, 1983. 95p.
Summarizes the building industry's views, production changes and energy
supplies, its role within the national economy, and future research needs. A
useful introduction to present and future directions in the housing industry.

487 **New towns and old: housing and services in Sweden.**
Edited by Hans-Erland Heineman, translated from the Swedish by
Keith Bradfield. Stockholm: Swedish Institute, 1975. 183p. maps.

The editor and five other authors contribute essays discussing the development of
town and urban planning, transport networks, and especially of housing during
the last century. A concise and cogent study for all readers.

488 **The Swedish housing model: an assessment.**
Thomas S. Nesslein. *Urban Studies*, vol. 19, no. 3 (1982),
p. 235–46. bibliog.

Surveys post-war Swedish housing policy and examines its strengths and
weaknesses. An excellent, concise, critical summary.

489 **European housing subsidy systems.**
Irving H. Welfeld. Washington, DC: US Department of Housing
and Urban Development, 1972. 52p.

Includes a brief (p. 36–43) description of Swedish housing programmes. A helpful
introduction but in need of revision.

Health and medicine

490 **Dental health care in Scandinavia: achievements and future
strategies.**
Edited by Asger Frandsen. Chicago, Illinois: Quintessence
Publishing Co., 1982. 259p.

Seven major papers presented at a symposium. 'Dental health care in
Scandinavia' in Oslo, January 1981, and shorter items. The main articles discuss
the nature of present health care systems in Scandinavia, common dental diseases
and assessments of preventive dental programmes for various age groups. An
important introduction to a subject infrequently surveyed in English.

491 **Controlling medical technology in Sweden.**
Erik H. L. Gaensler, Egon Jonsson, Duncan vB. Nauhauser. In:
*The management of health care technology in nine countries (United
Kingdom, Canada, Australia, Japan, France, West Germany,
Netherlands, Sweden, United States).* Edited by H. David Banta,
Kerry Britten Kemp, foreword by Kerr L. White. New York:
Springer, 1982, p. 167–92. bibliog. (Springer Series on Health Care
and Society, vol. 7).

Describes the development of Sweden's health care system and, by the use of case
studies, the options available to Swedish planners for the control of medical
technology and innovations. Of value to those wishing to study such control

mechanisms or as an introduction to the Swedish health care system and the use of modern medical technology in the country. For a detailed discussion of hospital administration, see Eric Rhenman, *Managing the community hospital: systems analysis of a Swedish hospital* (Lexington, Massachusetts: Lexington Books; Westmead, England: Saxon House, 1973).

492 Health: a major issue.
Scandinavian Review, vol. 63, no. 3 (1975), 63p. bibliog.
The entire issue of the journal is devoted to articles on health care in Scandinavia. It includes statistical data and discussion of doctors, hospitals, consumerism, and other related topics.

493 The shaping of the Swedish health system.
Edited by Arnold J. Heidenheimer, Nils Elvander, assisted by Charly Hultén. New York: St. Martin's Press, 1980. 245p.
Nine essays by leading scholars on the nature and development of Sweden's health care programmes. These articles address such topics as the development of Swedish health care in comparison to Norway and Denmark's experiences during the 19th and 20th centuries, health care as a political and governmental issue, its impact on the medical profession; and medical results in comparison to financial expenditure. Some knowledge of the subject is presumed but the essays are cogent, professional, and non-polemical.

494 National and regional health planning in Sweden.
Vincente Navarro. Washington, DC: US Department of Health, Education, and Welfare; Public Health Service; National Institute of Health, 1974. 244p. bibliog. (DHEW Publication, No. (NIH) 74–240).
A detailed description of the Swedish health care system and the government planning process by which it is organized and administered. A basic work in this field.

495 Mental health systems in Scandinavia.
David J. Vail, special comments by Christian Astrup. Springfield, Illinois: Charles C. Thomas, 1968. 157p. bibliog.
The section on Sweden (p. 73–115) outlines mental health programmes available in the country. In need of revision to reflect changes since the book was published, but still a valuable introduction for scholars in the field.

Swedish life and landscape.
See item no. 45.
Sweden: holiday guide for the disabled.
See item no. 111.
Sweden's development from poverty to affluence, 1750–1970.
See item no. 151.

The Scandinavian countries, 1720–1865: the rise of the middle classes.
See item no. 159.

The Viking achievement: a survey of the society and culture of early medieval Scandinavia.
See item no. 175.

The Viking world.
See item no. 176.

The Norsemen.
See item no. 183.

The Viking world.
See item no. 186.

Social Scandinavia in the Viking age.
See item no. 190.

Les peuples scandinaves au moyen âge. (The Scandinavian people in the Middle Ages.)
See item no. 196.

Nordic slavery in an international setting.
See item no. 199.

Rise and decline of an aristocracy: the Swedish social and political élite in the 17th century.
See item no. 200.

Gustavus Adolphus: a history of Sweden 1611–1632.
See item no. 215.

Sweden as a great power 1611–1697: government: society: foreign policy.
See item no. 219.

Sweden's Age of Greatness 1632–1718.
See item no. 220.

Europe and Scandinavia: aspects of the process of integration in the 17th century.
See item no. 224.

Sweden in the 1760s.
See item no. 236.

Sweden.
See item no. 240.

The *Mittelstand* in Swedish class society, 1870–1914.
See item no. 246.

Ideology and social policy in the mid-nineteenth century.
See item no. 247.

Causes of poverty in Sweden in the nineteenth century.
See item no. 256.

Recent developments in Swedish social history of the period since 1800.
See item no. 293.

More children of better quality?: aspects of Swedish population policy in the 1930s.
See item no. 301.

Population policy in Western Europe: responses to low fertility in France, Sweden, and West Germany.
See item no. 303.

Aristocrats, farmers, proletarians: essays in Swedish demographic history.
See item no. 306.

Sweden.
See item no. 308.

Social and economic aspects of Swedish population movements 1750–1933.
See item no. 313.

Social science research in Sweden.
See item no. 431.

Early child care in Sweden.
See item no. 435.

Sweden's day nurseries: focus on programs for infants and toddlers.
See item no. 436.

Social welfare and handicap policy in Sweden.
See item no. 496.

Limits of the welfare state: critical views on post-war Sweden.
See item no. 501.

Sweden and the price of progress.
See item no. 508.

Politics in the post-welfare state: responses to the new individualism.
See item no. 520.

Governing Greater Stockholm: a study of policy development and system change.
See item no. 567.

Legal values in modern Sweden.
See item no. 577.

Law and the weaker party: an Anglo–Swedish comparative study.
See item no. 582.

Society. Health and medicine

Stockholm: the politics of crime and conflict, 1750 to the 1970s.
See item no. 584.

'Police and the social order': contemporary research perspectives.
See item no. 585.

Sweden: choices for economic and social policy in the 1980s.
See item no. 652.

Full employment and public policy: the United States and Sweden.
See item no. 682.

The suburban environment: Sweden and the United States.
See item no. 759.

Acta Sociologica.
See item no. 927.

Kulturtidskriften: 1986 katalog över kulturtidskrifter i Sverige. (The
cultural journal: 1986 catalogue of cultural journals in Sweden.)
See item no. 955.

Föräldrar och barn: en kommenterad litteraturlista. (Parents and
children: an annotated bibliography.)
See item no. 966.

Scandinavia in social science literature: an English-language bibliography.
See item no. 972.

Women and men in Swedish society: research projects supported by the
Bank of Sweden Tercentenary Foundation.
See item no. 981.

Culture for Swedish children.
See item no. 1000.

The Social Welfare State

496   **Social welfare and handicap policy in Sweden.**
Barbro Folke Carlsson, translated from the Swedish by Victor J.
Kayfetz.   Stockholm: Swedish Institute, 1982. 54p.
A broad overview of the development and scope of policies regarding
handicapped people in Sweden. An excellent introduction to the subject.

497   **Sweden: the middle way.**
Marquis W. Childs.   New Haven, Connecticut; London: Yale
University Press, 1963. 199p. map.
First published in 1936, re-published several times, and issued as a new, revised
edition in 1947, it was one of the first and most influential works to point out the
beginnings of Sweden's social programmes during the 1930s. It deals primarily
with many of the state's regulatory functions and is best known for its discussion
of the cooperative movement. A landmark work on the subject. See also Childs's
later consideration of the subject in his *Sweden: the middle way on trial* (q.v.).

498   **Politics against markets: the Social Democratic road to power.**
Gösta Esping-Andersen.   Princeton, New Jersey: Princeton
University Press, 1985. 366p. bibliog.
Studies the development of the Social Democratic parties in the Scandinavian
countries and of the social welfare policies they created. A critical, penetrating
work of greatest interest to economists and political scientists but also to all
serious students of contemporary Scandinavia. See also his *Social class, social
democracy and state policy: party policy and party decomposition in Denmark and
Sweden* (Copenhagen: New Science Monographs, 1980).

499 **Suède: la réforme permanente.** (Sweden: the permanent reform.)
Edited by Guy de Faramond, Claude Glagman, Micheline Jérôme,
Dan Franck. Paris: Éditions Stock, 1977. 400p. map. bibliog.
(Livre-dossier).

A collection of articles and interviews by both Swedes and foreigners on aspects
of Swedish social democracy. Prepared against the background of the 1976
electoral victory of the non-socialist parties over the Social Democrats, the
articles represent many points of view on the nature and effect of the welfare
state.

500 **The evolution of social welfare policy in Sweden.**
Mats Forsberg, translated from the Swedish by Victor J. Kayfetz.
Stockholm: Swedish Institute, 1984. 80p. bibliog.

Describes the historical roots of Sweden's social welfare policy from the late 19th
century until the 1930s. It is also a topical study of the various sectors of the social
welfare system since then. A concise survey for the general reader and useful
introduction for those wishing to study further. For a briefer study, now out of
print, see Leif Holgersson and Stig Lundström's *The evolution of Swedish social
welfare* (Stockholm: Swedish Institute, 1975).

501 **Limits of the welfare state: critical views on post-war Sweden.**
Edited by John Fry. Westmead, England: Saxon House, 1979.
234p.

A collection of twelve essays by Swedes on contemporary politics, society and
economics. Representative of the New Left view of the social welfare state and
clearly controversial in its own right, as indicated by the review of it by Richard F.
Tomasson in *Scandinavian Studies*, vol. 53, no. 2 (1981), p. 232–33.

502 **The case for the welfare state: from social security to social equality.**
Norman Furniss, Timothy A. Tilton. Bloomington, Indiana;
London: Indiana University Press, 1977. 249p.

Discusses the development of social welfare policies in Britain, Sweden and the
United States. Four chapters examine common developments with later chapters
on each country. That on Sweden (p. 122–52) is a thorough, clear sketch of social
welfare programmes, the disadvantages and achievements that have resulted. Of
interest both to the specialist and the general reader.

503 **The welfare state and beyond: success and problems in Scandinavia.**
Gunnar Heckscher. Minneapolis, Minnesota: University of
Minnesota Press, 1984. 271p. bibliog. (Nordic Series, vol. 11).

A well-balanced view of the roots of the Scandinavian welfare state, its ideals,
general character, and the political processes involved in governing a state based
on these principles. The author, a former leader of the Swedish Conservative
Party, also provides a critique of the imagined and real problems facing the
welfare state, particularly the problems created by stagflation, a new era of
political confrontation after decades of consensus, and current political issues. An

explanation and criticism of the welfare state by an active participant in its construction. For a briefer discussion of some of his views, see 'Ideals of the welfare state', *Scandinavian Review*, vol. 70, no. 3 (1982), p. 6–16.

504 **Modern social politics in Britain and Sweden: from relief to income maintenance.**
Hugh Heclo. New Haven, Connecticut; London: Yale University Press, 1974. 349p. bibliog.
Compares the development of unemployment insurance and old-age pensions programmes in Britain and Sweden from the early 20th century until the late 1960s. A thorough, well-respected study presented in non-technical terminology, of value both to the scholar and interested general reader.

505 **Public policy comparisons: Scandinavia.**
Edited by Arnold J. Heidenheimer. *West European Politics*, vol. 3, no. 3 (1980), p. 293–430.
An entire issue of the journal devoted primarily to comparative studies of social welfare programmes in Scandinavia, changes in their operation, and influence on programmes elsewhere. Most valuable for social scientists but also for other interested readers.

506 **Beyond welfare capitalism: issues, actors and forces in societal change.**
Ulf Himmelstrand, Göran Ahrne, Leif Lundberg, Lars Lundberg. London: Heinemann, 1981. 370p. bibliog.
Discusses the breakdown of the mixed economy and the evolution of new economic solutions by business and labour forces, particularly employee investment funds. A detailed study of greatest interest to social scientists.

507 **The new totalitarians.**
Roland Huntford. New York: Stein & Day, 1972. 354p.
A critical, New Right description of Swedish society as the fulfilment of Aldous Huxley's *Brave new world* and George Orwell's *1984*. One of the earliest and most influential negative discussions of the impact of social welfare programmes on Sweden. As one-sided and biased as works that blindly praise Sweden's progress and development.

508 **Sweden and the price of progress.**
David Jenkins. New York: Coward-McCann, 1968. 286p.
Examines Swedish society and the welfare state for the influence which they have on the Swedish character. It is perceptive, mildly critical, and the work of a writer with an extensive knowledge of the country.

The Social Welfare State

509 **The growth of social insurance programs in Scandinavia: outside influences and internal forces.**
Stein Kuhnle. In: *The development of welfare states in Europe and America.* Edited by Peter Flora, Arnold J. Heidenheimer.
New Brunswick, New Jersey; London: Transaction Books, 1982, p. 125–50. bibliog.

A scholarly discussion on a comparative basis of the external and internal factors which led to the development of the first social welfare legislation in the Scandinavian countries during the late 19th and early 20th centuries. It is analytical rather than descriptive, with some knowledge presumed of Scandinavian history or of social welfare programmes, but also a very cogent work by an expert. For other works by Kuhnle on the same subject, see 'The beginnings of the Nordic welfare state: similarities and differences', *Acta Sociologica*, vol. 21, supplement (1978), p. 9–35; and in *Nordic democracy* (q.v.), p. 399–415. For a comparative study of public policy in many countries, including Sweden, of education, health, social welfare programmes, and economic policy, see Arnold J. Heidenheimer, Hugh Heclo, Carolyn Adams's, *Comparative public policy: the politics of social change in Europe and America* (New York: St. Martin's Press, 1983), 2nd ed.

510 **The debate on economic planning in Sweden.**
Leif Lewin. In: *Sweden's development from poverty to affluence, 1750–1970.* Edited by Steven Koblik, translated by Joanne Johnson. Minneapolis, Minnesota: University of Minnesota Press, 1975, p. 282–302.

Summarizes the debate in Sweden in this controversial subject from the 1920s until the late 1960s. It emphasizes the contribution of Ernst Wigforss in particular as well as Prime Minister Tage Erlander and Gösta Rehn to Social Democratic ideology on this issue and the role of Herbert Tingsten as the spokesman for the non-socialist camp. Another important article in the same work on this subject is Kurt Samuelsson's 'The philosophy of Swedish welfare policies', p. 335–53.

511 **Beyond the welfare state: economic planning and its international implications.**
Gunnar Myrdal. New Haven, Connecticut: Yale University Press, 1960. 287p. (Storrs Lectures in Jurisprudence).

Examines the tendency towards economic planning followed by many Western nations and its international implications. Swedish examples are frequent and also reflect the work of one of Sweden's most influential modern economists.

512 **The wages of success.**
Gösta Rehn. *Daedalus*, vol. 113, no. 2 (1984), p. 137–68.

Sketches the social insurance programmes of the five Nordic governments and employment policies with an even-handed discussion of the benefits and disadvantages of Swedish policy in particular. An excellent introduction. For other perceptive assessments of the Scandinavian social welfare state in the same work with a special emphasis on Sweden, see Bernt Hagtvet and Erik Rudeng's

138

'Scandinavia: achievements, dilemmas, challenges' (p. 227–56); in the companion volume, *Daedalus*, vol. 113, no. 1 (1984) see Per Olov Enquist's 'On the art of flying backward with dignity' (p. 60–73), translated by Verne Moberg; Hans L. Zetterman's, 'The rational humanitarians' (p. 75–92); Hans F. Dahl's, 'Those equal folk' (p. 93–107); and Bengt Roald Andersen's, 'Rationality and irrationality of the Nordic welfare state' (p. 109–39).

513   **The social programs of Sweden: a search for security in a free**
      society.
      Albert H. Rosenthal.   Minneapolis, Minnesota: University of
      Minnesota Press, 1967. 193p. bibliog.
A detailed description of Sweden's social welfare programmes and administration as they existed when the book was written. In need of revision but worthwhile as a guide for the policies and programmes up to that point. See also Carl G. Uhr's *Sweden's social security system: an appraisal of its economic impact in the postwar period* (Washington, DC: US Department of Health, Education and Welfare, Social Security Administration, Office of Research and Statistics, 1966).

514   **The welfare state in Sweden: a study in comparative social**
      administration.
      Dorothy Wilson.   London: Heinemann, 1979. 173p. bibliog.
      (Studies in Social Policy and Welfare).
A thorough, unbiased description of Swedish social welfare programmes. An excellent introduction to more analytical or less impartial works. Includes a detailed bibliography of additional works in English on the subject.

Sweden.
See item no. 7.

The Scandinavians.
See item no. 16.

Scandinavia.
See item no. 23.

A clean, well-lighted place: a private view of Sweden.
See item no. 51.

Sweden: model for a world.
See item no. 56.

Recent developments in Swedish population policy.
See item no. 297.

Sweden.
See item no. 300.

More children of better quality?: aspects of Swedish population policy in
the 1930s.
See item no. 301.

Report from a Swedish village.
See item no. 456.

Mothers at work: public policies in the United States, Sweden, and China.
See item no. 468.

Swedish women on the move.
See item no. 484.

Sweden: the middle way on trial.
See item no. 517.

The social democratic image of society: a study of the achievements and origins of Scandinavian social democracy in comparative perspective.
See item no. 528.

A Swedish road to socialism: Ernst Wigforss and the ideological foundations of social democracy.
See item no. 540.

Scandinavia at the polls: recent political trends in Denmark, Norway, and Sweden.
See item no. 544.

Post-industrial society.
See item no. 646.

Trouble in Eden: a comparison of the British and Swedish economies.
See item no. 654.

The transition from capitalism to socialism.
See item no. 655.

Planning and productivity in Sweden.
See item no. 660.

Reformist programmes in the planning for post-war economic policy during World War II.
See item no. 664.

Trade union strategies and social policy in Italy and Sweden.
See item no. 692.

Scandinavian government and politics: a bibliography of materials in English.
See item no. 983.

Sweden: focus on post-industrialism.
See item no. 1004.

Politics

General

515 **Olof Palme: the socialist aristocrat.**
Leif Björkman. *American–Scandinavian Review*, vol. 62, no. 2 (1974), p. 117–27.
Sketches Palme's early life and political career until he became Prime Minister and head of Sweden's Social Democratic party in 1969. Few works are available at present on the late Swedish leader. For brief works published after his death, see Gunnar Fredriksson's *Swedish portraits: Olof Palme* (Stockholm: Swedish Institute, 1986), a short pamphlet; and a special issue of *Inside Sweden*, vol. 2, no. 2 (1986).

516 **Scandinavia: the politics of stability.**
Francis G. Castles. In: *Modern political systems: Europe*. Edited by Roy C. Macridis. Englewood Cliffs, New Jersey: Prentice-Hall, 1983. 5th ed. p. 387–434. map. bibliog.
Surveys factors significant to the political development of Scandinavia, political parties and groups, and the imposing influence of the Scandinavian Social Democratic parties on the politics of the region. A thorough and helpful introduction to the subject, first published in 1963.

517 **Sweden: the middle way on trial.**
Marquis W. Childs.   New Haven, Connecticut; London: Yale University Press, 1980. 179p.
In part a revision of Marquis W. Childs' *Sweden: the middle way* (q.v.), it contains also the reminiscences of a person who knows Sweden and many Swedes as well, and a discussion of Swedish politics and problems during the 1970s. These include consideration of prominent politicians such as Olof Palme and Torbjörn

Fälldin and subjects such as the weakness in social welfare programmes, the nuclear power debate, and Swedish–American relations. An important study of contemporary Sweden.

518 **Welfare states in hard times: problems, policy, and politics in Denmark and Sweden.**
Erin Einhorn, John Logue.   Kent, Ohio: Kent Popular Press, 1982. rev. ed. 72p. bibliog.

Examines the governments and political parties of the two countries and their responses to the economic and political crises of the late 1970s. A very useful, concise introduction to contemporary developments in both countries.

519 **The consensual democracies?: the government and politics of the Scandinavian states.**
Neil Elder, Alastair H. Thomas, David Arter.   Oxford, England: Martin Robertson, 1982. 244p. map. bibliog.

A study of modern politics and government in the Nordic states. The authors discuss the establishment of the 'five party' model for politics in these countries during the first half of the 20th century, the structure of government and the factors that threaten 'consensual' democracy as they define the term.

520 **Politics in the post-welfare state: responses to the new individualism.**
Edited by M. Donald Hancock, Gideon Sjöberg.   New York; London: Columbia University Press, 1972. 335p.

A collection of essays assessing contemporary economic, social, and political conditions in the United States, Britain, and Sweden regarding the role of the individual in society. The section on Sweden (p. 223–324) contains essays by Hancock, Kaj Björk, Erik Annars, Lars Gyllensten, and Nils Elvander which discuss the quest for economic and political change, conservatism, radicalism during the 1960s, the nature of a 'new individualism' in Sweden, and the relationship of the individual to the large number of interest groups that exist in Sweden. A pertinent work still relevant to modern Swedish politics and society.

521 **Patterns of social and political mobilization: a historical analysis of the Nordic countries.**
Stein Kuhnle.   London; Beverly Hills, California: Sage Publications, 1975. 75p. bibliog. (Sage Professional Papers in Contemporary Political Sociology).

A very broad theoretical introduction to Scandinavian politics, political development, and political participation, of greatest interest to social scientists.

522 **The aftermath of the Palme assassination.**
Ingemar Lindahl. *Scandinavian Review*, vol. 75, no. 1 (1987),
p. 15–21.
Assesses Palme's impact on Swedish politics during his lifetime and the effect his
death may have on immediate political developments. Both a sympathetic and a
critical treatment.

523 **Western European party systems: trends and prospects.**
Edited by Peter H. Merkl. New York: Free Press; London:
Collier-Macmillan, 1980. 676p.
A chapter by M. Donald Hancock (p. 185–204) discusses political events and
issues during the 1970s. References to Sweden are frequently made in the
chapters on comparative politics that follow. Useful for students of both topics.

524 **Political science research in Sweden 1960–1975: an overview.**
Olof Ruin. *Scandinavian Political Studies*, vol. 12 (1977),
p. 157–84.
Examines the basic fields of research and chief scholars in Swedish political
science research during the period. This paper and an article by Nils Elvander
entitled 'The growth of the profession 1960–1975: Sweden' (p. 75–82) were
contributions to a special issue of the journal on 'Political science in the Nordic
countries 1960–1975'.

525 **Scandinavia: the experiment in social democracy.**
James L. Waite. In: *The other Western Europe: a political
analysis of the small democracies.* Edited by Earl H. Fry, Gregory
A. Raymond. Santa Barbara, California; Oxford: ABC-Clio
Information Services, 1983. 2nd rev. ed. p. 195–233. bibliog.
(Studies in International and Comparative Politics).
First published in 1980, this is a concise summary of government, political parties,
interest groups, and recent political developments. A useful introduction for those
planning further study of these subjects.

Political parties

526 **The conservative dilemma: ideology and vote maximisation in
Sweden.**
Sten Berglund, Ulf Lindström. In: *Conservative politics in
Western Europe.* Edited by Zig Layton-Henry. New York:
St. Martin's Press, 1982, p. 68–82.
Examines the background of Sweden's Moderata Samlingspartiet (Moderate
Conservative Party), electoral strategies, and support. A helpful discussion of an
important party.

527 **The Scandinavian party system(s): a comparative study.**
Sten Berglund, Ulf Lindström. Lund, Sweden: Studentlitteratur,
1978. 203p. maps. bibliog.
A discussion of the political party systems of the Scandinavian countries and their
relative conformity to the 'five party model'. Topics considered are the evolution
of the different political parties, their relative strengths, social bases of support,
and their activity within the national parliamentary bodies. The final chapter
describes the significant changes during the 1970s that occurred among these
political parties. For a briefer article by Berglund on the same subject, see his
article in *Nordic Democracy* (q.v.), p. 80–125.

528 **The social democratic image of society: a study of the achievements
and origins of Scandinavian social democracy in comparative
perspective.**
Francis G. Castles. London; Henley, England; Boston,
Massachusetts: Routledge & Kegan Paul, 1978. 162p. bibliog.
Investigates the origins of Social Democratic parties in the Scandinavian states
during the 20th century, the development of the welfare state as defined by four
basic criteria, and the means by which the Scandinavian Social Democratic parties
successfully dominated politics until the late 1970s.

529 **Democratic Socialism: the mass left in advanced industrial societies.**
Edited by Bogdan Denitch, foreword by Michael
Harrington. Montclair, New Jersey: Allanheld, Osmun, 1981.
180p.
Two essays discuss different aspects of Sweden's Social Democratic Party. John
D. Stephens' 'The ideological development of the Swedish Social Democrats'
(p. 136–48) analyses aspects of the debate that have developed regarding the early
history of the party, and considers more recent questions. Ulf Himmelstrand's
'Sweden: paradise in trouble' (p. 149–62) deals with the party while it was out of
power in the late 1970s, and the prospects for its revival. Useful works by noted
scholars.

530 **The Centre parties of Norway and Sweden.**
Neil C. M. Elder, Rolf Gooderham. *Government and
Opposition*, vol. 13, no. 2 (1978), p. 218–35.
A comparative study of the origins, changes in, and success of the parties. An
excellent introduction to parties often overlooked in analyses of Scandinavian
politics from the outside.

531   **In search of new relationships: parties, unions, and salaried employees' associations in Sweden.**
Nils Elvander.   *Industrial and Labor Relations Review*, vol. 28, no. 1 (1974), p. 60–74.

Important for its discussion of the cooperative relationship between Sweden's Social Democratic Party and Landsorganisation (LO, Trade Union Federation) and of the more independent unions for salaried employees, Tjänstemännens Centralorganisation (TCO, Central Organization of Salaried Employees) and Sveriges Akademikers Centralorganisation (SACO, Central Organization of Swedish Academics). A useful introduction to the subject.

532   **Scandinavian social democracy: its strengths and weaknesses.**
Nils Elvander.   Uppsala, Stockholm: Almqvist & Wiksell, 1979. 35p. (Acta Universitatis Upsaliensis: Skrifter rörande Uppsala Universitet: C. Organisation och historia, vol. 39).

A comparative study of the Danish and Swedish Social Democratic parties and the Labour party in Norway. Consideration is also given to the development of the issue of employee investment funds by these parties and the labour unions they represent. A concise survey of development to the late 1970s.

533   **Communism in the Nordic countries: Denmark, Norway, Sweden and Iceland.**
Trond Gilberg.   In: *The changing face of Western Communism*. Edited by David Childs. London: Croom Helm, 1980, p. 205–59.

A convincing interpretative summary of Scandinavian Communism up to the late 1970s.

534   **Sweden's emerging labor socialism.**
M. Donald Hancock.   In: *Eurocommunism and Eurosocialism: The Left confronts modernity*. Edited by Bernard E. Brown. New York; London: Cyrio Press, 1979, p. 316–37.

Sketches the party's role in politics during the 1960s and 1970s and underlines the importance of the Meidner Report of 1976 calling for the creation of the wage-earner funds as a distinctive example of the influence of the LO (Trade Union Federation) on the party and as a means of economic reform. A concise assessment of recent developments within the Social Democratic Party.

535   **The dilemma of Social Democratic Labor parties.**
Erling Olsen.   *Daedalus*, vol. 113, no. 2 (1984), p. 169–94.

Provides a survey of the origins and development of the Social Democratic parties in the Nordic countries, the problems posed by the New Left and New Right to their domination of politics during the 1970s, and the problems they are likely to face in the near future.

Politics. Political parties

536   **Scandinavian party politics re-examined: social democracy in decline.**
Diane Sainsbury.   *West European Politics*, vol. 7, no. 4 (1984), p. 67–102.

Examines the decline of factors which have contributed in the past to the success of Scandinavian Social Democratic parties. A cogent analysis by an expert in the field. Part of a special issue of the journal on 'Party politics in contemporary Western Europe'. For another article by the author dealing with the same subject, see 'Functional hypotheses of party decline: the case of the Scandinavian Social Democratic parties', *Scandinavian Political Studies*, new series, vol. 6, no. 4 (1983), p. 241–60.

537   **Swedish Social Democratic ideology and electoral politics 1944–1948: a study of the functions of party ideology.**
Diane Sainsbury.   Stockholm: Almqvist & Wiksell, 1980. 192p. bibliog. (Stockholm Studies in Politics, vol. 17).

Considers the origins and nature of Social Democratic ideology in the mid-1940s and its impact on the party's approach to the Swedish elections of 1946 and 1948. A scholarly account for students of Sweden and modern politics.

538   **Social democracy in capitalist society: working-class politics in Britain and Sweden.**
Richard Scase.   London: Croom Helm; Totowa, New Jersey: Rowman & Littlefield, 1977. 184p. bibliog.

Examines the impact of trade unions and labour parties in Sweden (Social Democratic Party) and Britain on class inequalities and political attitudes. A detailed, scholarly study primarily for social scientists. See also his 'Social democracy in Sweden', in *Social Democratic parties in Western Europe*, edited by William E. Paterson, Alastair H. Thomas (London: Croom Helm, 1979), p. 316–41.

539   **The Communist Party of Sweden.**
Åke Sparring.   In: *The Communist parties of Scandinavia and Finland*. Edited by Anthony F. Upton. London: Weidenfeld & Nicolson, 1973, p. 61–101.

Sketches the party's development and difficulties from its split with the Social Democrats during the First World War until the late 1960s. A knowledgeable, clear introduction. For another article by Sparring on the same subject, see his contribution in *Communism in Europe: continuity, change, and the Sino-Soviet dispute*, edited by William E. Griffith (Oxford: Pergamon Press, 1967), vol. 2, p. 287–319.

540 **A Swedish road to socialism: Ernst Wigforss and the ideological foundations of Swedish social democracy.**
Timothy A. Tilton. *American Political Science Review*, vol. 73, no. 2 (1979), p. 505–20. bibliog.
Discusses the influence of Ernst Wigforss (1881–1977) on the ideology and programmes of the Social Democratic Party from the 1920s to the 1960s. An excellent introduction by an expert.

541 **The Swedish Social Democrats: their ideological development.**
Herbert Tingsten, foreword by Richard Tomasson, translated from the Swedish by Greta Frankel, Patricia Howard-Rosen. Totowa, New Jersey: Bedminster Press, 1973. 719p.
First published in Swedish, *Den Svenska Socialdemokratins idéutveckling* (Stockholm: Tidens Forlag, 1941), it studies the party's development from the late 19th century until the 1930s. Written by an ex-Social Democrat, for many years the editor of *Dagens Nyheter*, Sweden's most influential newspaper, it is a detailed, critical study which now has its own critics but remains the most comprehensive study of the party in any language.

Interest groups and elections

542 **Political value patterns and parties in Sweden.**
Gunnar Boalt, Ulla Bergryd. Stockholm: Almqvist & Wiksell, 1981. 134p.
Describes the result of a research project linking party preference to the promises made by politicians and the needs and demands of voters. Of greatest interest to social and political scientists. For a more theoretical work developed from the same research project, see Gunnar Boalt's *The political process: a sociological approach* (Stockholm: Almqvist & Wiksell, 1984).

543 **Democracy and elections: electoral systems and their political consequences.**
Edited by Vernon Bogdanor, David Butler. Cambridge, England: Cambridge University Press, 1983. 267p. bibliog.
The essay by Bo Särlvik on Scandinavia (p. 122–48) discusses the use of proportional representation in the elections for Scandinavian parliaments. A concise and useful summary of the topic.

544 **Scandinavia at the polls: recent political trends in Denmark, Norway, and Sweden.**
Edited by Karl H. Cerny. Washington, DC: American Enterprise Institute for Public Policy Research, 1977. 304p.

Nine essays discuss different aspects of the current Scandinavian economic and political scene. The volume is divided into three sections that deal with parties and elections, social discontent and the mass media, and business and welfare in the welfare state. See particularly Bo Särlvik's 'Recent electoral trends in Sweden' (p. 73–129). For an earlier work by the author of the same subject, see his 'Political stability and change in the Swedish electorate', *Scandinavian Political Studies*, vol. 1 (1966), p. 188–222.

545 **The Scandinavian states.**
Neil C. M. Elder. In: *Adversary politics and electoral reform.* Edited by S. E. Finer. London: Anthony Wigram, 1975, p. 185–202.

Discusses the electoral practice of proportional representation as a positive factor in politics.

546 **Organizations and pressure groups.**
Kjell A. Eliassen. In: *Nordic democracy: ideas, issues, and institutions in politics, economy, education, social and cultural affairs of Denmark, Finland, Iceland, Norway, and Sweden.* Edited by Erik Allardt, Nils Andrén, Erik J. Friis, Gylfi T. Gislason, Sten Sparre Nilson, Henry Valen, Frantz Wendt, Folmer Wisti. Copenhagen: Det Danske Selskab, 1981, p. 609–26.

A comparative study of the structure and historical development of the many interest groups in the Nordic nations, the degree of structural centralization within them, and their relationship to the state. For a related study in the same work, see Eliassen's 'Political parties and public participation' (p. 126–37).

547 **Interest groups in Sweden.**
Nils Elvander. *Annals of the American Academy of Political and Social Science*, vol. 413 (1974), p. 26–43.

Examines both the specific interest groups which are influential and the governmental system by which they are consulted during the legislative process.

548 **The Swedish electorate 1887–1968.**
Leif Lewin, Bo Jansson, Dag Sörbom, translated from the Swedish by Carol Waldén. Stockholm: Almqvist & Wiksell, 1972. 293p. maps. (Publications of the Political Science Association in Uppsala, vol. 60).

A detailed study of Swedish voting patterns discussing methods as much as outcomes. An important study primarily for social scientists.

549 **The 1985 Swedish election: the conservative upsurge is checked.**
Diane Sainsbury. *West European Politics*, vol. 9, no. 2 (1985),
p. 293–97.

Describes and analyses the election. A cogent summary and a rare contribution
on so recent an event. For brief studies of the 1982 election, see Svante Ersson,
Jan-Erik Lane's 'Polarisation and political economy crisis: the 1982 Swedish
election', *West European Politics*, vol. 6, no. 3 (1983), p. 287–96; and Olof Ruin's
'The 1982 Swedish election: the re-emergence of an old pattern in a new
situation', *Electoral Studies*, vol. 2, no. 2 (1983), p. 166–71.

550 **The changing Swedish electorate: class voting, contextual effects,
and voter volatility.**
John D. Stephens. *Comparative Political Studies*, vol. 14, no. 2
(1981), p. 163–204. bibliog.

An analytical article examining recent changes in party control of the *Riksdag*
(Parliament) on the basis of shifts in traditional voting patterns. Primarily of
interest to political scientists.

The second new nation: the mythology of modern Sweden.
See item no. 10.

Atlas över Sverige/National Atlas of Sweden.
See item no. 93.

Sweden's development from poverty to affluence, 1750–1970.
See item no. 151.

**Russia, England, and Swedish party politics 1762–1766: the interplay
between Great Power diplomacy and domestic politics during Sweden's
Age of Liberty.**
See item no. 238.

**The first 'modern' party system?: political parties, Sweden's Age of
Liberty and the historians.**
See item no. 239.

**Agrarian structure and peasant politics in Scandinavia: a comparative
study of rural response to economic change.**
See item no. 254.

Years of crisis, 1906–1914.
See item no. 255.

Parliamentary reform in Sweden, 1866–1921.
See item no. 257.

Economic policy in Scandinavia during the inter-war period.
See item no. 263.

Sweden: the neutral victor: Sweden and the Western Powers 1917–1918: a study of Anglo–American relations.
See item no. 266.

Gustav V and Swedish attitudes toward Germany, 1915.
See item no. 272.

The crisis agreement and the Social Democratic road to power.
See item no. 274.

Parliamentary politics during World War II.
See item no. 282.

Social science research in Sweden.
See item no. 431.

Sweden's power elite.
See item no. 455.

Sweden.
See item no. 471.

Swedish women on the move.
See item no. 484.

Politics against markets: the Social Democratic road to power.
See item no. 498.

Suède: la réforme permanente. (Sweden: the permanent reform.)
See item no. 499.

Limits of the welfare state: critical views on post-war Sweden.
See item no. 501.

Public policy comparisons: Scandinavia.
See item no. 505.

Sweden: the politics of postindustrial change.
See item no. 551.

Administered elites: elite political culture in Sweden.
See item no. 555.

Stable democracy without majorities? Scandinavian parliamentary democracy today.
See item no. 560.

Coping with budget deficits in Sweden.
See item no. 564.

The politics of compromise: a study of parties and cabinet government in Sweden.
See item no. 565.

System 37 Viggen: arms, technology and the domestication of glory.
See item no. 626.

Economic development and the response of labor in Scandinavia: a multi-level analysis.
See item no. 687.

Trade union strategies and social policy in Italy and Sweden.
See item no. 692.

White collar power: changing patterns of interest group behavior in Sweden.
See item no. 693.

The rights of labor.
See item no. 704.

The strategy of gradualism and the Swedish wage-earner funds.
See item no. 705.

The hare and the tortoise: clean air policies in the United States and Sweden.
See item no. 756.

Scandinavian Political Studies.
See item no. 939.

Scandinavian Studies.
See item no. 942.

Scandinavia: a bibliographic survey of literature.
See item no. 958.

A selective bibliography of Scandinavian politics and policy.
See item no. 967.

Scandinavian political institutions and political behavior 1970–1980: an annotated bibliography.
See item no. 968.

Scandinavia in social science literature: an English-language bibliography.
See item no. 972.

Government and the Constitution

General

551 **Sweden: the politics of postindustrial change.**
M. Donald Hancock.   Hinsdale, Illinois: Dryden Press, 1972.
298p. map. bibliog. (Modern Comparative Politics Series).

A survey primarily of Swedish government and politics with some consideration
of topics such as foreign policy and the problem of post-industrial change. No
current survey of Swedish government is available that adequately considers the
constitutional changes of 1970 which created a unicameral legislature and an
entirely new constitution in 1975. Works written before then that are still relevant
include Nils Andrén's *Government and politics in the Nordic countries: Denmark,
Finland, Iceland, Norway, Sweden* (Stockholm: Almqvist & Wiksell, 1968), 2nd
rev. ed. (first published in 1961); and Joseph B. Board, Jr.'s *The government and
politics of Sweden* (Boston, Massachusetts: Houghton Mifflin, 1970).

Constitution

552 **Constitutional documents of Sweden: the Instrument of
Government, the Riksdag Act, the Act of Succession, the Freedom
of the Press Act.**
Introduction by Erik Holmberg, Nils Stjernquist, translated from
the Swedish by Ulf K. Nordenson, Frank O. Finney.   Stockholm:
Swedish Riksdag, 1981. 164p.

The official translation of the constitutional documents passed by the *Riksdag*
(Parliament) which became effective in 1975.

152

553 **The new Swedish constitution.**
Olle Nyman. *Scandinavian Studies in Law*, vol. 26 (1982),
p. 171–99.
Summarizes and analyses basic features of the 1975 Instrument of Government. A
very useful discussion.

National government

554 **The Swedish institution of ombudsman: an instrument of human
rights.**
Ibrahim al-Wahab, foreword by Ulf Lundvik. Stockholm: Liber
Förlag, 1979. 190p. bibliog.
Examines the organization and functions of the office. A concise, clear summary
regarded as a major reference work on the subject. For a briefer study, see Frank
Stacey, *Ombudsmen compared* (Oxford: Clarendon Press, 1978), p. 1–17.

555 **Administered elites: elite political culture in Sweden.**
Thomas J. Anton. Boston, Massachusetts; The Hague, The
Netherlands; London: Martinus Nijhoff, 1980. 203p.
A detailed study of the character and attitudes of Swedish senior civil service
officials and their interaction with members of Sweden's *Riksdag* (Parliament). A
serious study primarily for social scientists.

556 **The Nordic parliaments: a comparative analysis.**
David Arter. New York: St. Martin's Press, 1984. 421p.
Compares the parliaments in the five Nordic nations and studies the Nordic
Council. Three basic processes of policy formulation, adoption and implementa-
tion are discussed from the standpoint of the 'decline of parliament' thesis.
Extensive endnotes provide information on the important literature on the
subject. For a comparative study of a more detailed aspect of this topic, see the
author's 'The Nordic parliaments: patterns of legislative influence', *West
European Politics*, vol. 8, no. 1 (1985), p. 55–70.

557 **Government in Sweden: the executive at work.**
Neil C. M. Elder, foreword by Nevil Johnson. Oxford; New
York: Pergamon Press, 1970. 210p. bibliog. (Governments in
Western Europe).
Studies the executive branch of government, including its departments and
boards, the civil service, and controls over it. Some aspects have been modified by
recent legislation and the book deals only peripherally with the *Riksdag*
(Parliament) and the changes which occurred in its structure when it was being
written. Still regarded as the chief work on this subject.

558 **The first decade of the unicameral Riksdag: the role of the Swedish Parliament in the 1970s.**
Magnus Isberg. Stockholm: Stockholms Universitet Statsvetenskapliga Institutionen, 1982. 110p. bibliog.
A descriptive and analytical work assessing the impact of the new *Riksdag* (Parliament). A unique work on an important subject.

559 **The Swedish parliamentary system: how responsibilities are divided and decisions are made.**
Eric Lindström, foreword by Nils G. Rosenberg, translated from the Swedish by Victor J. Kayfetz. Stockholm: Swedish Institute, 1982. 98p. (Sweden Books).
Considers basic features of Sweden's *Riksdag* (Parliament) after the constitutional changes of 1970 and 1975. An excellent introduction for all readers. First published as *Riksdag och regering* (Parliament and government).

560 **Stable democracy without majorities? Scandinavian parliamentary government today.**
John Logue. *Scandinavian Review*, vol. 73, no. 3 (1985), p. 39–47.
A concise description of Scandinavian parliamentary government and factors in contemporary politics. A perceptive 'quick study' for all readers.

561 **The Swedish parliamentary ombudsmen.**
Leif Lundvik, Gunner Thyresson, Bertil Wennergren. Stockholm: Liber, 1976. 37p.
A survey by the three holders of the office. Useful, concise, authoritative. For other worthwhile works on this subject, see Walter Gellhorn's *Ombudsmen and others: citizen's protectors in nine countries* (Cambridge, Massachusetts: Harvard University Press, 1966) and 'The Swedish justitieombudsman', *Yale Law Review*, vol. 75, no. 1 (1965), p. 1–58; *Ombudsmen for American government?*, edited by Stanley V. Anderson (Englewood Cliffs, New Jersey: Prentice-Hall, 1968); and William B. Gwyn's 'The discovery of the Scandinavian ombudsman in English-speaking countries', *West European Politics*, vol. 3, no. 3 (1980), p. 317–38. The latter is part of a special issue on 'Public policy comparison' (q.v.).

562 **Direct democracy in national politics.**
Sten Sparre Nilson. In: *Nordic democracy: ideas, issues, and institutions in politics, economy, education, social and cultural affairs of Denmark, Finland, Iceland, Norway, and Sweden.* Edited by Erik Allardt, Nils Andrén, Erik J. Friis, Gylfi T. Gislason, Sten Sparre Nilson, Henry Valen, Frantz Wendt, Folmer Wisti. Copenhagen: Det Danske Selskab, 1981, p. 138–59. bibliog.
Studies the referendum as a means by which Scandinavian voters can directly influence governmental policy. A useful survey of the subject as it has been employed throughout Scandinavia in the 20th century.

563 **Government and central administration.**
Gustaf Petrén.   In: *Nordic democracy: ideas, issues, and institutions in politics, economy, education, social and cultural affairs in Denmark, Finland, Iceland, Norway, and Sweden.* Edited by Erik Allardt, Nils Andrén, Erik J. Friis, Gylfi T. Gislason, Sten Sparre Nilson, Henry Valen, Frantz Wendt, Folmer Wisti. Copenhagen: Det Danske Selskab, 1981, p. 163–81.

A comparative study of the executive and legislative bodies of the national government with secondary consideration given to their relationship to the judicial system and the civil service agencies that implement policy.

564 **Coping with budget deficits in Sweden.**
Rune Premfors.   *Scandinavian Political Studies*, new series, vol. 7, no. 4 (1984), p. 261–84. bibliog.

Discusses the causes for the rapid growth of governmental budget deficits during the late 1970s and early 1980s and the strategies devised by both non-socialist and Social Democratic governments. A clear discussion of the subject for all readers.

565 **The politics of compromise: a study of parties and cabinet government in Sweden.**
Dankwart A. Rustow.   Princeton, New Jersey: Princeton University Press, 1955. 257p.

Discusses political parties, the legislative process, and cabinet government from the parliamentary reforms of the 1860s to the early 1950s. Constitutional changes of the 1970s have deprived this work of its immediacy but it is still regarded as a major study of the time and subjects. For a more theoretical article by the author on the same subject, see 'Sweden's transition to democracy: some notes toward a generic theory', *Scandinavian Political Studies*, vol. 6 (1971), p. 9–26.

566 **Swedish government administration: an introduction.**
Peter Vinde, Gunnar Petri, translated from the Swedish by Patrick Hort.   Stockholm: Bokförlaget Prisma, Swedish Institute, 1978. 91p.

First published in Swedish, *Den svenska statsförvaltningen*, and in English in 1971, it outlines the organization and procedures of the Swedish central government. An appendix briefly describes the divisions and functions of seventy-five governmental agencies and institutions. A very useful reference work. For a related work by the same author, see *The Swedish civil service* (Stockholm: Ministry of Finance, 1967).

Local government

567 **Governing Greater Stockholm: a study of policy development and system change.**
Thomas J. Anton, foreword by Stanley Scott, Victor Jones.
Berkeley; Los Angeles, California: University of California Press, 1975. 237p. maps.

Examines the policy-making and decision-making processes of Stockholm from 1945–70, particularly in the fields of planning, housing, and transport. A major work in the field. For other views of the same topic, see Hans Calmfors, Francine F. Rabinovitz, Daniel J. Alesch, *Urban government for Greater Stockholm* (New York: Frederick A. Praeger, 1968); and Hjalmar Mehr, 'Stockholm', in *Great cities of the world: their government, politics, and planning*, edited by William A. Robson, D. E. Regan (London: George Allen & Unwin, 1972), 3rd ed., vol. 2, p. 873–901.

568 **Local government in Sweden.**
Agne Gustafsson, translated from the Swedish by Roger G.
Tanner. Stockholm: Swedish Institute, 1983. 139p. maps. bibliog.

Describes the organization, functions, financing and other issues related to local governmental administration in Sweden. A basic introduction to the subject for all readers. For a comparison with local government throughout Scandinavia, see Krister Ståhlberg's 'Local government', p. 182–95 in *Nordic democracy* (q.v.).

569 **Local government reform in Sweden.**
Gunnel Gustafsson. Lund, Sweden: C. W. K. Gleerup, 1980. 187p. bibliog. (Umeå Studies in Politics and Administration, vol. 5).

Assesses the effects of 1962 local government reform legislation on efficiency, democracy, and regional self-government. A critical, scholarly discussion of the subject. See also the author's 'Modes and effects of local government mergers in Scandinavia', *West European Politics*, vol. 3, no. 3 (1980), p. 339–57. The article is part of a special issue on Scandinavia, 'Public policy comparisons' (q.v.).

570 **Comparing urban service delivery systems: structure and performance.**
Edited by Vincent Ostrom, Frances Pennell Bish. Beverly Hills, California; London: Sage, 1977. 304p. bibliog.

Contains two articles on Swedish local government. Bengt Owe Birgersson's 'The service paradox: citizen assessment of urban services in 36 Swedish communes' (p. 243–67) discusses citizens' perceptions of services provided by local governments. Lars Stromberg's 'Electors and the elected in Sweden' (p. 269–302) concerns the representative character of local government officials. Primarily for political scientists and interested general readers. For similar studies of Swedish local government, see Thomas J. Anton's 'The pursuit of efficiency: values and

156

Government and the Constitution. Local government

structure in the changing politics of Swedish municipalities' (p. 87–110) and Jörgen Westerståhl's 'Decision making in thirty-six Swedish communes' (p. 141–62) in *Comparative community politics*, edited by Terry Nichols Clark (New York: John Wiley, 1974).

The Swedes: how they live and work.
See item no. 2.

Scandinavia.
See item no. 24.

Sweden's development from poverty to affluence, 1750–1970.
See item no. 151.

Sweden as an aristocratic republic.
See item no. 197.

Council, king and estates in Sweden, 1713–1714.
See item no. 212.

On aristocratic constitutionalism in Swedish history 1520–1720.
See item no. 217.

Sweden as a great power 1611–1697: government: society: foreign policy.
See item no. 219.

Sweden's Age of Greatness 1632–1718.
See item no. 220.

Europe and Scandinavia: aspects of the process of integration in the 17th century.
See item no. 224.

Russia, England and Swedish party politics 1762–1766: the interplay between Great Power diplomacy and domestic politics during Sweden's Age of Liberty.
See item no. 238.

Parliamentary reform in Sweden, 1866–1921.
See item no. 257.

Svensk–engelsk fackordbok: for näringsliv, förvaltning, undervisning och forskning. (Swedish–English technical dictionary: for economics, administration, education and research.)
See item no. 379.

National and regional health planning in Sweden.
See item no. 494.

Sweden: the middle way.
See item no. 497.

Government and the Constitution. Local government

Public policy comparisons: Scandinavia.
See item no. 505.

Welfare states in hard times: problems, policy, and politics in Denmark and Sweden.
See item no. 518.

The consensual democracies?: the government and politics of the Scandinavian states.
See item no. 519.

Scandinavia: the experiment in social democracy.
See item no. 525.

Interest groups in Sweden.
See item no. 547.

Elements of Nordic public law.
See item no. 575.

'Police and the social order': contemporary research perspectives.
See item no. 585.

Scandinavian Political Studies.
See item no. 939.

Scandinavia: a chronology and fact book.
See item no. 960.

A selective bibliography of Scandinavian politics and policy.
See item no. 967.

Scandinavia in social science literature: an English-language bibliography.
See item no. 972.

Scandinavian government and politics: a bibliography of materials in English.
See item no. 983.

Sveriges statliga publikationer: bibliografi. (Sweden's official publications: bibliography).
See item no. 996.

Law and the Legal System

General

571 **Anglo–Scandinavian law dictionary of legal terms used in professional and commercial practice.**
Ralph J. B. Anderson.   Oslo: Universitetsforlaget, 1977. 137p.
Separate sections define English, Norwegian, Swedish, and Danish legal terms. In each section, concise definitions are provided for each term as well as equivalent terms in the other languages where applicable. The preface presents brief sketches of the judicial systems of civil law in each country.

572 **Justice in modern Sweden: a description of the components of the Swedish criminal justice system.**
Harold K. Becker, Einar O. Hjellmo, foreword by Donald R. Cressey.   Springfield, Illinois: Charles C. Thomas, 1976. 145p. bibliog.
A survey of the chief elements in the administration of criminal justice in Sweden: the Ministry of Justice, the police, the judiciary and the correction system. An important introduction to the subject.

573 **Philosophy of law in the Scandinavian countries.**
Frede Castberg.   *American Journal of Comparative Law*, vol. 4, no. 3 (1955), p. 388–400.
Discusses the main trends in legal philosophy during the first half of the 20th century. An excellent survey of the topic but in need of revision to incorporate developments since mid-century.

574 **Human rights in Sweden.**
Hans Danelius. Stockholm: Swedish Institute, 1981. 68p.
First published in 1970, it summarizes Swedish legislation on human rights. A helpful introduction to the subject.

575 **Elements of Nordic public law.**
Nils Herlitz, foreword by H. W. R. Wade. Stockholm: P. A. Norstedt & Söner, 1969. 287p. bibliog.
Examines constitutional and administrative law, the governmental institutions involved in its creation and implementation, and the nature of Nordic cooperation in this field. Some details relating to governmental organization have changed since its publication but it remains a major study of the subject.

576 **The growth of Scandinavian law.**
Lester Bernhardt Orfield, foreword by Benjamin F. Boyer. Philadelphia, Pennsylvania: University of Pennsylvania Press for Temple University Publications, 1953. 363p. bibliog.
Developments in each country are treated separately in this work. The chapter on Sweden (p. 227–326) discusses aspects of criminal law and civil procedure. Still a significant survey of Sweden's legal past although more recent works must be consulted for current legal developments.

577 **Legal values in modern Sweden.**
Folke Schmidt, Stig Strömholm. [Totowa, New Jersey]: Bedminster Press, 1964. 87p. bibliog.
Examines specific values such as civil rights, the status of women, labour relations, and the establishment of law which are the foundations for the Swedish legal system. A concise summary still valuable today.

578 **An introduction to Swedish law.**
Edited by Stig Strömholm. Deventer, The Netherlands: Kluwer; Stockholm: P. A. Norstedt & Söner, 1981. 2 vols. bibliog.
This work contains fourteen specific chapters on different aspects of Swedish law and an introductory essay by the editor. It fulfils admirably its avowed purpose of providing a basic survey of Swedish law. Pertinent bibliographies conclude most chapters. An essential work for all libraries with an interest in law or Scandinavia.

Civil and criminal law

579 **The Swedish code of judicial procedure.**
Edited by Anders Bruzelius, Krister Thelin, translation and
introduction of first edition by Anders Bruzelius, Ruth Bader
Ginsburg, introduction to second edition by John Delaney.
Littleton, Colorado: Fred B. Rothman; London: Sweet &
Maxwell, 1979. rev. ed. 253p. (American Series of Foreign Penal
Codes, vol. 24).
First published in 1968 as volume 15 in the series, the work provides a translation
of the Swedish code of judicial procedure in both civil and criminal cases. An
essential work on the subject.

580 **Civil procedure in Sweden.**
Ruth Bader Ginsburg, Anders Bruzelius, preface by Hans
Smit.   The Hague, The Netherlands: Martinus Nijhoff, 1965.
491p. bibliog. (Columbia University School of Law, Project on
International Procedure).
A detailed description of the Swedish civil process by experts on the subject.

581 **The Swedish penal code (the translation is that of the wording of the
penal code as at July 1, 1984).**
Translated from the Swedish by John Hogg, foreword by Bo
Svensson.   Stockholm: Liber Förlag, 1984. 109p. (The National
Council for Crime Prevention, Report no. 13).
A complete translation in English of the Swedish penal code. Supersedes *The
penal code of Sweden as amended January 1st, 1972* (South Hackensack, New
Jersey: Fred B. Rothman; London: Sweet & Maxwell, 1972).

Special studies

582 **Law and the weaker party: an Anglo–Swedish comparative study.**
Edited by Steve Anderman, Alan C. Neal, Tore Sigeman, Anders
Victorin.   Abingdon, England: Professional Books, 1981–83.
5 vols.
A major study of English and Swedish law on the subjects of housing, consumer,
employment and labour relations law. The first volume contains a series of essays
on Swedish law on these topics, the third volume consists of translations of
Swedish statutes, and the last two contain comparative studies of English and
Swedish law in these areas. An important work for scholars in this field.

Law and the Legal System. Special studies

583 **Labour law in Sweden: a brief outline.**
Reinhold Fahlbeck. Lund, Sweden: Juridiska Föreningen i Lund,
1981. 66p. bibliog. (Acta Societatis Juridicae Lundensis: Skrifter
utgivna av Juridiska Föreningen i Lund).
Surveys the general nature of Swedish law relating to labour, trade unions and
individual employment. A concise, clear introduction to this subject.

584 **Stockholm: the politics of crime and conflict, 1750 to the 1970s.**
Peter N. Grabosky, Leif Persson, Sven Sperlings. In: *The politics
of crime and conflict: a comparative history of four cities.* Edited by
Ted Robert Gurr, Peter N. Grabosky, Richard C. Hula. Beverly
Hills, California; London: Sage Publications, 1977, p. 215–320.
A chronological account of crime, the police and the administration of justice in
Sweden's capital during the period. An excellent survey for all interested readers.

585 **'Police and the social order': contemporary research perspectives.**
Edited by Johannes Knutsson, Eckart Kühlhorn, Albert Reiss, Jr.,
preface by Kurt Lindroth. Stockholm: Liber, 1979. 387p. bibliog.
(National Swedish Council for Crime Prevention, Research and
Development Division, Report no. 6).
The reports of an international conference in 1977 on police research. Most of the
articles deal with Scandinavian or Swedish topics such as the historical
organization of the police in Scandinavia, crime prevention, the use of the police
in different situations, and current research in the field. A worthwhile
contribution to an area infrequently covered in English. For a similar work, see
'Policing Scandinavia', edited by Ragnar Hauge, *Scandinavian Studies in
Criminology*, vol. 7 (1980).

586 **The law of labour relations in Sweden.**
Folke Schmidt. Cambridge, Massachusetts: Harvard University
Press; Uppsala, Sweden: Almqvist & Wiksell, 1962. 343p.
An account of the regulatory system which has been developed between labour
and management in Sweden during the 20th century. A detailed discussion of the
topic by an expert.

Meet Sweden.
See item no. 12.

**The Viking achievement: a survey of the society and culture of early
medieval Scandinavia.**
See item no. 175.

Nordic slavery in an international setting.
See item no. 199.

Europe and Scandinavia: aspects of the process of integration in the 17th century.
See item no. 224.

Tyrannicide and the right of resistance, 1792–1809: a study of J. J. Anckarström.
See item no. 237.

The Sami national minority in Sweden.
See item no. 323.

Svensk–engelsk fackordbok: for näringsliv, förvaltning, undervisning och forskning. (Swedish–English technical dictionary: for economics, administration, education and research.)
See item no. 379.

Social science research in Sweden.
See item no. 431.

Deviant behavior in Sweden.
See item no. 462.

Limits to pain.
See item no. 463.

Drinking and driving in Scandinavia.
See item no. 464.

Everyday violence in contemporary Sweden: situational and ecological aspects.
See item no. 467.

Consumer protection in Sweden: legislation, institutions and practice.
See item no. 656.

Sweden's system to resolve consumer disputes: especially the Public Complaints Board and the small claims procedure.
See item no. 657.

The Swedish Companies Act 1975 with excerpts from the Accounting Act 1976.
See item no. 711.

Scandinavian Political Studies.
See item no. 939.

Scandinavian Studies in Criminology.
See item no. 943.

Scandinavian Studies in Law.
See item no. 944.

Scandinavia in social science literature: an English-language bibliography.
See item no. 972.

Law and the Legal System. Special studies

Svenska författninger översätta till främmande språk: en förteckning.
(Swedish statutes translated into foreign languages: a catalogue.)
See item no. 977.

Scandinavian legal bibliography.
See item no. 980.

Foreign Relations and National Security

General

587 **Sweden's foreign policy.**
Samuel Abrahamsen, introduction by Alvin Johnson.
Washington, DC: Public Affairs Press, 1957. 99p. bibliog.
Surveys Sweden's exercise of neutrality from the First World War to the 1950s. A concise and useful historical introduction to modern Swedish foreign policy.

588 **Sweden and the Cold War: the structure of a neglected field of research.**
Wilhelm Agrell. *Scandinavian Journal of History*, vol. 10, no. 3 (1985), p. 239–53.
A concise survey of Swedish foreign relations 1945–63, suggesting a further chronological division of the subject, perspectives on the topic which can be developed, and a valuable analysis of resources available and research which has been done. A very useful, thoughtful introduction.

589 **Power-balance and non-alignment: a perspective on Swedish foreign policy.**
Nils Andrén. Stockholm: Almqvist & Wiksell, 1967. 212p. bibliog.
Discusses Sweden's policy of non-alignment as applied to a number of 20th-century situations. The work also contains government documents pertinent to the cases studied. An important work by an expert.

590   **Sweden's policy of neutrality.**
      Sverker Åström.   Stockholm: Swedish Institute, 1983. 2nd rev. ed.
      20p.

First published in 1976, it is a statement by an experienced and prominent member of Sweden's diplomatic corps of the motives and limits of Swedish neutrality and its application to important recent situations. A concise, authoritative view of the keystone of Swedish foreign policy.

591   **Sweden in world society: thoughts about the future: a report prepared for the Swedish Secretariat for Future Studies.**
      Bo Huldt, Thomas Hörberg, Svante Iger, Rune Johansson, Lars
      Nieléhn, Sven Tägil, translated from the Swedish by Michael F.
      Metcalf.   Oxford; New York: Pergamon Press, 1980. 227p. map.
      bibliog. (Pergamon International Library of Science, Technology,
      Engineering and Social Studies).

An interdisciplinary study presenting four projections of the world's future and Sweden's response to them. Of interest to all readers, particularly students of foreign policy and the world's future. For a study of the Swedish Secretariat for Future Studies, see Björn Wittrock's 'Long-range forecasting and policy-making: options and limits in choosing a future', *The uses and abuses of forecasting* (London: Macmillan; New York: Holmes & Meier, 1979, p. 267–88).

592   **Neutrality and defence: the Swedish experience.**
      Revue Internationale d'Histoire Militaire, no. 57 (1984), 216p.

This volume was prepared by the Swedish Commission on Military History, chaired by Göran Rystad. It contains eight articles by experts on many aspects of Swedish security policy during the 20th century, including Sweden's policy of neutrality, Swedish foreign policy during the Second World War, and the country's participation in United Nations peace-keeping operations in the Middle East. A valuable single-volume contribution to the field. Articles in English on Swedish military history can also be found occasionally in the *Militärhistorisk Tidskrift* (Swedish Journal of Military History).

With other Scandinavian countries

593   **The Nordic Council: a study of Scandinavian regionalism.**
      Stanley V. Anderson.   Seattle, Washington: University of
      Washington Press, 1967. 194p.

An examination of Scandinavian regionalism as exemplified by the nature of the Nordic Council and its results. Anderson outlines the development of cooperation by the Nordic Interparliamentary Union after the Second World War, the structure of the Nordic Council, the procedures followed during its sessions, and other forms of intergovernmental cooperation. The negotiations during the 1950s to create a Nordic common market are studied closely as an example of the limits to integration.

594 **Nordic integration and cooperation: illusion and reality.**
Nils Andrén. *Cooperation and Conflict*, vol. 19, no. 4 (1984), p. 251–62.
Presents up-to-date, critical examination of Nordic cooperation at all levels. A helpful addition to earlier studies.

595 **The future of the Nordic balance.**
Nils Andrén, with Katarina Brodin, Bo Dreiwitz, Ingemar N. H. Dörfer, Maria Nyberg. Stockholm: Ministry of Defence, 1978. 161p. bibliog.
Examines the problems of Swedish security as they are related to the rest of Scandinavia. A concise discussion of Sweden's diplomatic and military policy and of the concept of 'Nordic balance' developed by specialists in the field. For a recent assessment of Sweden's security policy, see Andrén's 'Sweden's defence doctrines and changing threat perceptions', *Cooperation and Conflict*, vol. 17, no. 1 (1982), p. 29–39.

596 **The Scandinavian option: opportunities and opportunity costs in postwar Scandinavian foreign policies.**
Barbara G. Haskel, foreword by Johan Jørgen Holst. Oslo: Universitetsforlaget, 1976. 266p. bibliog. (Norwegian Foreign Policy Series, no. 15).
Studies aspects of the 'Scandinavian option' of greater cooperation or integration: a common defence pact in the late 1940s; economic integration from 1947–59; and cooperation in communications and the labour movement. All are studied by the 'costing' process by which each state is shown to have evaluated the comparative advantages of the proposals.

597 **The pattern of Nordic security.**
Johan Jørgen Holst. *Daedalus*, vol. 113, no. 2 (1984), p. 195–225.
A concise and critical assessment of the security pattern created by the five Nordic nations since the Second World War. It emphasizes the military and geopolitical factors in Nordic foreign policy and discusses the nuclear options these countries possess. An important work by an expert in the field.

Foreign Relations and National Security. With other Scandinavian countries

598 **The military buildup in the high North: American and Nordic perspectives.**
Edited by Sverre Jervell, Kare Nyblom, foreword by Samuel P. Huntington. Lanham, Maryland; London: Center for International Affairs, Harvard University; University Press of America, 1986. 159p.

Brief essays by Nordic and American scholars and government officials on defence and security policy in Northern Europe. Two articles deal directly with Sweden: Anders Thunborg's 'The need to maintain Sweden's defense efforts' (p. 67–73), and Kjell Goldman's 'The challenge to Sweden' (p. 107–24). Particularly useful in conjunction with more detailed surveys of the subject.

599 **Nordic cultural cooperation: joint ventures 1946–1972.**
Ingeborg Lyche, foreword by Leif J. Wilhelmsen. Olso: Universitetsforlaget, 1974. 171p. bibliog. (Scandinavian University Books).

Describes official organs for cultural cooperation established by governments of the Scandinavian countries and the cooperative efforts established unofficially by the media and educational institutions. A valuable contribution to a field generally confined to discussing governmental policy.

600 **Winning the peace: vision and disappointment in Nordic security policy 1945–49.**
Karl Molin. In: *Scandinavia during the Second World War.* Edited by Henrik Nissen. Minneapolis, Minnesota: University of Minnesota Press, 1983, p. 324–82.

Briefly discusses domestic developments in the Scandinavian countries and provides a clear, detailed analysis of the military and defence policies followed by the Scandinavian states during the period. Particular emphasis is given to the discussions between Sweden, Norway and Denmark about a neutral alliance among themselves or with the Western powers (NATO). One of the clearest and most important studies to date of the events of this period.

601 **'Scandinavianism'.**
Scandinavian Journal of History, vol. 9, no. 3 (1984), p. 171–253.

An entire issue of the journal devoted to Scandinavianism. Articles discuss: mid-19th-century Scandinavianism; the relationship between the turn-of-the-century Nordic Inter-Parliamentary Union and the post-Second World War Nordic Council; post-Second World War attempts to create a Nordic economic union, and a review of conferences of Nordic historians from 1965 to 1983.

Foreign Relations and National Security. With other Scandinavian
countries

602 **At gun point: a critical perspective on the attempts of the Nordic
governments to achieve unity after the Second World War.**
Bernt Schiller. *Scandinavian Journal of History*, vol. 9, no. 3
(1984), p. 221–38.
An analytical discussion, particularly of the unsuccessful Nordek (Scandinavian
economic union) negotiations of the 1960s. A critical, provocative work by an
expert in the field. Part of an issue of the journal on Scandinavianism.

603 **The Nordic Council and Scandinavian integration.**
Erik Solem, foreword by Frantz Wendt. New York; London:
Praeger, 1977. 197p. map. bibliog. (Praeger Special Studies in
International Politics and Government).
Studies the development of the Nordic Council after the Second World War, the
areas in which the countries have developed common policies after the Council
was established, the organizational reforms needed to create a greater degree of
integration, and the ways in which the Nordic Council conforms to current
integration theory.

604 **Nordic industry and Nordic economic co-operation: the Nordic
industrial federations and the Nordic customs unions negotiations
1947–1959.**
Bo Stråth. Stockholm: Almqvist & Wiksell, 1978. 334p. bibliog.
(Bulletin of the Department of History, University of Gothenburg,
no. 15. Research section: Post War History: Interest Organizations
and Internationalism).
Outlines the discussions of 1947–57 between business and government leaders in
Denmark, Finland, Norway and Sweden regarding a Nordic customs union in the
light of other options for greater Western European unity that developed at that
time. The position of each of the national federations of industrial firms on this
question is studied, particularly in the light of the possibility of the formation of
EFTA (European Free Trade Association) in 1958. A final section summarizes
the position of the federations and Nordic cooperation as demonstrated during
the period.

605 **Foreign policies of Northern Europe.**
Edited by Bengt Sundelius. Boulder, Colorado: Westview Press,
1982. 239p. bibliog. (Westview Special Studies in International
Relations).
Eight essays by leading scholars on different aspects of Nordic foreign policy. The
essays are on a comparative basis and concern such subjects as the 20th-century
background, domestic decision-making processes, changing strategic perspectives,
and Nordic policy towards international organizations, the Third World, and each
other as cooperating partners. An up-to-date, excellent introduction to the
subject.

606 **Managing transnationalism in Northern Europe.**
Bengt Sundelius. Boulder, Colorado: Westview Press, 1978. 127p.

A study of the most common forms of contact and communication between the Nordic countries, and an evaluation of the methods and success of the Nordic Council in managing them. An introductory chapter contains an essay discussing some of the earlier literature on the broader subject of Scandinavian integration.

607 **The other European community: integration and co-operation in Nordic Europe.**
Barry Turner with Gunilla Nordquist. London: Weidenfeld & Nicolson, 1982. 307p. maps. bibliog.

Contains studies of political and economic developments in the Scandinavian states on a country-by-country basis, and longer accounts of efforts since 1945 towards regional economic cooperation. The summaries of Swedish developments are clear and useful, and Sweden's involvement in discussions for a Scandinavian economic union (Nordek) and EFTA (European Free Trade Association) are lucidly described.

608 **Cooperation in the Nordic countries: achievements and obstacles.**
Frantz Wendt. Stockholm: Almqvist & Wiksell for the Nordic Council, 1981. 408p. bibliog.

A detailed description of the many forms of cooperation that have developed among the Nordic countries after the Second World War and some of the impediments that have retarded further advances in some fields, especially the unsuccessful attempts from 1945 to 1970 to establish a Nordic Common Market (Nordek). A revision of the author's earlier work, *The Nordic Council and cooperation in Scandinavia* (Copenhagen: Munksgaard, 1959) and many other publications on the same subject.

609 **Nordic cultural cooperation with the world at large.**
Folmer Wisti. In: *Nordic democracy: ideas, issues and institutions in politics, economy, education, social and cultural affairs of Denmark, Finland, Iceland, Norway, and Sweden.* Edited by Erik Allardt, Nils Andrén, Erik J. Friis, Gylfi T. Gislason, Sten Sparre Nilson, Henry Valen, Frantz Wendt, Folmer Wisti. Copenhagen: Det Danske Selskab, 1981, p. 709–42.

Discusses some of the means and purveyors of Nordic culture throughout the world. The author outlines some of the official and unofficial channels developed by each country to extend information about itself abroad. Special consideration is given to universities that provide instruction in the Nordic languages, journals that deal especially with the Nordic region, and the role of the American–Scandinavian Foundation. For an article in the same book that describes support by the Nordic countries for domestic cultural programmes, see Finn Jor's 'Public support for culture and the arts' (p. 504–16).

With the Superpowers

610 **Soviet Baltic strategy and the Swedish submarine crisis.**
Wilhelm Agrell. *Cooperation and Conflict*, vol. 18, no. 4 (1983),
p. 269–81.

Discusses the strategic implications of the Soviet submarine incursions into
Swedish territorial waters. Analytical rather than descriptive, and a rare and
useful study of the subject. For a more descriptive article in the same journal, see
Milton Leitenberg's 'The stranded USSR submarine and the question of a Nordic
nuclear-free zone', vol. 17, no. 1 (1982), p. 17–28.

611 **Great Britain and the problem of bases in the Nordic areas
1945–1947.**
Knut Einar Eriksen. *Scandinavian Journal of History*, vol. 7,
no. 2 (1982), p. 135–63.

A study of British diplomatic and military policy during the period with respect to
three issues of the time: revision of the treaty between Norway and the USSR
regarding Spitsbergen (Svalbard); the Soviet occupation of Bornholm; and free
Soviet naval access to the Baltic. The article is representative of the growing
research interest in this period of Scandinavian history.

612 **Sweden between the power blocs: a new strategic position?**
Gunnar Jervas, translated from the Swedish by Marina Lange,
foreword by Anders Clason. Stockholm: Swedish Institute, 1986.
48p. maps. bibliog.

A provocative analysis of Sweden's strategic position as a result of events during
the 1980s. Assumes some knowledge of Swedish foreign policy and recent events
but can and should be read by any interested person.

613 **America, Scandinavia and the Cold War 1945–1949.**
Geir Lundestad. New York: Columbia University Press, 1980.
434p.

A detailed account of US relations with the Scandinavian countries from the end
of the Second World War until the creation of the North Atlantic Treaty
Organization (NATO). Much of the emphasis is on US policy towards Norway
and Denmark because of their support for NATO but the book also reveals the
contrasting view taken by Washington of Sweden's refusal to abandon her
neutrality and join the Western alliance.

614 **China and the Nordic countries, 1950–1970.**
Marita Siika. *Cooperation and Conflict*, vol. 18, no. 2 (1983),
p. 101–13.

Examines an important subject in need of continued research.

171

615 **Sweden and Eastern Europe: a study in European co-operation.**
Carl-Einar Stålvant. In: *Co-operation in Europe*. Edited by Johan
Galtung, assisted by Sverre Lodgaard. Oslo: Universitetsforlaget,
1970, p. 232–58. (Peace Research Monographs from the
International Peace Research Institute, Oslo, vol. 3).

Sketches the forms of Swedish cooperation and communications with the USSR
and the other states of Eastern Europe. In need of revision but a useful
background work on the subject.

616 **An agent in place: the Wennerström affair.**
Thomas Whiteside. New York: Viking Press, 1966. 150p.

A general account of the activities of Colonel Stig Wennerström, a Swedish Air
Force officer, who was a Soviet spy from 1948 to 1963.

With the UN, EFTA and the EEC

617 **Sweden, the United Nations, and decolonization: a study of Swedish
participation in the Fourth Committee of the General Assembly
1946–69.**
Bo Huldt. Stockholm: Esselte Studium, 1974. 228p. bibliog.
(Scandinavian University Books; Lund Studies in International
History, vol. 5).

A cliometrical study of the Swedish position on several issues relating to the Third
World. Primarily for social scientists.

618 **Dilemmas of the Atlantic alliance: two Germanys, Scandinavia,
Canada, NATO and the EEC.**
Peter Christian Ludz, H. Peter Dreyer, Charles Pentland, Lother
Ruhl, foreword by Curt Gasteyger. New York: Praeger, 1975.
255p. (Praeger Special Studies in International Politics and
Government/Atlantic Studies, vol. 1).

Published for the Atlantic Institute for International Studies, it contains a section
by Dreyer on Scandinavia (p. 73–149) discussing the strategic importance of the
North, the dilemmas of separate national policies towards NATO and the EEC,
and future options for the region. A thoughtful, concise summary of these
subjects.

619 **The reluctant Europeans: the attitudes of the Nordic countries**
towards European integration.
Toivo Miljan. Montreal: McGill-Queen's University Press, 1977.
325p. bibliog.
A study of the specific political and economic interests of Finland, Sweden,
Norway and Denmark, including their many successful attempts to cooperate with
each other, and the difficulties they have had in extending this mutual cooperation
to wider European economic and political associations. Extensive consideration is
therefore given to the abortive efforts to create Nordek, a Nordic free trade
association, the establishment of the European Free Trade Association (EFTA),
and in particular the policies each country established towards the EEC in the
early 1970s.

With other states

620 **The Nordic countries and North–South relations.**
Nils Andrén. In: *Nordic democracy: ideas, issues, and institutions*
in politics, economy, education, social and cultural affairs of
Denmark, Finland, Iceland, Norway, and Sweden. Edited by Erik
Allardt, Nils Andrén, Erik J. Friis, Gylfi T. Gislason, Sten Sparre
Nilson, Henry Valen, Frantz Wendt, Folmer Wisti. Copenhagen:
Det Danske Selskab, 1981, p. 691–708.
An examination of Nordic reactions to five major aspects of North–South
confrontation: decolonization; developmental assistance; trade; effects on security;
and the impact of the North–South crisis on Nordic countries in the form of
immigrants to Scandinavia.

621 **Refugees: the Scandinavian response.**
Nadia Christensen, Neil Hollander, Harald Mertes.
Scandinavian Review, vol. 70, no. 1 (1982), p. 9–32.
Outlines the involvement of the Scandinavian states, including Sweden, in aiding
refugees. Particular attention is focused on the work of various Scandinavian
agencies in Hong Kong and Thailand.

622 **The political economy of Sweden's development policy in Africa.**
L. Adele Jinadu. *Cooperation and Conflict*, vol. 19, no. 3 (1984),
p. 177–96.
Examines the ideological foundations of Sweden's development policy in Africa
during the 1970s and 1980s. A critical survey for all readers. For another study of
this topic in the same journal, see Björn Beckman's 'Aid and foreign investments:
the Swedish case', vol. 14, nos 2–3 (1979), p. 133–48.

623 **As others see us.**
Göran Palm, translated from the Swedish by Verne Moberg.
Indianapolis, Indiana; New York: Bobbs-Merrill, 1968. 249p.
First published in Swedish as *En orättvis betraktelse* (An unfair view) (Stockholm: P. A. Norstedt & Söner, 1966). An indictment of Western, including Swedish, exploitation of the Third World. An example of the critical self-appraisal of modern Sweden.

624 **Sweden as a partner in development.**
Lars Rylander, preface by Lennart Wohlgemuth. Stockholm: SIDA, 1983. 142p.
An extensive reference work outlining the public and private organizations in Sweden engaged in cooperative enterprises with developing countries. A useful work on the subject.

Defence

625 **Citizens in arms: the Swedish model.**
Nils Andrén, Einar Lyth. In: *Armed forces and the welfare societies: challenges in the 1980s: Britain, the Netherlands, Germany, Sweden and the United States.* Edited by Gwyn Harries-Jenkins. London: Macmillan, 1982, p. 124–57.
Examines the social, professional and institutional changes facing the Swedish military system in the 1980s. A concise, analytical work. The volume was published for the International Institute for Strategic Studies.

626 **System 37 Viggen: arms, technology and the domestication of glory.**
Ingemar N. H. Dörfer. Oslo: Universitetsforlaget, 1973. 258p. bibliog. (Norwegian Foreign Policy Series, vol. 6).
Discusses the development of the Viggen fighter plane in Sweden during the late 1950s and the 1960s from the standpoints of military technology and planning, and political decision-making. A well-written, critical study.

627 **Nordic security today: Sweden.**
Ingemar N. H. Dörfer. *Cooperation and Conflict*, vol. 17, no. 4 (1982), p. 273–85.
A current assessment of Swedish defence spending and military forces and the perceptions of Swedish security policy at the beginning of the 1980s which motivated this defence policy. A concise, critical summary by an expert on the subject.

628 **Nation in arms: the theory and practice of territorial defence.**
Adam Roberts. London: Chatto & Windus; Toronto: Clarke,
Irwin, 1976. 288p. maps. (Studies in International Security,
vol. 18).

Published for the International Institute for Strategic Studies, it compares
Swedish and Yugoslav defence programmes as elements of their countries' foreign
policies and of the concept of 'territorial defence'. A useful discussion of these
issues.

629 **Nordic defense: comparative decision making.**
Edited by William J. Taylor, Jr., Paul M. Cole. Lexington,
Massachusetts: Lexington Books/D. C. Heath, 1985. 218p.

In the chapter on Sweden (p. 127–86), Taylor discusses the components of
Sweden's armed forces, the response by Swedes to several public opinion polls on
defence and foreign policy issues, the decision-making structure of the Swedish
government relating to defence matters, and recent defence issues and
developments. An excellent introduction for all readers to the subject of Swedish
defence. On this subject, see also *The defence forces of Sweden*, edited by C. H.
Stainforth (Tavistock, England: West England Press, 1975).

Count Folke Bernadotte

630 **Count Folke Bernadotte: his life and work.**
Ralph Hewins. London: Hutchinson, 1950. 264p.

Concentrates in particular on Bernadotte's work for the International Red Cross,
which saved thousands of Jews from the Holocaust in 1945, and his mission to the
Middle East for the United Nations that led to his death in September 1948. A
fair, thorough treatment.

631 **Mediation and assassination: Count Bernadotte's mission to
Palestine in 1948.**
Sune O. Persson. London: Ithaca Press, 1979. 354p. maps.
bibliog.

Describes Count Bernadotte's efforts in 1948 to resolve the struggle over
Palestine and analyses his work in the context of the decision-making process. An
important and detailed work on Bernadotte's role in the Middle Eastern conflict.
For Bernadotte's own 'diary report' of his peace efforts in 1948 prior to his death,
see *To Jerusalem* (Westport, Connecticut: Hyperion Press, 1976), translated from
the Swedish by Joan Bulman, with a foreword by Ragnar Svanström. It is a part
of the 'Rise of Jewish Nationalism and the Middle East' series, first published in
Swedish as *Till Jerusalem*, and a reprint of an earlier English edition (London:
Hodder & Stoughton, 1951).

Dag Hammarskjöld

632 Dag Hammarskjöld.
Nicholas Gillett, foreword by Courtlandt Canby. London: Heron, 1970. 302p. (Great Nobel Prizes).

A perceptive summary of Hammarskjöld's career before his selection as Secretary-General of the United Nations and a more detailed study of his work in that capacity until his death. An excellent study for the general reader.

633 Markings.
Dag Hammarskjöld, translated from the Swedish by Leif Sjöberg, W. H. Auden. New York: Alfred Knopf, 1964. 222p.

Hammarskjöld was undoubtedly the best-known Swede of his day, as Secretary-General (1953–61) of the then recently formed United Nations. There was considerable surprise, after his death in that office, that he should have also kept an aphoristic diary of his 'spiritual' relationship with God and man. A good commentary on this book is Gustaf Aulén's *Dag Hammarskjöld's White Book: an analysis of Markings* (Philadelphia: Fortress Press, 1969).

634 Dag Hammarskjold: custodian of the brushfire peace.
Joseph P. Lash. Garden City, New York: Doubleday, 1961. 304p.

One of the most frequently cited biographies of Hammarskjöld. In progress during 1960, it contains only a brief epilogue on Hammarskjöld's death and, like most works, gives little attention to his career prior to 1953. However, it does provide valuable insights into Hammarskjöld's career and personal characteristics.

635 Hammarskjold.
Brian Urquhart. New York: Harper & Row, 1984. 655p. maps.

First published in 1972 by a member of the United Nations Secretariat, it is a thorough study of Hammarskjöld's activities as Secretary-General. For an analytical study of Hammarskjöld as Secretary-General, see Mark W. Zacher's *Dag Hammarskjöld's United Nations* (New York; London: Columbia University Press, 1970).

636 Dag Hammarskjöld: the statesman and his faith.
Henry P. Van Dusen. New York: Evanston, Illinois; London: Harper & Row, 1967. 240p.

A thorough study of the diplomat's early career in Sweden and later at the United Nations, particularly on the basis of *Markings* (q.v.). Other important works on Hammarskjöld include astute personal views by Bo Beskow, *Dag Hammarskjöld: strictly personal* (Garden City, New York: Doubleday, 1969); and Sven Stolpe's *Dag Hammarskjöld: a spiritual portrait*, translated from the Swedish by Naomi Walford (New York: Charles Scribner's, 1966).

Raoul Wallenberg

637 **With Raoul Wallenberg in Budapest: memories of the war years in Hungary.**
Per Anger, translated from the Swedish by David Mel Paul, Margareta Paul, introduction by Elie Wiesel. New York: Holocaust Library, 1981. 191p. maps. bibliog.
Describes the efforts made by the Swedish legation in Budapest during 1944 in which Wallenberg played a leading role to save Hungarian Jews from the Germans and the Hungarian Arrow Cross militia. In the second half of the work Anger describes Wallenberg's separation from the Swedish legation in early 1945, and the realization that Wallenberg was being held in Soviet custody. More important for the details Anger can provide of Wallenberg's activities in Budapest than for its depth.

638 **Righteous Gentile: the story of Raoul Wallenberg, missing hero of the Holocaust.**
John Bierman. New York: Viking Press, 1981. 218p. bibliog.
Treats Wallenberg's life prior to 1944 in greater detail than some works and discusses the evidence for Wallenberg's continued imprisonment by the Russians after 1945 more analytically than, for example, *Lost hero* (q.v.).

639 **Wallenberg.**
Kati Marton. New York: Random House, 1982. 243p.
An account of Wallenberg's life, efforts in 1944 to save Hungarian Jews from the Nazis, his seizure by the Russians, and efforts until 1972 to learn of his fate. A well-written work for the general reader.

640 **Raoul Wallenberg: angel of rescue: heroism and torment in the Gulag.**
Harvey Rosenfeld, foreword by Jack Kemp, afterword by Per Anger. Buffalo, New York: Prometheus Books, 1982. 261p. maps. bibliog.
Places Wallenberg's work in Hungary within the context of the assistance given by other neutral nations and an extensive treatment of the problem of Wallenberg's fate since 1945. A thorough, less dramatic account than most other works.

641 **Lost hero: the mystery of Raoul Wallenberg.**
Frederick E. Werbell, Thurston Clarke. New York: New American Library, 1985. 268p. bibliog.
Focuses on Wallenberg's efforts to save Hungarian Jews in Budapest 1944–45, the evidence for his continued detention by the Soviets after 1945, and efforts by his family and others to secure his release. It is also a highly controversial work because it claims that Wallenberg died in 1965. First published in 1982 (New York: McGraw-Hill).

Foreign Relations and National Security. Raoul Wallenberg

The second new nation: the mythology of modern Sweden.
See item no. 10.

Meet Sweden.
See item no. 12.

The Scandinavians.
See item no. 16.

Scandinavia.
See item no. 20.

Scandinavia.
See item no. 23.

Scandinavia.
See item no. 24.

A journal of the Swedish embassy in the years 1653 and 1654.
See item no. 58.

Problems of Norden.
See item no. 70.

Scandinavians: selected historical essays.
See item no. 160.

Gustavus Adolphus: a history of Sweden 1611–1632.
See item no. 215.

Sweden as a great power 1611–1697: government: society: foreign policy.
See item no. 219.

Russia and the problem of Sweden–Finland, 1721–1809.
See item no. 233.

Russia, England and Swedish party politics 1762–1766: the interplay between Great Power diplomacy and domestic politics during Sweden's Age of Liberty.
See item no. 238.

British views on Norwegian–Swedish problems 1880–1895: selections from diplomatic correspondence.
See item no. 250.

Scandinavia in great power politics 1905–1908.
See item no. 251.

Norway–Sweden: union, disunion and Scandinavian integration.
See item no. 252.

The Aland Islands question: its settlement by the League of Nations.
See item no. 260.

The Scandinavian states and the League of Nations.
See item no. 264.

Sweden: the neutral victor: Sweden and the Western Powers 1917–1918: a study of Anglo–American relations.
See item no. 266.

The decline of neutrality 1914–1941, with special reference to the United States and the Northern neutrals.
See item no. 271.

Gustav V and Swedish attitudes toward Germany, 1915.
See item no. 272.

The debate on the foreign policy of Sweden 1918–1939.
See item no. 275.

Swedish foreign policy during the Second World War.
See item no. 276.

Diplomat: memoirs of a Swedish envoy in London, Paris, Berlin, Moscow, Washington.
See item no. 279.

Sweden's ambiguous neutrality.
See item no. 280.

Scandinavia between the Great Powers: attempts at mediation in the first year of the Second World War.
See item no. 281.

The strategy of phoney war: Britain, Sweden and the iron ore question 1939–1940.
See item no. 283.

German coal and Swedish fuel 1939–1945.
See item no. 285.

Sweden's attempts to aid Jews, 1939–1945.
See item no. 333.

Sweden's power elite.
See item no. 455.

Sweden: the middle way on trial.
See item no. 517.

Sweden: the politics of postindustrial change.
See item no. 551.

The Nordic parliaments: a comparative analysis.
See item no. 556.

Foreign Relations and National Security. Raoul Wallenberg

Elements of Nordic public law.
See item no. 575.

Cooperation and Conflict.
See item no. 929.

Documents on Swedish Foreign Policy.
See item no. 930.

Scandinavia: a bibliographic survey of literature.
See item no. 958.

Scandinavia in social science literature: an English-language bibliography.
See item no. 972.

Dag Hammarskjöld.
See item no. 1014.

Economy

General

642 **Trademark Scandinavia.**
Barbara Bader. New York: Greenwillow Books, 1976. 91p.
A concise description of the many important sections of the economy of the
Scandinavian countries, including mining and manufacturing in Sweden. A useful
introduction for young adults and the general reader.

643 **Wages in Sweden 1860–1930.**
Gösta Bagge, Erik Lundberg, Ingvar Svennilson. Stockholm:
P. A. Norstedt & Söner; London: P. S. King, 1933–35. 2 vols.
maps. (Stockholm Economic Studies, vol. 3a–b).
Prepared as part of the series on 'Wages. cost of living and national income in
Sweden 1860–1930' by the Institute for Social Sciences, University of Stockholm,
the volumes present detailed data of wages in various sectors of the economy
during the period. An important resource for study of late 19th-century and early
20th-century economics.

644 **The Swedish economy.**
Edited by Barry T. Bosworth, Alice M. Rivlin. Washington, DC:
Brookings Institution, 1987. 338p.
Thorough, thoughtful essays on Sweden's adjustment during the 1970s to a slower
economic growth and budget deficits, as well as a consideration of the solutions to
these problems developed during the 1980s.

Economy. General

645   **The Swedish economy: facts and figures 1986.**
Edited by Åke Burstedt, Tomas Franzén, Sven Hegelund, Dick
Kling, Åke Zettermark.   Stockholm: Swedish Institute, 1986. 31p.
maps.

A brief survey of the Swedish economy, covering such topics as employment,
gross national product, investment patterns, industry, foreign trade, energy, and
income. Well illustrated with many graphs and charts. A most useful introduction
to basic elements of the economy.

646   **Post-industrial society.**
Edited by Bo Gustafsson.   New York: St. Martin's Press;
London: Croom Helm, 1979. 238p.

The product of a symposium held to commemorate the 500th anniversary of the
University of Uppsala. Three of the eight articles discuss the development of the
service industry and the public sector in the modern economy. These
contributions are Karl-Gustaf Hildebrand's 'The new industrial structure: the
Scandinavian experience' (with comments by Francis Sejersted) (p. 48–79); Erik
Höök's 'The role of the public sector in Scandinavia' (comment by P. Norregaard
Rasmussen) (p. 101–18), and as an appendix, 'The expansion of the public sector
in Sweden in the post war period' (p. 194–235) by Anders Forsman, Lennart
Waara, Enrique Rodriguez and Kurt Wickman. A concise examination of these
aspects of the Scandinavian economy.

647   **Sweden: the road to stability.**
Ingemar Hansson, Lars Jonung, Johan Myhrman, Hans T:son
Söderström.   Stockholm: Studieförbundet Näringsliv & Samhälle,
1985. 48p.

Published for the SNS (Business and Social Research Institutes) by its Economic
Policy Group 1985. A short introduction describes the work of the SNS, followed
by an analysis of economic conditions in Sweden and current policy proposals. A
concise, professional discussion of monetary and fiscal policy.

648   **An economic history of Sweden.**
Eli F. Heckscher, translated from the Swedish by Göran Ohlin.
Cambridge, Massachusetts: Harvard University Press, 1968. 308p.
map.

The classic survey of Swedish economic history. First published in Swedish in 1951
as *Svenskt arbete och liv*, and in English in 1954, it concentrates on developments
since 1600. Included in the work is a tribute to Heckscher by Alexander
Gerschenkron (xiii–xlii) and a supplementary chapter by Gunnar Heckscher, 'The
disintegration of nineteenth-century society' (p. 268–83). Bertil Boëthius provides
a detailed critique of the second part of this work as it was first published in
Swedish in 'New light on eighteenth century Sweden', *Scandinavian Economic
History Review*, vol. 1, no. 2 (1953), p. 143–77.

649 **The gross domestic product of Sweden and its composition
1861–1955.**
Östen Johansson.   Stockholm: Almqvist & Wiksell, 1967. 190p.
(Acta Universitatis Stockholmiensis: Stockholm Economic Studies,
new series, vol. 8).

The work contains brief methodological prefaces and postscripts and extensive
tables of statistical data.

650 **A history of prices in Sweden 1732–1914.**
Lennart Jörberg.   Lund, Sweden: C. W. K. Gleerup, 1972. 2 vols.
maps.

Includes detailed tables listing prices of many agricultural and non-agricultural
commodities during the period, a description of Sweden's monetary system, and
an analysis of these factors. A rich resource for any researcher of this topic or
historical period.

651 **OECD Economic Survey: Sweden.**
Paris: Organisation for Economic Cooperation and Development,
1968–. annual.

A regular report on recent economic developments, government policy and
statistical data.

652 **Sweden: choices for economic and social policy in the 1980s.**
Edited by Bengt Rydén, Villy Bergström, translated from the
Swedish by Peter Landelius.   London: Allen & Unwin, 1982.
257p.

First published in Swedish as *Vägval i Svensk politik*, it contains fifteen essays on
the prospects and problems of Sweden's economy and the country's society.
Presupposes some knowledge of contemporary developments in these subjects,
but a balanced, solid study. Most of the essays contain notes or reading lists
helpful to those wishing to read more. Of special interest is Olof Palme's
'Sweden's role in the world' (p. 234–53).

653 **The economy of Sweden: a study of the modern welfare state.**
Martin Schnitzler.   New York; Washington, DC; London:
Praeger, 1970. 252p. map. (Praeger Special Studies in International
Economics and Development).

A survey of Sweden's economic and fiscal programmes and policies. Specific
topics discussed include stabilization policies, income redistribution, money and
credit, labour management relations, government regulation and planning of the
economy, and the ways in which Sweden's economy is a model for others,
particularly the United States. A fundamental work on the topic, although now
needing revision because of changes since its publication.

654 **Trouble in Eden: a comparison of the British and Swedish economies.**
Eli Schwartz, foreword by Milton Friedman.   New York: Praeger, 1980. 143p.

A scholarly comparative study of the economies of both countries. Based on the thesis that Britain's economy demonstrated the harmful effects of socialist economic policies relatively soon after their inception while the damage done to Sweden's economy for the same reasons has taken much longer to manifest itself but may be much more serious in the long run. A much more technical study than *New totalitarians* (q.v.), for example, but also a more serious criticism by conservatives of Sweden's economic development.

655 **The transition from capitalism to socialism.**
John D. Stephens.   Basingstoke, England; London: Macmillan Press, 1979. 231p. bibliog. (New Studies in Sociology).

A comparative study of the evolution of socialism in modern society. The author cites Swedish evidence frequently, particularly regarding labour organization, the pension controversy of the 1950s, industrial democracy, and the recent employee investment funds debate. A theoretical work primarily of interest to scholars in the field.

Consumer cooperation and protection

656 **Consumer protection in Sweden: legislation, institutions and practice.**
Ulf Bernitz, John Draper.   Stockholm: Liber, 1981. 366p. (Publications by the Institute of Intellectual Property and Market Law at Stockholm University, no. 12).

A detailed description of the laws and procedures of consumer protection. Of greatest interest to students in the field.

657 **Sweden's system to resolve consumer disputes: especially the Public Complaints Board and the small claims procedure.**
Bernadette Demeulenaere.   Stockholm: Liber Förlag, 1983. 96p. bibliog. (Publications by the Institute for Intellectual Property and Market Law, University of Stockholm, no. 22).

A specialized study of a single governmental agency dealing with consumer protection. For specialists in law and consumer studies.

658 Consumer owned: Sweden's cooperative democracy.
W. T. Lundberg.   Palo Alto, California: Consumer's Cooperative
Publishing Association, 1978. 86p. bibliog.

Discusses the origins and nature of the Kooperativa Förbundet (Cooperative
Union) and its 180 local Konsum (cooperative societies). A sympathetic, readable
introduction to the subject.

659 The cooperative movements.
Herman Stolpe.   In: *Nordic democracy: ideas, issues, and
institutions in politics, economy, education, social and cultural
affairs of Denmark, Finland, Iceland, Norway, and Sweden.* Edited
by Erik Allardt, Nils Andrén, Erik J. Friis, Gylfi T. Gislason, Sten
Sparre Nilson, Henry Valen, Frantz Wendt, Folmer Wisti.
Copenhagen: Det Danske Selskab, 1981, p. 359–83. bibliog.

Provides an outline of the cooperative activities within each of the Nordic states.
The brief section on Sweden (p. 377–82) provides a summary of the formation of
consumers' and agricultural cooperatives and their present status.

Economic policy and planning

660 Planning and productivity in Sweden.
H. G. Jones.   London: Croom Helm; Totowa, New Jersey:
Rowman & Littlefield, 1976. 212p.

Examines in particular the Labour Market Board as a major force in Swedish
economic planning, industrial relations, industrial democracy, and investment. A
positive but also critical view of key elements in the Swedish economy.

661 Planning in a mixed economy: the case of Sweden.
Abdul Khakee.   Stockholm: Liber Tryck, 1979. 94p. maps.
bibliog.

Describes the development and forms of planning in Sweden since 1945, including
physical, regional, municipal and social planning. A critical work sponsored by
the Swedish Council for Building Research.

662 Swedish economic policy.
Assar Lindbeck.   Berkeley, California; Los Angeles: University
of California Press, 1974. 268p. bibliog.

First published as *Svensk economisk politik* (Stockholm, 1968), it concerns
Swedish economic policy since 1945 in the areas of stability, growth, resource
allocation, and income distribution. A major reference work for the subject by a
past spokesman for Sweden's Social Democratic Party on economic affairs.

663 **Eurosclerosis: the case of Sweden.**
Per-Martin Meyerson, translated from the Swedish by Victor J. Kayfetz. Stockholm: Federation of Swedish Industries, 1985. 118p.
A business view of Sweden's current economic problems and their solution. See also his *The welfare state in crisis: the case of Sweden: a critical examination of some central problems in the Swedish economy and political system* (Stockholm: Federation of Swedish Industries, 1982).

664 **Reformist programmes in the planning for post-war economic policy during World War II.**
Tapani Paavonen. *Scandinavian Economic History Review*, vol. 31, no. 3 (1983), p. 178–200.
Includes an extensive discussion of the planning done in Sweden by individuals such as Gunnar Myrdal, and organizations such as the labour unions and the Social Democratic and Liberal parties to prepare for the economic contingencies of the post-war period. Provides interesting background information on the evolution of recent Swedish economic policy.

665 **Le modèle suédois.** (The Swedish model.)
Jean Parent. Paris: Calmann-Lévy, 1970. 308p. map.
A masterly survey of the Swedish economy discussing Sweden's industrial development, investment and business enterprise with reference particularly to the Wallenberg family, labour unions, and cooperatives up to the late 1960s.

666 **A long-term perspective on regional economic development in Sweden, ca. 1580–1914.**
Johan Söderberg. *Scandinavian Economic History Review*, vol. 32, no. 1 (1984), p. 1–16.
A concise view of economic development surveyed over a long chronological period and on a regional basis. For a different approach by Söderberg to the same subject, see his 'Regional economic disparity and dynamics, 1840–1914: a comparison between France, Great Britain, Prussia, and Sweden', *Journal of European Economic History*, vol. 14, no. 2 (1985), p. 273–96.

Taxation

667 **A fiscal history of Sweden.**
Stellan Dahlgren. Stockholm: National Swedish Tax Board, 1982. 16p.
Describes some forms of taxation from Sweden's past in a well-illustrated introduction for the general reader.

668 **Trends in Scandinavian taxation.**
Gustaf Lindencrona. Deventer, The Netherlands: Kluwer, 1979.
46p.

An excellent summary of various forms of taxation and fiscal policy in the Scandinavian countries.

Study and research

669 **The life of Knut Wicksell.**
Torsten Gårdlund, translated from the Swedish by Nancy Adler.
Stockholm: Almqvist & Wiksell, 1958. 355p. (Acta Universitatis Stockholmiensis: Stockholm Economic Studies, new series, vol. 2).

An abridged version of *Knut Wicksell, rebell i det nya riket* (Knut Wicksell: rebel in the new land) (Stockholm: Bonniers, 1956), it provides a biography of the Swedish economist (1851–1926), known for his studies of capital and taxation and his social radicalism. Well written, and for all interested readers.

670 **The Stockholm School and the development of dynamic method.**
Björn A. Hansson. London: Croom Helm, 1982. 286p.

A technical study of the 'Stockholm School' of economists which developed during the late 1920s and 1930s. Specific studies are made of Gunnar Myrdal, Bertil Ohlin, Erik Lindahl, Dag Hammarskjöld and Erik Lundberg. Of greatest interest to students of economic theory.

671 **A survey of economic thought in Sweden, 1875–1950.**
Eli F. Heckscher. *Scandinavian Economic History Review*, vol. 1, no. 1 (1953), p. 105–25.

Describes the main influences on Swedish economic thought during the period and some of the main contributors to the study of economics. An excellent introduction by an expert.

672 **Economics in modern Sweden.**
Karl-Gustav Landgren, foreword by Burton W. Adkinson, translated from the Swedish by Paul Gekker. Washington, DC: Library of Congress, Reference Department, 1957. 117p.

Surveys Swedish research on economics from the 1930s to the mid-1950s and Swedish journals and research institutions specializing in the study of economics. In need of revision, but still important as a background to contemporary studies.

673 **Economic doctrines of Knut Wicksell.**
Carl G. Uhr.   Berkeley, California; Los Angeles: University of
California Press, 1962. 356p. bibliog. (Publications of the Institute
of Business and Economic Research).
An explanation of and commentary on the economic theories of one of Sweden's
leading 19th-century economists. The classic work on Wicksell by an expert. For a
shorter study by the same author, see 'Knut Wicksell: a centennial evaluation',
American Economic Review, vol. 41, no. 5 (1951), p. 829–60.

The Swedes: how they live and work.
See item no. 2.

Sweden.
See item no. 7.

The second new nation: the mythology of modern Sweden.
See item no. 10.

Scandinavia.
See item no. 23.

Scandinavia.
See item no. 24.

An economic geography of the Scandinavian states and Finland.
See item no. 68.

The Scandinavian lands.
See item no. 71.

The Scandinavian world.
See item no. 73.

A geography of Norden: Denmark, Finland, Iceland, Norway, Sweden.
See item no. 74.

Economic geografical (sic) excursion to Middle Sweden.
See item no. 76.

Atlas över Sverige/National Atlas of Sweden.
See item no. 93.

Sweden's development from poverty to affluence, 1750–1970.
See item no. 151.

**From great power to welfare state: 300 years of Swedish social
development.**
See item no. 155.

The Scandinavian countries, 1720–1865: the rise of the middle classes.
See item no. 159.

The 'Price Revolution' in the sixteenth century: some Swedish evidence.
See item no. 205.

Gustavus Adolphus: a history of Sweden 1611–1632.
See item no. 215.

Sweden's Age of Greatness, 1632–1718.
See item no. 220.

Structural change and economic growth in nineteenth-century Sweden.
See item no. 248.

The economic development of continental Europe 1780–1870.
See item no. 253.

Economic policy in Scandinavia during the inter-war period.
See item no. 263.

Scandinavia 1914–1970.
See item no. 265.

How Sweden overcame the Depression 1930–1933.
See item no. 269.

The adaptable nation: essays in Swedish economy during the Second World War.
See item no. 278.

Sweden.
See item no. 308.

Pre-industrial economy and population structure: the elements of variance in early modern Sweden.
See item no. 309.

Social and economic aspects of Swedish population movements 1750–1933.
See item no. 313.

Social science research in Sweden.
See item no. 431.

Sweden: the middle way.
See item no. 497.

Limits of the welfare state: critical views on post-war Sweden.
See item no. 501.

Beyond welfare capitalism: issues, actors and forces in societal change.
See item no. 506.

Sweden and the price of progress.
See item no. 508.

Beyond the welfare state: economic planning and its international setting.
See item no. 511.

A Swedish road to socialism: Ernst Wigforss and the ideological foundations of Swedish social democracy.
See item no. 540.

Law and the weaker party: an Anglo–Swedish comparative study.
See item no. 582.

Scandinavian Economic History Review.
See item no. 935.

Scandinavian Journal of Economics.
See item no. 936.

Skandinaviska Enskilda Banken Quarterly Review.
See item no. 946.

Scandinavia in social science literature: an English-language bibliography.
See item no. 972.

Scandinavian social economics: 1850–1930: a bibliographic note.
See item no. 973.

Scandinavian government and politics: a bibliography of materials in English.
See item no. 983.

Finance, Banking and Investment

674 **Studies in Swedish post-war industrial investments.**
Villy Bergström. Uppsala, Sweden: Almqvist & Wiksell, 1982.
121p. (Acta Universitatis Upsaliensis: Studia Oeconomica
Upsaliensia, vol. 7).
A detailed, scholarly study of Sweden's taxation policy on business profits and
capital formation. Primarily for experts in the field.

675 **Business around the globe: the Wallenberg dynasty.**
Robert T. Elson. *Fortune*, vol. 65, no. 5 (May, 1962), p. 77–86.
Sketches the background and business operations of the Wallenbergs, the most
important banking and industrial dynasty in Sweden. An interesting sketch of a
powerful family which has shunned publicity.

676 **Sweden's capital imports and exports.**
Jucker Fleetwood, Erin Elver. New York: Arno Press, 1977.
223p. bibliog. (European Business: four centuries of foreign
expansion).
First published in 1947 (Stockholm: Natur & Kultur), it chiefly examines Swedish
investment abroad from 1850 to the immediate post-war years and analyses these
developments according to economic theory.

677 **History of Stockholm's Enskilda Bank to 1914.**
Olle Gasslander. Stockholm: Esselte, 1962. 643p. map. bibliog.
An abridged version of the two-volume *Bank och industriellt genombrott:
Stockholms Enskilda Bank kring sekelskiftet 1900* (Bank and industrial break-
through: Stockholm's Enskilda Bank around the turn of the century in 1900)
(Stockholm, 1956–60) published to honour the Bank's centenary in 1956.
Discusses the bank's development during the period, the financial activities of the
Wallenberg family which were instrumental in its success, and much of Sweden's

economic life during the last half of the 19th century. For a review of the work, see J. Potter's 'The role of a Swedish bank in the process of industrialisation', *Scandinavian Economic History Review*, vol. 11, no. 1 (1963), p. 60–72.

678 **The Bank of Sweden in its connection with the Bank of Amsterdam.**
Eli F. Heckscher. In: *History of the principal public banks accompanied by extensive bibliographies of the history of banking and credit in eleven European countries.* Edited by J. G.
Van Dillen. New York: Augustus M. Kelley, 1965, p. 160–99.
bibliog. (Reprints of Economics Classics).

First published in 1934 (The Hague: Martinus Nijhoff), the essay sketches the history of the Bank of Sweden from its founding in the 17th century until the end of the 19th century. Heckscher also added a brief bibliography (p. 457–63) of works on the same subject. A unique and informative survey.

679 **Banking in a growing economy: Svenska Handelsbanken since 1871.**
Karl-Gustaf Hildebrand, translated from the Swedish by D. Simon Harper. Stockholm: Svenska Handelsbanken, 1971. 72p. map.

First published as *I omvandlingens tjänst: Svenska Handelsbanken 1871–1955* (In the service of change: Svenska Handelsbanken 1871–1955) (Stockholm, 1972), it sketches the bank's history on the occasion of its centenary with emphasis on activities from the early 20th century up to the Second World War.

680 **The role of large deposit banks in the financial systems of Germany, France, Italy, the Netherlands, Switzerland, Sweden, Japan and the United States.**
Edited by Dimitri Vittas, foreword by Ian Morison. London: Inter-Bank Research Organisation, 1981. 347p. bibliog.

Contains a chapter on Sweden (p. 235–66), prepared by Tim Hindle and Roger Brown, outlining the organizational structure of the Swedish banking system and the financial characteristics of major Swedish banks. A useful introduction to the subject.

Sweden, Norway, Denmark and Iceland in the World War.
See item no. 262.

Svensk–engelsk affärsordlista. (Swedish–English business glossary.)
See item no. 383.

Sweden: the road to stability.
See item no. 647.

A history of prices in Sweden 1732–1914.
See item no. 650.

The economy of Sweden: a study of the modern welfare state.
See item no. 653.

Skandinaviska Enskilda Banken Quarterly Review.
See item no. 946.

Labour Relations, Trade Unions and Employment

General

681 **Industrial relations and employment in Sweden.**
Lennart Forsebäck. Stockholm: Swedish Institute, 1980. 2nd rev.
ed. 135p.

First published in 1976, it outlines the development of labour and management
organizations and explains collective bargaining procedures, wage policy, and
labour market policy. An excellent introduction for all readers. See also *The trade
union situation in Sweden: report of a mission from the International Labour
Office* (Geneva, Switzerland: International Labour Office, 1961); Steven D.
Anderman, 'Sweden', in *International manual on collective bargaining for public
employees* (New York: Praeger, 1973), edited by Seymour P. Kaye, Arthur
Marsh, p. 264–99; and Stig Jägerskiöld, *Collective bargaining for state officials in
Sweden* (Ann Arbor, Michigan: Institute for Labor and Industrial Relations,
University of Michigan, Wayne State University, 1971).

682 **Full employment and public policy: the United States and Sweden.**
Helen Ginsburg. Lexington, Massachusetts; Toronto: Lexington
Books, 1983. 235p.

Includes a discussion of Sweden's full-employment programme and the problems
it created for some groups in society, such as women and immigrants. A highly
regarded, thorough work.

Labour Relations, Trade Unions and Employment. General

683 **Sweden: the quest for economic democracy.**
M. Donald Hancock, John Logue. *Polity*, vol. 17, no. 2 (1984),
p. 248–70.
Describes labour legislation of the last two decades, summarizes Swedish
experiments in industrial democracy during the 1970s, and provides a relatively
detailed discussion of the wage-earner fund controversy up to the eve of its
passage in 1983. An excellent summary of recent developments on these subjects.

684 **Labor mobility: studies of labor turnover and migration in the
Swedish labor market.**
Bertil Holmlund.   Stockholm: Almqvist & Wiksell, 1984. 279p.
bibliog.
A cliometrical study of these subjects most useful to social scientists and
economists.

685 **Strikes and industrial conflict: Britain and Scandinavia.**
Geoffrey K. Ingham.   London: Macmillan, 1974. 95p. bibliog.
(Studies in Sociology).
The section on Scandinavia (p. 45–65) emphasizes Swedish labour relations. A
useful summary of the topic to the early 1970s but in need of a more detailed
study which considers developments during the last decade. See also the section
on Sweden (p. 27–36) in *Industrial conflict: a comparative legal survey*, edited by
Benjamin Aaron, K. W. Wedderburn (New York: Crane, Russak, 1972).

686 **The Swedish approach to labor market policy.**
Bo Jangenäs, translated from the Swedish by Victor J. Kayfetz.
Stockholm: Swedish Institute, 1985. 69p. maps. bibliog.
A survey emphasizing the development of Sweden's labour market policy after
the Second World War, existing programmes, and current trends. A useful
introduction for all readers, including those wishing to proceed to more detailed
and specialized research on the topic. See also Bo Rothstein's 'The success of the
Swedish labour market policy: the organizational connection to policy', *European
Journal of Political Research*, vol. 13, no. 2 (1985), p. 153–65.

687 **Economic development and the response of labor in Scandinavia: a
multi-level analysis.**
William M. Lafferty.   Oslo: Universitetsforlaget, 1971. 360p.
bibliog.
Part one discusses industrial development in Scandinavia during the 19th century;
the second section describes the response of labour, with a historical overview of
pre-19th-century developments and a more detailed examination of the late 19th
and 20th centuries on a country-by-country basis. The final, more theoretical
section discusses the determining factors in party ideology.

Trade unions

688 Trade unions in Sweden.
Bo Carlson.   Stockholm: Tidens förlag, 1969. 176p.
Discusses the Landsorganisation (LO, or Trade Union Federation) and its work.
Clearly in need of revision but otherwise a singularly helpful introduction to this
influential organization.

689 Scandinavia.
Walter Galenson.   In: *Comparative labor movements*. Edited
by Walter Galenson.   New York: Russell & Russell, 1968,
p. 104–72.
Surveys the origins and development of the trade union movements in Denmark,
Norway and Sweden, and discusses union organization and structure, collective
bargaining, labour ideology, and the relationship of the unions to the labour
parties in these countries up to the late 1950s. For more recent developments, see
Galenson's 'Current problems of Scandinavian trade unionism', p. 267–96 in
Scandinavia at the polls (q.v.).

**690 The working class in welfare capitalism: work, unions and politics
in Sweden.**
Walter Korpi.   London; Boston, Massachusetts: Routledge &
Kegan Paul, 1978. 448p. bibliog. (International Library of
Sociology).
A socio-political study of Swedish trade unions and their membership. It discusses
the workplace environment, the effectiveness of trade unions, and the dynamics
of union politics. Of greatest interest to social scientists and serious students of
the topic.

691 Governing trade unions in Sweden.
Leif Lewin.   Cambridge, Massachusetts; London: Harvard
University Press, 1980. 180p.
A detailed, scholarly study emphasizing the centralized character of trade union
leadership and organization in Sweden. First published in Sweden as *Hur styrs
facket?* (How is the union governed?).

692 Trade union strategies and social policy in Italy and Sweden.
Marino Regini, Gösta Esping-Andersen.   *West European Politics*,
vol. 3, no. 1 (1980), p. 106–23.
Sketches the general wage policy of Sweden's Landsorganisation (LO) and social
welfare policy from the 1930s until the late 1970s by a comparison with similar
developments in Italy. A concise summary for all readers, and also valuable as an
introduction to current labour and political developments. A contribution to a
special issue, 'Trade unions and politics in Western Europe'.

693 **White collar power: changing patterns of interest group behavior in Sweden.**
Christopher Wheeler. Urbana, Illinois: University of Illinois Press, 1975. 210p.

Examines the political activities of the Tjänstemännens Centralorganisation (TCO, or Central Organization of Salaried Employees). Respected for its discussion of this distinctive group and as an interest-group study. Primarily for economists and political scientists.

Industrial democracy and technological change

694 **New factories: job design through factory planning in Sweden.**
Stefan Agurén, Jan Edgren, translated from the Swedish by David Jenkins. Stockholm: Swedish Employers Confederation, 1980. 108p.

Describes recent innovations in job design in several Swedish industries to eliminate the assembly line. Specific, detailed but readily understandable by all readers.

695 **Trade unions and technological change: a research report submitted to the 1966 Congress of Landsorganisationen: Sverige (The Swedish Federation of Trade Unions).**
Edited and translated by S. D. Anderman. London; Allen & Unwin, 1967. 258p.

A study by Landsorganisation (LO) economists of manpower and technological change. It represents the views of the trade union organization and is a valuable early study of an increasingly important economic question. Among those contributing to the report were Rudolf Meidner, Sven F. Bengtson, Gösta Dahlström, G. G. Karlsson, Eric Pettersson, Bo Jonsson and Evert Holmberg.

696 **Efficiency, satisfaction and democracy in work: ideas of industrial relations in post-war Sweden.**
Edmund Dahlström. In: *Work and power: the liberation of work and the control of political power.* Edited by Tom R. Burns, Lars-Erik Karlsson, Veljko Rus. Beverly Hills, California: Sage Publications, 1979, p. 15–47. (Sage Studies in International Sociology, vol. 18).

Examines industrial relations in Sweden from the Second World War to the mid-1970s, emphasizing demands for industrial democracy which have developed. Published in a somewhat different form in *Acta Sociologica*, vol. 20, no. 1 (1977), p. 25–53.

697 **Democracy on the shop floor: an American look at employee
influence in Scandinavia today.**
Edited by Eric S. Einhorn, John Logue.   Kent, Ohio: Kent
Popular Press, 1982. 80p.
Assesses recent programmes in industrial democracy. Emphasis is given to
Swedish developments and the impact such programmes may have on industry in
the United States. A concise and well-respected work.

698 **Industrial democracy and labour market policy in Sweden.**
Edited by John A. Fry.   Oxford; New York: Pergamon Press,
1979. 163p. (Pergamon International Library of Science,
Technology, Engineering and Social Studies).
Twenty-three essays on many aspects of these two topics; both descriptive and
critical assessments of Swedish policy and programmes. The authors presume
some background knowledge on the part of readers but the volume contains
perceptive, worthwhile studies of Swedish industrial relations.

699 **Job design and automation in Sweden: skills and computerisation.**
Bo Göranzon, Max Elden, Olle Hammarström, Jan Forslin, Birger
Viklund, Bo Hedberg, Åke Sandberg, Ingela Josefson, Tore
Nordenstam, Kalle Mäkilä.   Stockholm: Centre for Working Life,
1982. 110p.
Discusses the debates and experiments in the computerization of work in Sweden
during the 1970s. A useful, fair treatment of the subject.

700 **Industrial democracy approaches in Sweden: an Australian view.**
Doron Gunzburg, foreword by Ian MacPhee.   Melbourne,
Australia: Productivity Promotion Council of Australia, 1978. 90p.
Summarizes Swedish legislation and experiences in industrial democracy pro-
grammes during the 1970s. A sympathetic but fair introduction for all interested
readers.

701 **People at work.**
Pehr G. Gyllenhammer, introduction by Leonard Woodcock.
Reading, Massachusetts: Addison-Wesley, 1977. 164p.
The president of Volvo describes the work reforms established by his company
during the 1970s, which became a model for similar programmes in many
countries.

702 **The flight from work.**
Göran Palm, translated from the Swedish by Patrick Smith, introduction by Dorothy Wedderburn, foreword by Peter Docherty. Cambridge, England: Cambridge University Press, 1977. 204p.

An abridged, translated version of a two-volume work, *Ett år på LM* (A year at LM) (1972) and *Bokslut från LM* (Final account from LM) (1974). It is a critical, first-person account from the political left of Swedish industry, working conditions and labour–management relations.

703 **Industrial democracy.**
Edited by Martin Peterson, John Logue. *Scandinavian Review*, vol. 65, no. 1 (1977), 89p.

The issue is devoted to a discussion of many aspects of this topic such as worker participation in management boards, wage-earner funds, and women as a part of the labour force. A useful introduction for all readers. See also Bjørn Gustavsen's 'Industrial democracy', p. 324–58 in *Nordic democracy* (q.v.).

Wage-earner investment funds

704 **The rights of labor.**
Bengt Abrahamsson, Anders Broström. Beverly Hills, California; London: Sage Publications, 1980. 299p. bibliog.

First published in Swedish as *Om arbetets rätt: vägar till ekonomisk demokrati* (The rights of labour: ways to economic democracy) (Stockholm: Almqvist & Wiksell, 1979), it discusses the early development of Sweden's Social Democratic Party and the current debate in Sweden over wage-earner investment funds. Useful for its technical framework and its presentation of these aspects of Swedish politics and economics.

705 **The strategy of gradualism and the Swedish wage-earner funds.**
Peter Aimer. *West European Politics*, vol. 8, no. 3 (1985), p. 43–55.

Sketches the nature of the wage-earner funds programme established by the *Riksdag* (Parliament) in 1983, the political struggle which ensued prior to its passage, and the changes it portends for Swedish politics. A useful description of the political struggle over this issue, and a good supplement to earlier discussions of the inception of this measure.

706 **Industrial and economic democracy in Sweden: from consensus to
confrontation.**
Erik Åsard. *European Journal of Political Research*, vol. 14,
nos 1–2 (1986), p. 207–19. bibliog.
Discusses the background of the wage-earner investment fund proposal and the
controversy surrounding this issue from 1975 to 1980. An excellent introduction to
the topic.

707 **Employee investment funds: an approach to collective capital
formation.**
Rudolf Meidner, Anna Hedborg, Gunnar Fond. London: Allen
& Unwin, 1978.
First published as *Kollektiv kapitalbildning genom löntagarfonder* (Collective
capital formation through wage-earner funds) (Stockholm: Prisma, 1978).
Explains the plan to use company profits for the purchase of investments to be
held by Sweden's labour unions. The author is the chief economist of Sweden's
Landsorganisation (LO), and the original author of the proposal that has been the
chief political issue in Sweden for several years and was made law by the Social
Democratic government in 1983.

The Scandinavians.
See item no. 16.

Swedish sociology: contemporary concerns.
See item no. 458.

Mothers at work: public policies in the United States, Sweden, and China.
See item no. 468.

Sex roles in transition: a report on a pilot program in Sweden.
See item no. 478.

Sweden's 'right to be human' sex-role equality: the goal and the reality.
See item no. 480.

Swedish women on the move.
See item no. 484.

Beyond welfare capitalism: issues, actors and forces in societal change.
See item no. 506.

The wages of success.
See item no. 512.

**In search of new relationships: parties, unions, and salaried employees'
associations in Sweden.**
See item no. 531.

Scandinavian social democracy: its strengths and weaknesses.
See item no. 532.

Trade and Business

708 **Company policies for international expansion: the Swedish experience.**
Sune Carlson. In: *Multinationals from small countries*. Edited by Tamir Agmon, Charles P. Kindleberger. Cambridge, Massachusetts; London: MIT Press, 1977, p. 49–76.
Examines the main Swedish firms organized on an international basis and their expansion policies. A basic introduction to the subject.

709 **Multinational corporations in the Nordic countries.**
Olav Knudsen. In: *Nordic democracy: ideas, issues, and institutions in politics, economy, education, social and cultural affairs of Denmark, Finland, Iceland, Norway, and Sweden*. Edited by Erik Allardt, Nils Andrén, Erik J. Friis, Gylfi T. Gislason, Sten Sparre Nilson, Henry Valen, Frantz Wendt, Folmer Wisti. Copenhagen: Det Danske Selskab, 1981, p. 384–98. bibliog.
Studies the impact of multi-national corporations on the economic mechanisms of the different Nordic states and on democracy in economic life. Among the subjects discussed are the degree of centralization in the decision-making of these corporations and their effects on employment, sales and specific industries.

710 **Patterns of barriers to trade in Sweden: a study in the theory of protection.**
Lars Lundberg. Washington, DC: World Bank, 1981. 24p. bibliog. (Staff Working Paper, no. 494).
A technical study of the forms of protection and the industries affected by such programmes in Sweden. Of greatest interest to economists.

711   **The Swedish Companies Act 1975, with excerpts from the Accounting Act 1976.**
Stockholm: Sveriges Industriförbund, 1976. 144p.

Elements of Swedish law pertaining to the establishment of businesses in Sweden. Most useful for foreigners interested in this process.

712   **Retailing and the competitive challenge: a study of retail trends in the Common Market, Sweden and the USA.**
Jennifer Tanburn.   London: Lintus, 1974. 111p. map.

Surveys marketing practices in the different countries, which places Swedish practices in a comparative perspective. An interesting introduction to the subject.

713   **Public enterprise in Sweden.**
Douglas V. Verney.   Liverpool, England: Liverpool University Press, 1959. 132p.

Describes the nature, organization, and accountability of public-owned businesses in Sweden. Although dated, it remains a solid and respected study.

Swedes as others see them: facts, myths or a communications complex?
See item no. 9.

Meet Sweden.
See item no. 12.

Swedish know-how in the 80s.
See item no. 30.

A guide to the industrial archaeology of Europe.
See item no. 108.

Working and living in Sweden: a guide to important measures applicable to foreigners assigned to Sweden.
See item no. 115.

The Viking achievement: a survey of the society and culture of early medieval Scandinavia.
See item no. 175.

Les peuples scandinaves au moyen âge. (The Scandinavian people in the Middle Ages.)
See item no. 196.

Salt and cloth in Swedish economic history.
See item no. 207.

The incredible Ivar Kreuger.
See item no. 261.

Sweden, Norway, Denmark and Iceland in the World War.
See item no. 262.

Kreuger: genius and swindler.
See item no. 273.

Engelsk–svensk teknisk ordbok. (English–Swedish technical dictionary.)
See item no. 377.

Engelsk–svensk ordbok i teknik. (English–Swedish dictionary of technology.)
See item no. 380.

Svensk–engelsk affärsordlista. (Swedish–English business glossary.)
See item no. 383.

**Nordic industry and Nordic economic co-operation: the Nordic industrial
federations and the Nordic customs unions negotiations 1947–1959.**
See item no. 604.

Industry

714 **Entrepreneurial activity and the development of Swedish industry, 1919–1939.**
Erik Dahmén, translated from the Swedish by Axel Leijonhufvud.
Homewood, Illinois: Richard D. Irwin; Georgetown, Ontario:
Irwin-Dorsey, 1970. 440p. maps. (The American Economic
Association Translation Series).
A translation of the first volume (of two) of *Svensk industriell företagarsverk-samhet: kausalanalys av den industriella utvecklingen 1919–1939* (Swedish entrepreneurial activity: causal analysis of industrial development 1919–1939) (Uppsala: Almqvist & Wiksell, 1950). It is primarily an historical study of industrial development during the inter-war period and an analytical and statistical study of many representative industrial firms. A detailed study of greatest interest to economists.

715 **Vem äger vad i svensk näringsliv/Who owns what in Swedish industry.**
Birgitta Forsgren, Olof Forsgren, foreword by Sune Carlson.
Stockholm: Almqvist & Wiksell, 1967. 523p.
A dual-language listing of the ownership structure of Swedish companies. Clearly in need of revision but an informative and useful work.

716 **The small giant: Sweden enters the industrial era.**
Carl G. Gustavson. Athens, Ohio; London: Ohio University
Press, 1986. 364p. maps. bibliog.
A thorough, informative study of the impact of the Industrial Revolution. It deals primarily with the technical developments and inventions of the 19th and 20th centuries, with much less emphasis on economic theory. It also contains an excellent bibliography of both Swedish and English works on the subject.

204

717 **Swedish industry faces the 80s.**
Mats Hallvarsson, edited and translated from the Swedish by
Victor J. Kayfetz, preface by Lars Nasbeth. Stockholm:
Federation of Swedish Industries, Swedish Institute, 1981. 212p.
bibliog.

Summarizes the history of Swedish industry, social and economic factors affecting
industrial development, and Sweden's major industrial sectors. A readable,
thorough introduction that supersedes *Industry in Sweden*, edited by Marie and
Christian Norgren (Stockholm: Swedish Institute, Federation of Swedish Industries,
1971). For another study of this subject, see Lennart Jörberg's *Growth and
fluctuations of Swedish industry 1869–1912: studies in the process of industrialisation* (Stockholm: Almqvist & Wiksell, 1961).

718 **Technology policy and industrial development in Scandinavia:
proceedings from a workshop held in Copenhagen, Denmark, May
20–21, 1981.**
Edited by Peer Hull Kristensen, Rikard Stankiewicz. Malmö,
Sweden: Research Policy Institute and Institute of Economics and
Planning, 1982. 217p.

Fourteen essays discussing the relationship between economic growth, technological change and governmental policy. Of special interest regarding Sweden are
Lennart Lübeck's 'Recent development in industrial and R & D policies of the
Swedish government' (p. 129–37) and Staffan Håkansson's 'The early development in Sweden of support to technical research and development' (p. 138–60).

719 **The rise of modern industry in Sweden.**
G. Arthur Montgomery. London: P. S. King & Son, 1939. 287p.
map. (Stockholm Economic Studies, vol. 8).

Describes the process of industrialization in Sweden from its origins during the
19th century to the beginning of the First World War. Despite its age, it is still
regarded as the major work on this subject. An interesting contrast in style and
approach to the much newer *The small giant: Sweden enters the industrial era*
(q.v.).

Scandinavia 1914–1970.
See item no. 265.

The creation of a modern arms industry: Sweden 1939–1974.
See item no. 286.

**Nordic industry and Nordic economic co-operation: the Nordic industrial
federations and the Nordic customs unions negotiations 1947–1959.**
See item no. 604.

Post-industrial society.
See item no. 646.

Industry

Le modèle suédois. (The Swedish model.)
See item no. 665.

Energy in Swedish manufacturing.
See item no. 738.

L. M. Ericsson: 100 years.
See item no. 739.

SAAB: the innovator.
See item no. 742.

Agriculture and Forestry

Agriculture

720 **Agricultural policy in Sweden.**
Paris: Organisation for Economic Cooperation and Development, 1974. 58p. map. (Agricultural Policy Reports).
Examines existing agricultural conditions in Sweden and the nature of the government's agricultural policy. In need of revision but a basic work in the study of this subject.

721 **Sweden's agricultural policy.**
Marshal H. Cohen. Washington, DC: US Department of Agriculture, 1982. 34p. map. bibliog. (Foreign Agricultural Economic Report, no. 175).
Discusses the formulation of Swedish agricultural policy, developments during the early 1980s, and the implications for American agricultural exports to Sweden. A concise introduction to the subject.

722 **Swedish agriculture.**
Hugo Osvald, Lennart Gustafsson, translated from the Swedish by Eric Englund, Nils G. Sahlin. Stockholm: Swedish Institute, 1952. 103p. maps.
Although now out of print, the work remains an excellent introduction to the topic and to more recent works because of its extensive treatment of geographical conditions and climate, the history of farming and agricultural interest groups.

Forestry

723 **Swedish timber imports 1850–1950: a history of the Swedish timber trade.**
Edited by E. F. Söderlund. Stockholm: Almqvist & Wiksell, 1952. 383p. map.
Published for the Swedish Wood Exporters' Association, with contributions by the editor, Annagreta Hallberg, and Jan Sundin, the work concentrates on this aspect of the industry but also considers topics relating to production.

724 **Laws in the forests: a study of public direction of Swedish private forestry.**
Per Stjernquist. Lund, Sweden: C. W. K. Gleerup, 1973. 216p. maps. bibliog. (Skrifter utgivna av Kungl. Humanistiska Vetenskapssamfundet, Lund, vol. 69).
Discusses the many factors affecting the direction of privately owned forests in Sweden including 20th-century legislation and its implementation by *län* (county) officials. An important work on the subject.

725 **Swedish forestry: some facts.**
[Stockholm]: Forskningsstiftelsen Skogsarbeten, Logging Research Foundation, [1974]. 19p. maps.
An information pamphlet with data regarding the Swedish timber industry.

A geographical excursion through central Norrland.
See item no. 79.

From the Bothnian Gulf through southern and central Lapland to the Norwegian fiords.
See item no. 81.

Agricultural atlas of Sweden.
See item no. 91.

The Scandinavian countries, 1720–1865: the rise of the middle classes.
See item no. 159.

Large scale farming in Scandinavia in the seventeenth century.
See item no. 208.

Agrarian structure and peasant politics in Scandinavia: a comparative study of rural response to economic change.
See item no. 254.

Scandinavia 1914–1970.
See item no. 265.

A history of prices in Sweden 1732–1914.
See item no. 650.

Mining

726 **Swedish iron and steel, 1600–1955.**
Bertil Boëthius. *Scandinavian Economic History Review*, vol. 6,
no. 2 (1958), p. 144–75.
Surveys developments within the industry and describes the historical research
project by which an extensive study was made. An excellent, readable
introduction to the subject.

727 **Luleå and Narvik: Swedish ore ports.**
Lucile Carlson. *Journal of Geography*, vol. 52, no. 1 (1953),
p. 1–13. maps. bibliog.
Describes the use of Luleå in Sweden and Narvik in Norway as ports for the
transport of iron ore abroad.

728 **Scandinavian iron ore mining and the British steel industry
1870–1914.**
Michael Flinn. *Scandinavian Economic History Review*, vol. 2,
no. 1 (1954), p. 30–46.
Discusses the nature of Swedish iron-ore fields and their increasing value to the
British steel industry during the period, as technological changes were made in
the steel-making process.

729 The iron ores of Sweden.

Per Geijer, Nils H. Magnusson.   In: *Symposium sur les gisements der fer du monde (Symposium on the earth's deposits of iron).* Edited by F. Blondel, L. Marvier. Algiers: XIXe Congrès Géologique International, 1952, II, p. 475–99. bibliog.

A geological analysis of Swedish iron ores. For a different perspective on the same subject by the same authors, see their 'Geological history of the iron ores of central Sweden', *Report on the eighteenth session, Great Britain 1948* (London: International Geological Congress, 1951), edited by W. E. Swinton, pt. 13, p. 84–89.

730 Zinc and lead deposits of central Sweden.

Nils H. Magnusson.   In: *Report of the eighteenth session of the International Geological Congress, Great Britain 1948.* Edited by G. D. Hobson. (London: International Geological Congress, 1950), pt. 7, p. 371–79. maps.

Describes the varieties of these two metals found in central Sweden.

731 The origin of the iron ores in central Sweden and the history of their alterations.

Nils H. Magnusson.   *Sveriges Geologiska Undersökning: avhandlinger och uppsatser,* vol. 63, no. 6 (1970). 2 pts. maps.

A presentation consisting of one part of text (p. 1–126) discussing the topic and a second part of maps and illustrations (p. 132–364). A detailed geological study of Sweden's iron-ore mining region.

732 Stora Kopparberg: 1000 years of an industrial activity.

Sven Rydberg.   Stockholm: Gullers International, 1979. 93p. maps.

An introduction, designed for the general reader, to Stora Kopparberg (Great Copper Mountain) in Dalarna, Sweden's chief source of the metal. Readable and accompanied by many colour photographs, it is a popular work on a subject which demands a much fuller treatment.

Economic geografical (sic) excursion to Middle Sweden.
See item no. 76.

From the plains of Middle Sweden to the high mountains.
See item no. 77.

From the Bothnian Gulf through southern and central Lapland to the Norwegian fiords.
See item no. 81.

Geology of the European countries: Denmark, Finland, Iceland, Norway, Sweden.
See item no. 98.

Mining

A guide to the industrial archaeology of Europe.
See item no. 108.

Iron and man in prehistoric Sweden.
See item no. 127.

The Northmen.
See item no. 131.

The runes of Sweden.
See item no. 134.

A history of Scandinavian archaeology.
See item no. 135.

The world of the Norsemen.
See item no. 138.

Economic aspects of the Viking Age.
See item no. 191.

Trademark Scandinavia.
See item no. 642.

Energy and Natural Resources

733 **Scandinavia rejects the nuclear option.**
Dean Abrahamson, Thomas B. Johansson.
Scandinavian Review, vol. 70, no. 3 (1982), p. 64–71.
Discusses the interest originally shown by many of the Scandinavian countries in the non-military uses of nuclear energy and the factors that led them to reject this energy alternative.

734 **Sweden buries its radioactive waste problems.**
Andrew Blowers. *Geography*, vol. 71, pt. 3 (1986), p. 260–63.
map.
Sketches current plans for disposal of Sweden's radioactive waste materials.

735 **Energy: dilemma of the decade.**
Scandinavian Review, vol. 66, no. 3 (1978), 66p.
The entire issue of the journal is devoted to the subject. Topics considered include the nuclear power alternative, 'waste heat', and hydroelectricity. An excellent introduction for the general reader.

736 **Energy in transition: a report on energy policy and future options.**
Måns Lönnroth, Peter Steen, Thomas B. Johansson, Lee Schipper, preface by Måns Lönnroth, Lars Ingelstam. Berkeley, California; Los Angeles: University of California Press, 1980. 171p. bibliog.
Based on the work of a project for the Swedish Secretariat for Future Studies and published shortly before the 1980 referendum on the use of nuclear power. The work itself provides a conceptual framework for Sweden's long-term energy policy and the use of nuclear power. A reference work for the discussion of the Swedish energy debate during the 1970s and later policy.

737 **The politics of energy policy change in Sweden.**
Robert C. Sahr. Ann Arbor, Michigan: University of Michigan
Press, 1985. 267p. bibliog.

A technical but readable study of the recent shift in Swedish attitudes to energy –
towards conservation and away from nuclear power. Particularly valuable for its
perceptive, well-presented account of the 1980 nuclear energy referendum.

738 **Energy in Swedish manufacturing.**
Edited by Bengt-Christer Ysander, foreword by Gunnar Eliasson,
Rune Castenäs, Åse Sohlman. Stockholm: Almqvist & Wiksell,
1983. 260p. bibliog.

Published for the Industrial Institute for Economic and Social Research, the
Economic Research Institute, Stockholm School of Economics, and the Energy
System Research Group, University of Stockholm; the book contains seven essays
on past and future energy costs in Swedish manufacturing and suggested changes
in energy use in present-day Swedish industries. A technical study for experts in
the field.

Problems of Norden.
See item no. 70.

Economic geografical (sic) excursion to Middle Sweden.
See item no. 76.

A geographical excursion through central Norrland.
See item no. 79.

Public policy comparisons: Scandinavia.
See item no. 505.

Sweden: the middle way on trial.
See item no. 517.

Transport and
Communications

739 L. M. Ericsson: 100 years.
Artur Attman, Jan Kuuse, Ulf Olsson, Christian Jacobaeus,
foreword by Marcus Wallenberg. [Stockholm: L. M. Ericsson,
1977]. 3 vols.

A detailed study of a well-known and important Swedish industrial firm
specializing in the production of telephone equipment. The first two volumes
provide a chronological account (1876–1932 and 1932–76) of the company, and
the third is a more technical discussion of the evolution of the telephone and
other communication equipment the company produces. A thorough discussion of
interest to scholars and students of business and communications.

**740 The Scandinavian Airlines System (SAS): its origin, present
organization and legal aspects.**
Henrik Bahr. *Arkiv for Luftrett*, vol. 1 (1958–62), p. 199–253.

Studies the factors that led to the formation of the Scandinavian Airlines System
(SAS) in 1951, the legal points of the agreement forming the airline, its
administrative apparatus, and legal issues raised by the agreement.

741 Alternatives for local and regional radio: three Nordic solutions.
Donald R. Browne. *Journal of Communication*, vol. 34, no. 2
(1984), p. 36–55.

Studies the local and regional radio systems developed by Norway, Finland and
Sweden during the 1970s. A useful work on the subject.

215

742 **SAAB: the innovator.**
Mark Chatterton. Newton Abbot, England; North Pomfret, Vermont: David & Charles, 1980. 160p.

Discusses the development of the first SAAB automobile after the Second World War and successive models until 1980. A descriptive, uncritical work, well illustrated with photographs of interest to car-lovers and SAAB owners. For a similar work, see Graham Robson's *The story of Volvo cars* (Cambridge, England: P. Stephens, 1983).

743 **State–media relations in Sweden.**
Jan Ekecrantz. In: *The Nordic model: studies in public policy innovation*. Edited by Clive Archer, Stephen Maxwell. Farnborough, England: Gower, 1980, p. 140–61.

Examines aspects of Swedish public policy governing and influencing the country's media, especially *SR*'s (Sveriges Radio) monopoly of radio and television. A concise, critical view.

744 **Intercommunication technologies: the development of postal services in Sweden.**
Thomas Falk, Ronald Amber. *Geografiska Annaler*, vol. 67, series B, no. 1 (1985), p. 21–28. maps. bibliog.

Sketches the development, expansion, and use of the Swedish postal service from its beginnings in the 17th century until 1960. A useful introduction to a subject demanding much further research in English.

745 **The Swedish state railways 1856–1956.**
Vincent H. Malmström. *American–Scandinavian Review*, vol. 44, no. 4 (1956), p. 359–70.

Emphasizes in particular the beginnings of the Swedish railway system from the 1840s when plans were first made, and from 1856 with the opening of the first railway line. A concise, informative survey; but it is unfortunate that no work exists in English to carry the story beyond the mid-1950s.

746 **Beautiful, well-built Swedes: Volvo and Saab.**
Bill Siuru. *Scandinavian Review*, vol. 74, no. 3 (1986), p. 29–36.

A concise discussion of the origins and early models of both automobiles. A valuable introduction for all readers.

The Swedes: how they live and work.
See item no. 2.

Engelsk–svensk teknisk ordbok. (English–Swedish technical dictionary.)
See item no. 377.

New towns and old: housing and services in Sweden.
See item no. 487.

Governing Greater Stockholm: a study of policy development and system change.
See item no. 567.

The Scandinavian option: opportunities and opportunity costs in postwar Scandinavian foreign policies.
See item no. 596.

Luleå and Narvik: Swedish ore ports.
See item no. 727.

Statistics

747 **State, economy and society in Western Europe 1815–1975: a data handbook in two volumes.**
Compiled by Peter Flora, Jens Alber, Richard Eichenberg, Jürgen Kohl, Franz Kraus, Winfried Pfenning, Kurt Seebohm. Frankfurt, FRG: Campus Verlag; London: Macmillan; Chicago, Illinois: St. James Press, 1983, 2 vols.
Contains data from many European countries, including Sweden, of interest in the study of many fields, such as demography, politics, economics, society, the welfare state, labour and housing.

748 **Statistisk Årsbok för Sverige/Statistical Abstract of Sweden.**
Stockholm: Statistiska Centralbyrån, 1914– . annual. map.
A yearly, detailed statistical study on virtually all subjects. Almost all headings are given in both Swedish and English. An indispensable guide.

749 **Yearbook of Nordic Statistics.**
Stockholm: P. A. Norstedt & Söner, 1962– . annual.
The work contains data from the central statistical offices of all five Nordic nations and is published by the Office of the Praesidium of the Nordic Council in Stockholm and the Nordic Statistical Secretariat in Copenhagen. The data itself covers a wide variety of subjects with all of the tables labelled in both English and Swedish.

Wages in Sweden 1860–1930.
See item no. 643.

The Swedish economy: facts and figures 1986.
See item no. 645.

The gross domestic product of Sweden and its composition 1861–1955.
See item no. 649.

A history of prices in Sweden 1732–1914.
See item no. 650.

OECD Economic Survey: Sweden.
See item no. 651.

The Environment
and Planning

750 **Care of the environment in Scandinavia.**
Edited by Joseph B. Board, Jr., Joanne Wyman.
Scandinavian Review, vol. 64, no. 4 (1976), 69p.
This entire issue is devoted to the theme of environmental protection. Several articles discuss basic themes common to all the Nordic countries. A useful introduction to the subject.

751 **Urban systems: strategies for regulation: a comparison of policies in Britain, Sweden, Australia, and Canada.**
L. S. Bourne.   Oxford: Clarendon Press, 1975. 264p. maps. bibliog.
A descriptive and comparative study of urban planning programmes in Sweden and the other countries. A critical, useful study.

752 **Environmental policy in Sweden.**
Paris: Organisation for Economic Co-operation and Development, 1977. 144p. maps. bibliog.
Also published in French as *Politique de l'environnement en Suède*, it surveys Swedish legislation protecting the environment, national physical planning, and the repercussions such action has had on Swedish foreign trade and employment. A basic reference work on the subject.

753 **Growth and transformation of the modern city: the Stockholm conference September 1978.**
Edited by Ingrid Hammarström, Thomas Hall.   Stockholm:
Swedish Council for Building Research, 1979. 278p.

The published proceedings of a symposium held in 1978 on 'Stockholm – growth and transformation of a city' concerning Stockholm's growth and development in comparison to that of other European capitals and major cities. Five of the eighteen essays discuss Stockholm's development within the context of this theme.

754 **National, regional and local planning.**
Kai Lemberg.   In: *Nordic democracy: ideas, issues, and institutions in politics, economy, education, social and cultural affairs of Denmark, Finland, Iceland, Norway, and Sweden.* Edited by Erik Allardt, Nils Andrén, Erik J. Friis, Gylfi T. Gislason, Sten Sparre Nilson, Henry Valen, Frantz Wendt, Folmer Wisti.
Copenhagen: Det Danske Selskab, 1981, p. 239–76. bibliog.

Defines the contemporary concern in Scandinavia för physical (land-use) planning, provides a brief survey of the development and nature of the planning programmes in each country, and briefly compares several features of them. In the section on Sweden (p. 263–69) emphasis is given to the governmental statutes regulating physical planning and the administrative levels at which this planning takes place.

755 **Environmental impact assessment in Sweden: status, problems and proposals for change.**
Lennart J. Lundkvist.   *Policy and Politics*, vol. 7, no. 3 (1979), p. 245–68.

Emphasizes necessary changes in environmental impact procedures. A critical study by an expert in the field.

756 **The hare and the tortoise: clean air policies in the United States and Sweden.**
Lennart J. Lundkvist.   Ann Arbor, Michigan: University of Michigan Press; Roxdale, Canada: John Wiley, 1980. 236p.

A comparative study of the development of clean air policies in the two countries. Of as much interest to political scientists as to those readers with environmental interests and concerns. Also see his *Environmental policies in Canada, Sweden, and the United States: a comparative overview* (Beverly Hills, California; London: Sage Publications, 1974).

757 **Urbanization in Sweden: means and methods for the planning.**
Ella Ödmann, Gun-Britt Dahlberg, translated from the Swedish by
Victor Braxton.   Stockholm: Allmänna Förlaget, 1970. 256p.
maps. bibliog.

A detailed study of the development of Swedish urban centres during the last
century and of the physical planning programmes which have developed. Special
consideration is given to Sweden's three largest urban centres, Stockholm,
Gothenburg and Malmö, and the impact of planning on the building industry and
process. Particularly for those with an interest in planning or related studies.

758 **Planning Sweden: regional development-planning and management
of land and water resources.**
Stockholm: Ministry of Labour and Housing; Ministry of Physical
Planning and Local Government, 1973. 142p. maps.

Discusses the background and nature of governmental policy established in 1972
regarding regional development and the management of land and water resources
in Sweden. An informative introduction to fundamental decisions made on these
subjects.

759 **The suburban environment: Sweden and the United States.**
David Popenoe.   Chicago; London: University of Chicago Press,
1977. 275p. maps.   (Studies of Urban Society).

A comparative study of urban development and planning that concentrates
specifically on the Stockholm suburb of Vällingby. A highly regarded work of
greatest interest to social scientists but also appropriate for the concerned general
reader.

760 **Swedish pollution control agencies.**
J. J. Richardson.   London: Social Science Research Council,
1980. 47p.

Describes the work of the National Environment Protection Board and the
Franchise Board in Sweden and evaluates the success of Swedish environmental
policy. A concise, clear introduction to the subject.

761 **Stockholm: 300 years of planning.**
Göran Sidenbladh.   In: *World capitals: toward guided
urbanizations.* Edited by H. Wentworth Eldredge. Garden City,
New York: Anchor Press, Doubleday, 1975, p. 25–54. maps.
bibliog.

Emphasizes in particular planning done since the Second World War to revitalize
Stockholm's main business district and to cope with a drastic increase in its size
and the population it serves.

762 **National physical planning.**
Jan Strömdahl, translated from the Swedish by Martin Percivall.
Stockholm: Ministry of Housing and Physical Planning, National
Board of Physical Planning and Building, 1984. 52p. maps.

Describes the nature and organization of national physical planning from 1965 to
the mid-1980s. A useful introduction for all readers. For another booklet by the
same board, see *Planning and building in Sweden* (Stockholm, 1985) which also
contains lists of their publications in English and addresses of relevant
organizations.

Problems of Norden.
See item no. 70.

**Town planning in Sweden and Finland until the middle of the nineteenth
century.**
See item no. 249.

The elderly and their environment: research in Sweden.
See item no. 466.

New towns and old: housing and services in Sweden.
See item no. 487.

Controlling medical technology in Sweden.
See item no. 491.

**Governing Greater Stockholm: a study of policy development and system
change.**
See item no. 567.

**Sweden in world society: thoughts about the future: a report prepared for
the Swedish Secretariat for Future Studies.**
See item no. 591.

The economy of Sweden: a study of the modern welfare state.
See item no. 653.

Planning in a mixed economy: the case of Sweden.
See item no. 661.

Sweden buries its radioactive waste problems.
See item no. 734.

Recent developments in Swedish architecture: a reappraisal.
See item no. 832.

Science and Technology

763 **Christopher Polhem: the father of Swedish technology.**
Foreword by Torsten Althin, preface by Karl William Hallden,
translated from the Swedish and with a preface by William A.
Johnson. Hartford, Connecticut: Trustees of Trinity College,
1963. 259p. bibliog.

First published in 1911 as *Christopher Polhem, minnesskrift utgifven af Svenska
Teknologföreningen, 1911* (Christopher Polhem: a memorial published by the
Swedish Association of Technology), it contains four essays on Polhem's life and
work in mechanics, mining and construction as well as a detailed bibliography by
Samuel E. Bring of Polhem's published and unpublished works. A major work on
an important early Swedish engineer (1661–1751). For a briefer sketch by
Johnson, see 'Christopher Polhem: the father of Swedish technology', *American–
Scandinavian Review*, vol. 56, no. 2 (1968), p. 162–75.

764 **Swedish astronomers 1477–1900.**
Per Collinder. Uppsala, Sweden: Almqvist & Wiksell, 1970. 73p.
bibliog. (Acta Universitatis Upsaliensis, Skrifter rörande Uppsala
Universitet, C. Organisation och historia, vol. 19).

Summarizes the work of Swedish astronomers during the period and the
instruments they used. A useful introduction to a subject needing further research
in English.

765 **Swedish research: policy, issues, organization.**
Annagreta Dyring, translated from the Swedish by Roger G.
Tanner. Stockholm: Swedish Institute, 1985. 80p.

Examines the main problems of finance and direction now facing Swedish
scientific research.

224

766 **History of science in Sweden.**
Tore Frängsmyr. *Isis*, vol. 74, no. 274 (1983), p. 464–68.

Discusses the development of chairs in the history of science at Sweden's five universities since 1932 and the main currents of thought emphasized in this discipline. A short but pithy survey of the subject.

767 **Nordic research and development.**
Elisabeth Helander. *Scandinavian Review*, vol. 72, no. 2 (1984), p. 11–15.

Discusses the difficulties impeding Nordic cooperation in research in a number of fields such as electronics and biotechnology and some factors that may lead to future success.

768 **Research funding and scientific training in Finland and Sweden.**
Rio Howard. *Scandinavian Review*, vol. 74, no. 1 (1986), p. 12–18.

Discusses the nature of scientific and technological training in Sweden and its relationship to private industry. Among the issues examined is the need for qualified specialists that the educational system has difficulty in providing.

769 **Jac. Berzelius: his life and work.**
J. Erik Jorpes, translated from the Swedish by Barbara
Steele. Berkeley, California; Los Angeles: University of
California Press, 1970. 156p. maps.

Emphasizes Berzelius' (1779–1848) work in chemistry with special mention of the contributions made by other Swedish chemists of the 18th and 19th centuries. An excellent introduction to Berzelius' contribution to science. For a more detailed study of Berzelius' scientific work, see Evan M. Melhado's *Jacob Berzelius: the emergence of his chemical system* (Stockholm: Almqvist & Wiksell; Madison, Wisconsin: University of Wisconsin Press, 1981).

770 **Science policies of industrial nations: case studies of the United
States, Soviet Union, United Kingdom, France, Japan, and Sweden.**
Edited by T. Dixon Long, Christopher Wright. New York:
Praeger, 1975. 232p. bibliog.

Contains a contribution by Ingemar N. H. Dörfer, 'Science and technology policy in Sweden', (p. 169–90), which examines factors in the development of scientific policy in Sweden and changes during the 1970s. An interesting, critical, and non-technical approach.

771 **Anders Celsius: a matter of degree.**
Richard Peter. *Scandinavian Review*, vol. 65, no. 4 (1977), p. 4–8.

Sketches many of Celsius' scientific accomplishments but concentrates on his development of the centigrade scale thermometer.

772 **Science policy and organization of research in Sweden.**
Paris, UNESCO, 1974. 59p. bibliog. (Science Policy Studies and
Documents, no. 34).

Outlines particularly the organization of scientific and technical research. In need
of revision after the educational reforms in Sweden of the last decade but still a
helpful survey.

773 **Science policy and the challenge of the welfare state.**
Björn Wittrock. *West European Politics*, vol. 3, no. 3 (1980),
p. 358–72.

Studies Swedish scientific policy from the 1950s to the late 1970s. Critical and
particularly useful to supplement official expressions of policy and goals. Part of a
special issue of this journal entitled *Public policy comparisons: Scandinavia*.

Swedish know-how in the 80s.
See item no. 30.

German coal and Swedish fuel 1939–1945.
See item no. 285.

Engelsk–svensk teknisk ordbok. (English–Swedish technical dictionary.)
See item no. 377.

Engelsk–svensk ordbok i teknik. (English–Swedish dictionary of technology.)
See item no. 380.

Emanuel Swedenborg.
See item no. 417.

The Swedenborg epic: the life and works of Emanuel Swedenborg.
See item no. 425.

The Swedish academic marketplace: the case of science and technology.
See item no. 440.

Public policy comparisons: Scandinavia.
See item no. 505.

System 37 Viggen: arms, technology and the domestication of glory.
See item no. 626.

The small giant: Sweden enters the industrial era.
See item no. 716.

**Technology policy and industrial development in Scandinavia: proceed-
ings from a workshop held in Copenhagen, Denmark, May 20–21, 1981.**
See item no. 718.

Literature

General

774 Contemporary Swedish prose.
Ingemar Algulin, translated from the Swedish by Verne Moberg,
Linda Schenck. Stockholm: Swedish Institute, 1983. 96p. bibliog.
A brief but perceptive introduction to post-war prose, concentrating on the late
1960s and 1970s. A useful starting point for the interested reader, its bibliography
is complete to 1983.

775 Sju decennier: svensk teater under 1900-talet. (Seven decades:
Swedish theatre in the twentieth century.)
P. G. Engel, Leif Janzon. Stockholm: Forum, 1974. 212p.
bibliog. (När? Vär? Hur? Serien).
A concise survey of the Swedish stage decade by decade to 1970, which looks at
the theatre from a national perspective.

776 The Swedish writer and his rights.
Jan Gehlin, translated from the Swedish by Paul Britten Austin.
Stockholm: Swedish Institute, 1980. 69p.
Swedish writers are perhaps the most protected in the world, as this book makes
clear. This book is a summary of their relationship to the state.

777 **A history of Swedish literature.**
Alrik Gustafson. Minneapolis, Minnesota: University of
Minnesota Press, 1961. 708p. bibliog.

Still the standard reference work in English and useful up to its date, it has a large
bibliography which should be the starting point for an initial look at earlier
Swedish literature.

778 **The Swedish crime story:** *svenska deckare.*
Bo Lundin. Stockholm: Tidskriften Jury, 1981. 127p.

This charming little bilingual survey of the Swedish detective story is a good
introduction to a productive area of popular literature in Sweden. It might
usefully be complemented by the exhaustive bibliography edited by Ivan
Hedman, *Deckare och thrillers på svenska 1864–1973* (Strängnäs, Sweden: Dast,
1974, 377p.).

Anthologies

779 **Friends, you drank some darkness: three Swedish poets – Harry
Martinson, Gunnar Ekelöf and Tomas Tranströmer.**
Edited and translated from the Swedish by Robert Bly. Boston,
Massachusetts: Beacon Press, 1975. 267p.

This bilingual edition of three major modern Swedish poets is eccentric in its
choice of poems. Bly tends to choose those which sound most like his own poetry
but these are undeniably some of the most brilliant translations of Swedish poetry
into English.

780 **Scandinavian plays of the twentieth century: first series.**
Edited by Alrik Gustafson. Princeton, New Jersey: Princeton
University Press, 1944. 176p.

The four plays in this anthology, reprinted (New York: Kraus Reprint Company,
1971), represent theatrical trends in the second quarter of this century. The plays
are Runar Schildt's *The gallows man: a midwinter story*, Hjalmar Bergman's *Mr.
Sleeman is coming*, Pär Lagerkvist's *The man without a soul* and Ragnar
Josephson's *Perhaps a poet.*

781 **An anthology of Scandinavian literature.**
Edited by Hallberg Hallmundsson. New York: Collier Books,
1965. 362p. bibliog.

This is a good anthology of Scandinavian literature, excluding Finland, but
including Iceland. Its selections stop around the Second World War. The poetic
translations from Swedish vary from C. W. Stork's admirable if musty attempts to
C. D. Locock's rather timid versions. The brief introductions to each writer must

occasionally be taken with a grain of salt (Bellman, for instance, hardly ever wrote his own tunes), but the basic collection is sound. The bibliography, though dated, is a useful starting point.

782 **Modern Swedish poetry in translation.**
Edited by Gunnar Harding, Anselm Hollo. Minneapolis, Minnesota: University of Minnesota Press, 1979. 270p.

This anthology is representative of the 1960s and early 1970s. The translations are often quite good, though there is no end to argument about poetic translation. The brief introduction and briefer presentations of the authors are breezy, not to say chatty, as is some of the poetry.

783 **Modern Swedish prose in translation.**
Edited by Karl Erik Lagerlöf. Minneapolis, Minnesota: University of Minnesota Press, 1979. 280p.

This is a good collection of major prose writers of the 1960s and 70s, generally well translated and briefly, if intelligently and only slightly pretentiously, introduced.

784 **'Eleven Swedish poets'.**
Edited by Rainer Schulte. *Mundus Artium*, vol. 6, no. 1 (1973), p. 8–85.

A bilingual selection of works by the major Swedish poets of the mid-20th century, with one glaring exception, Erik Lindegren. The translations are generally of high quality and include Pär Lagerkvist, Gunnar Ekelöf, Harry Martinson, Werner Aspenström, Folke Isaksson, Tomas Tranströmer, Göran Palm, Östen Sjöstrand, Lars Gustafsson, Gösta Friberg and Göran Sonnevi.

785 **Svenska författare.** (Swedish writers.)
Stockholm: Svenska vitterhetssamfundet, 1910– . 80 volumes.

This huge anthology presents standard, reliable texts for twenty-two major authors, mostly of the 17th and 18th centuries. Some are merely represented by one work; most have their complete works available.

786 **An anthology of modern Swedish literature.**
Edited by Per Wästberg. Merrick, New York: Cross-Cultural Communications, 1979. 217p. (International P.E.N. Books).

An anthology deriving mostly from the 1970s in translations by many hands, this is a good survey of Swedish prose and poetry of the period.

Literary criticism and trends

787 **Det moderna genombrottet i nordens litteratur.** (The modern
breakthrough in Nordic literature.)
Gunnar Ahlström. Stockholm: Rabén & Sjögren, 1974. 307p.
(First edition, Stockholm: KFs förlag, 1947).

The period from about 1880 to about 1910 is thought by many scholars to have
been the most critical for the development of modern Scandinavian literature.
This is the pioneering study of the period. Though written from a Marxist
perspective, the book is undogmatic in its exploration and tempered in its
judgement.

788 **The Old Norse element in Swedish romanticism.**
Adolph Burnett Benson. New York: AMS Press, 1966. 192p.
bibliog.

A study of the 'Gothic' movement in Swedish literature, an idea of great
importance for the early Romantic writers, especially Esaias Tegnér and Erik
Gustaf Geijer.

789 **Forays into Swedish poetry.**
Lars Gustafsson, translated from the Swedish by Robert Rovinsky.
Austin, Texas: University of Texas Press, 1978. 116p.

Fifteen brief, but splendid, essays on major Swedish poets of all periods, this
book also contains a sixteenth essay by the translator on the author. Gustafsson, a
major writer in all genres, is possibly the best literary essayist in Sweden.

790 **Den dubbla scenen: muntlig diktning från eddan till ABBA.** (The
double stage: oral poetry from the Edda to ABBA.)
Lars Lönnroth. Stockholm: Bokförlaget Prisma, 1978. 432p.

This is a study of the Swedish song-type called the *visa*, a blend of poetry and
music not unique to Sweden but cultivated with especial care and enjoyment
there. Lönnroth wears his erudition lightly, but this is not a book for everyone. Its
one major gap is the omission of Birger Sjöberg (1885–1929).

791 **Linjer i svensk prosa.** (Directions in Swedish prose.)
Edited by Kjerstin Norén. Lund, Sweden: Pax förlag, 1977. 431p.

Covering the decade 1965–75, this collection of thirteen essays deals with twelve
writers prominent in the period. All the novelists concerned shared a strong social
commitment which brings them together in this anthology.

792 **The hero in Scandinavian literature: from Peer Gynt to the present.**
Edited by John M. Weinstock, Robert T. Rovinsky. Austin,
Texas: University of Texas Press, 1975. 226p.

These proceedings of a thematic symposium held at the University of Texas in
1972 form an interesting collection of essays, whose Swedish component deals
mainly with August Strindberg and Ingmar Bergman.

Major authors

August Strindberg

793 **Structures of influence: a comparative approach to August Strindberg.**
Edited by Marilyn Johns Blackwell. Chapel Hill, North Carolina: University of North Carolina Press, 1981. 306p. (University of North Carolina Studies in the Germanic Languages, no. 98).

The seventeen essays in this *Festschrift* for Walter Johnson, the doyen of American Strindberg scholars, cover a great many areas from comparisons with other writers to a study of Strindberg and opera.

794 **Strindberg and the poetry of myth.**
Harry G. Carlson. Berkeley, California: University of California Press, 1982. 240p.

This study takes eight of Strindberg's greatest plays and reads them in the light of their relationship to ancient myths and archetypes, a new approach to Strindberg, who has mainly been looked at from the perspective of biography.

795 **The novels of August Strindberg: a study in theme and structure.**
Eric O. Johannesson. Berkeley, California: University of California Press, 1968. 317p. bibliog.

In Strindberg's vast output, his prose has not generally received as much attention as his plays. This book admirably rectifies this omission and concludes that Strindberg's strongest prose fiction is to be found in his shorter novels, such as *Utveckling* (Progress, 1883) or *Syndabocken* (The scapegoat, 1907).

796 **Strindberg and the historical drama.**
Walter Johnson. Seattle, Washington: University of Washington Press, 1963. 326p. bibliog.

Almost the only study of this part of Strindberg's large body of work. Strindberg's aspirations as an historical dramatist were considerable, and Johnson makes the best case for their worth.

797 **The Washington Strindberg.**
Edited, introduced and translated by Walter Johnson. Seattle, Washington: University of Washington Press, 1955–1979. 11 vols.

These volumes comprise the largest set of translations into English of Strindberg's plays by one hand. There are thirty-three plays and the famous *Open letters to the intimate theatre*. Johnson's translations have achieved a justifiable authority.

798 **August Strindberg.**
Olof Lagercrantz, translated from the Swedish by Anselm
Hollo. New York: Farrar, Straus, Giroux, 1979. 399p.

This detailed and well-written biography puts Strindberg's works into the context
of his life. What is new about the interpretation is that, unlike most Swedish
scholars, Lagercrantz does not see the so-called 'Inferno crisis' as the great
turning-point in Strindberg's writing. Instead, Lagercrantz stresses the continuing
experimentation in Strindberg's work.

799 **August Strindberg.**
Martin Lamm, translated from the Swedish and edited by Harry G.
Carlson. New York: Benjamin Blom, 1971. 561p. bibliog.

This is the classic study of Strindberg's life and works (first published 1940/41,
revised 1948). Lamm spent the better part of a lifetime trying to understand his
subject, and the resulting integration of life, work, psychology and period make a
masterful and influential biography.

800 **Strindberg: a biography.**
Michael Meyer. London: Secker & Warburg, 1985. 651p.

The newest large-scale biography; Meyer takes the laundry-list approach. This is a
detailed, almost day-by-day narrative, with liberal quotations from Strindberg's
diaries and letters. Meyer's strength as a biographer is that he has an absolute
command of the peripheral detail such as references by contemporaries to
Strindberg as well as the main events. His weakness is that he is not very critical
of the subject or his work.

801 **The Strindberg reader.**
Edited and translated from the Swedish by Arvid Paulson.
New York: Phaedra, 1968. 467p. bibliog.

Perhaps the best single introduction to the work of this complicated genius
(1849–1912), this is a selection that cuts across Strindberg's work, in intelligent
translation. Strindberg was much more than a playwright; he was a novelist of
considerable stature, an essayist of polemical weight, a short-story writer of great
notoriety, an average poet, a startling painter, and an egocentric photographer.

802 **Essays on Strindberg.**
Edited by Carl Reinhold Smedmark. Stockholm: Beckmans,
1966. 175p.

Nine essays on various aspects of Strindberg's life and works, of which several
focus on the intimate plays.

803 **Strindberg as dramatist.**
Evert Sprinchorn. New Haven, Connecticut: Yale University
Press, 1982. 332p.
Strindberg is a consistently modern playwright, whose work constantly shatters
convention. Sprinchorn views the plays almost as part of Strindberg's personality,
as one 'galvanized' into writing by some 'emotional storm'.

804 **August Strindberg.**
Birgitta Steene. Stockholm: Almqvist & Wiksell International,
1982. (Second, revised edition of *The greatest fire: a study of
August Strindberg*, Carbondale, Illinois: Southern Illinois
University Press, 1973), 173p. bibliog.
This is a fine study of the plays, which sees Strindberg as the 'cool observer' of life
around him, in an attempt to refute the more popular view of Strindberg as
voluble madman.

805 **Samlade verk.** (Collected works.)
August Strindberg. Stockholm: Strindbergssällskapet, 1981– .
This is the new critical edition of Strindberg's complete works, the so-called
'national edition' (*Nationalupplagan*). It will run to over seventy-five volumes, of
which only fifteen have so far appeared. Each is meticulously edited, and has a
commentary and glossary. All the volumes will also be accompanied by
commentary volumes and a microform edition of the manuscripts, as well as a
complete concordance.

806 **Strindbergian drama: themes and structures.**
Egil Törnqvist. Stockholm: Almqvist & Wiksell International,
1982. 259p.
This excellent book takes eleven important plays by Strindberg and examines
them for various details (e.g., plot in *Erik XIV*, the opening of *The Dance of
Death*). Törnqvist's scholarship is matched by his good theatrical sense.

807 **Strindberg on stage.**
Edited by Donald K. Weaver. Stockholm: Svensk teaterunion,
1983. 175p.
This collection of papers derives from a 1981 Strindberg symposium. The essays
cover a wide variety of topics from the staging of plays to their translation.

Carl Jonas Love Almqvist

808 **Carl Jonas Love Almqvist.**
Bertil Romberg, translated from the Swedish by Sten Liden.
Boston, Massachusetts: Twayne, 1977. 203p. (Twayne World
Authors Series, no. 401).

This is a fine, rapid introduction to the work of Sweden's most important
Romantic writer. Almqvist was an advanced thinker in his own day, and he
remains our contemporary. This book is especially useful as there is almost
nothing by or about Almqvist in English.

Carl Michael Bellman

809 **Carl Michael Bellman: genius of the Swedish rococo.**
Paul Britten Austin.   Malmö, Sweden: Allhems Förlag, 1967.
181p. bibliog.

The best biography to date in any language of Carl Michael Bellman. Austin's
first chapter, on 18th-century Stockholm, is a minor masterpiece of atmosphere in
itself. Austin has also translated many Bellman songs into English, some of which
have been recorded recently by Martin Best (NIMBUS 45019).

810 **Carl Michael Bellmans skrifter.** (Carl Michael Bellman's writings.)
Stockholm: Albert Bonniers, 1927– . (*Standardupplagan*, standard
edition).

Bellman is surely one of Sweden's most beloved poets, despite a complete lack of
sentimentality in his major work. This is the standard critical edition of his work,
in thirteen volumes to date. Each volume has a large commentary and includes
music to all song texts.

Hjalmar Bergman

811 **Hjalmar Bergman.**
Erik Hjalmar Linder, translated from the Swedish by Catherine
Djurklou.   Boston, Massachusetts: Twayne, 1975. 197p. (Twayne
World Authors Series, no. 356).

This is the best short introduction in English to Bergman, one of Sweden's finest
writers of psychological comedy. Linder is the main expert on this versatile and
troubled comic genius. The list of works even includes translations into Serbian.

Stig Dagerman

812 **Stig Dagerman.**
Laurie Thompson. Boston, Massachusetts: Twayne, 1983. 167p.
(Twayne World Authors Series, no. 676).
Dagerman was undoubtedly the most gifted of the Swedish writers who emerged in the 1940s. His suicide at 31 intensified Swedish interest in him, an interest that has not spread much beyond Sweden owing to lack of translations. Thompson's fine introduction places Dagerman well in his time for English-speaking readers.

Eyvind Johnson

813 **Eyvind Johnson.**
Gavin Orton. New York: Twayne, 1972. 160p. (Twayne World Authors Series, no. 150).
An introduction to a novelist who won the Nobel Prize in 1973, this study contains many plot summaries.

Pär Lagerkvist

814 **Pär Lagerkvist.**
Robert Donald Spector. New York: Twayne, 1973. 196p.
(Twayne World Authors Series, no. 267).
An introductory study that puts the main weight on Lagerkvist's major novels and plays, but less on his work as a poet and playwright.

815 **Modern theatre: seven plays and an essay.**
Pär Lagerkvist, translated from the Swedish by Thomas R. Buckman. Lincoln, Nebraska: University of Nebraska Press, 1966. 305p.
Apart from the plays, a side of Lagerkvist less well known to English-speaking audiences, this book contains the important essay, 'Modern theatre: points of view and attack', one of the milestones in the art of drama criticism and as central to the issue today as when it was written in 1918.

Selma Lagerlöf

816 **Selma Lagerlöf.**
Vivi Edström, translated from the Swedish by Barbara Lide.
Boston: Massachusetts: Twayne, 1984. 151p. bibliog. (Twayne World Authors Series, no. 741).
The most recent English study of this much-studied author, this book provides a sensible if rapid survey of Lagerlöf's major work. Readers interested in one of her greatest novels might find Elsa Olson-Buckner's *The epic tradition in Gösta Berlings saga* (Brooklyn, New York: Gaus, 1978, 144p.) useful.

Harry Martinson

817 **Harry Martinson: myter, målningar, motiv.** (Harry Martinson: myths, paintings, motifs.)
Ingvar Holm. Stockholm: Aldus, 1974. 386p.

This is the third, revised edition (first edition, 1960) of the best study of Martinson's work up to and including *Aniara* (1956). Martinson won the Nobel prize in 1973.

Vilhelm Moberg

818 **Vilhelm Moberg.**
Philip Holmes. Boston, Massachusetts: Twayne, 1980. 191p.
(Twayne World Authors Series, no. 584).

This excellent introduction to Moberg's large and rich output concentrates, properly, on the novels. Holmes is thoroughly aware of the background of Moberg's fiction and of the literary context within which he wrote.

Johan Ludvig Runeberg

819 **J. L. Runeberg.**
Tore Wretö, translated from the Swedish by Zelek S.
Herman. Boston, Massachusetts: Twayne, 1980. 186p. (Twayne World Authors Series, no. 503).

Although Finnish, Runeberg (1804–1877) wrote in Swedish. His impact upon Swedish poetry was enormous and Swedes consider him among their own. Though he is now less highly valued, much of his poetry is still readable and important today, not least for the many musical settings of it.

Edith Södergran

820 **Edith Södergran: modernist poet in Finland.**
George C. Schoolfield. Westport, Connecticut: Greenwood Press, 1984. 175p. (Contributions to the Study of World Literature, no. 3).

Södergran was a Swedish Finn whose work, together with that of J. L. Runeberg (q.v.), had a powerful effect on Swedish poetry. Most of Swedish modernism stems from her. In this, the finest English study of her poetry, Schoolfield has described hers as 'a life on the edge'.

The Russian Primary Chronicle.
See item no. 170.

The Vikings.
See item no. 174.

The Viking achievement: a survey of the society and culture of early medieval Scandinavia.
See item no. 175.

The Vikings and America.
See item no. 189.

Markings.
See item no. 633.

Das schwedische Theater: von den Gauklern bis zum Happening. (The Swedish theatre: from the travelling players to the happening.)
See item no. 847.

Swedish theatre.
See item no. 848.

Scandinavian Studies.
See item no. 942.

Scandinavica.
See item no. 945.

Swedish plays in English translation from Strindberg to the present.
See item no. 969.

Norse sagas translated into English: a bibliography.
See item no. 971.

Scandinavian literature in English translation 1928–1977.
See item no. 988.

The Arts

General

821 **Den svenska konstens historia.** (The history of Swedish art.)
Henrik Cornell.   Stockholm: Bonniers, 1959. 2 vols.
This is the standard history of Swedish art, including architecture, up to 1909. It consists mainly of brief biographies and a few words about the artist's importance to the history at large. It does not contain detailed analyses of specific works.

822 **Cultural policy in Sweden.**
Carl-Johan Kleberg.   Stockholm: Statens Kulturråd, [n.d. 1984?].
53p.
An article (intended for a book, *Government and the Arts in the Modern World*, edited by Milton Cummings, Richard Katz. Baltimore, Maryland: Johns Hopkins University Press, not yet published) which gives a summary of the post-war discussion and then looks quite closely at the policy debate after 1974. Available from Statens Kulturråd, Box 7843, S–103 98 Stockholm.

823 **Swedish cultural policy in the 20th century.**
Nils Gunnar Nilsson, translated from the Swedish by Paul Britten Austin.   Stockholm: Swedish Institute, 1980. 96p.
A good summary of official policy as it affects the whole range of Swedish culture, from the media to music and museums.

Visual arts

General

824 **The art of Scandinavia.**
Peter Anker, Aron Andersson.   London: Paul Hamlyn, 1970.
2 vols.

Despite their title, these two richly-illustrated volumes cover this area of art only from the Viking period to the early Middle Ages, ca. 400–1200 AD. The text is not for the beginner in either art history or things Scandinavian but it is comprehensive.

825 **Thought and form: studies in 18th century art.**
Edited by Per Bjurström, Nils-Göran Hökby.   Stockholm:
National Museum, 1979. 264p.

The essays in this collection all have some connexion with Sweden and the 18th century, the great age of Sweden's cultural flowering under its enlightened despot, Gustav III. One essay is in French, the rest are in English.

Painting

826 **The world of Carl Larsson.**
Görel Cavalli-Björkman, Bo Lindwall, Allan Lake Rice.
La Jolla, California: Green Tiger Press, 1982. 193p.

The largest, and best, survey of the work of Sweden's best-known painter, whose genial depictions of his home and family have made their way around the world. Much misunderstood in his own day, he nevertheless helped to define the new national-Romantic style that brings tears to the eyes of Swedes anywhere in the world today. This book is sumptuously illustrated, and is blessed with an intelligent text.

827 **Another light: Swedish art since 1945.**
Olle Granath.   Stockholm: Swedish Institute, 1982. 223p.

This trilingual book (English, French, German) is generously illustrated in colour as well as black-and-white. These are the main assets of the book, whose text covers the period only until the late 1970s.

828 **Northern light: realism and symbolism in Scandinavian painting 1880–1910.**
Kirk Varnedoe.   New York: The Brooklyn Museum, 1982. 240p.

This exhibition catalogue is an intelligently devised representation of the first major exhibition of Scandinavian painting to be shown in North America. The exhibit was organized around the theme of light and proved to be a great success. The discussions of the paintings are mainly historical.

Architecture

829   **Swedish architecture: drawings 1640–1970.**
Henrik O. Andersson, Fredric Bedoire, translated from the
Swedish by Kerstin Westerlund, H. O. Andersson, Alison
Woodward, Eva Raldon.   Stockholm: Byggförlaget, 1986. 257p.
maps. bibliog.

Wonder of wonders, a coffee-table book with a text worth reading! This
sumptuous survey is organized around the colour drawings of buildings by
Sweden's most famous architects, together with black-and-white photographs of
the buildings as they were actually constructed. This is preceded by a
photographic historical survey of Swedish architecture which, though concise, is
well done.

830   **Asplund.**
Claes Caldenby, Olof Hultin, translated from the Swedish by
Roger G. Tanner.   Stockholm: Arkitektur Förlag, 1985. 131p.

A fine, thoroughly illustrated, monograph in English on the most important
Swedish architect of this century, Gunnar Asplund (1885–1940). His monument
will always be the Stockholm Public Library, a building combining a vast sense of
space with a wealth of delicate detail to soften the view.

831   **Carl Larsson's home.**
Ulf Hård af Segerstad, Karl-Erik Granath, translated from the
Swedish by Pearl Lönnfors.   Stockholm: Swedish Booksellers'
Association, 1975. 103 [not paginated].

This picture book of the best-known home in Sweden will give those who know it
only from Carl Larsson's paintings a view of what he worked from in his famous
collections, *A Home, Our Farm* and others. (A useful complement is Eva von
Zweigbergk's *Hemma hos Carl Larssons* (At home with Carl Larsson) (Stockholm: Albert Bonniers, 1968, 183p., bibliog.), for a detailed discussion of the
development of the house itself.)

832   **Recent developments in Swedish architecture: a reappraisal.**
Edited by Gunilla Lundahl, translated from the Swedish by Patrick
Smith.   Stockholm: Swedish Institute, 1983. 192p.

This is a brief illustrated survey of issues in modern Swedish architecture,
including the re-use of old buildings, school buildings, care facilities and other
related matters. It suggests only directions, but has many fruitful ideas.

833 **Drottningholm: the palace by the lakeside.**
Jan Mårtenson, Gunnar Brusewitz, translated from the Swedish by
Eric Dickens.   Stockholm: Wahlström & Widstrand, 1985. 180p.

This is a very personal view of this famous palace, by one who lived there briefly.
Mårtenson's text is historically accurate but, as even he admits, somewhat
sentimental. Brusewitz' drawings are mostly decorations for the text. Nonetheless, this is a good history of the palace and those who have shaped it.

834 **The architecture of Erik Gunnar Asplund.**
Stuart Wrede.   Cambridge, Massachusetts: Massachusetts
Institute of Technology, 1980. 258p. bibliog.

A formal study with many illustrations of Asplund's (1885–1940) complete work.
This is the first and still the best academic view of this important modern
architect.

Textiles

835 **Svensk textilkonst: Swedish textile art.**
Edna Martin, Beate Sydhoff, translated from the Swedish by
William Barrett.   Stockholm: Liber, 1979. 151p.

Textiles, which here means art textiles, such as wall hangings and church
paraments, are an important Swedish craft often overlooked by those who think
in terms only of *rya* rugs. The pictures and parallel text of this book show the
extent of this art, with the emphasis on its state today.

836 **Contemporary textile art in Scandinavia.**
Charles S. Talley.   Uppsala, Sweden: Carmina, 1982. 200p.

A fine book of colour pictures and commentary on specific artists and textile
groups from all five Nordic countries. This shows the whole range of this
essentially conservative art.

Glass

837 **Swedish glass: awarded design.**
Rune B. Axelsson.   Stockholm: National Swedish Industrial
Board, 1984. 75p.

This full-colour book is also a catalogue of the exhibition of the winners of a glass
competition in 1983. There is a brief introduction to the glass district of Sweden.
Thereafter, the pictures and their captions do the rest. This is a good view of the
best current examples of an art in which the Swedes have always excelled.

838 **Orrefors: a Swedish glassplant.**
   Ann Marie Herlitz-Gezelius, translated from the Swedish by Susan
   M. Davis. Stockholm: Atlantis, 1984. 144p.

A history of one of Sweden's most famous glassworks. The text is rather thin, but the photographs and the design of the book are sumptuous.

839 **Swedish glass.**
   Elisa Steenberg, translated from the Swedish by Lillian Ollen.
   New York: Gramercy Publishing Co., 1950. 128p.

This little book is a handy guide to earlier Swedish glassworks and designers. It is sensibly written and the few illustrations are well chosen.

Photography

840 **The frozen image: Scandinavian photography.**
   Edited by Anne Hoene Hoy. New York: Abbeville Press, 1982.
   208p. bibliog.

This generous exhibition catalogue covers the whole field of Scandinavian photography, and in so doing provides a visual history hard to surpass.

841 **Den svenska fotografins historia, 1840–1940.** (The history of
   Swedish photography, 1840–1940.)
   Rolf Söderberg, Pär Rittsel. Stockholm: Albert Bonniers, 1983.
   344p. bibliog.

The most detailed study of the subject, with an especially good bibliography.

Design

842 **Scandinavian design: objects of a lifestyle.**
   Eileene Harrison Beer. New York: American–Scandinavian
   Foundation, 1975. 214p.

A somewhat superficial text is supplemented by many excellent photographs covering what is generally referred to as 'Scandinavian modern'. This is a coffee-table book that deserves some serious attention.

843 **Design in Sweden.**
   Edited by Monica Boman, translated from the Swedish by Roger
   G. Tanner. Stockholm: Swedish Institute, 1985. 142p.

This book is a complement to an earlier one of the same name (q.v.) and brings Swedish design into the 1980s. It covers briefly but usefully the whole area of design as it touches our everyday lives.

844 **Scandinavian modern design 1880–1980.**
Edited by David Revere McFadden. New York: Abrams, 1982.
287p. bibliog.

A book with numerous pictures and an intelligent text, this is the best recent survey in the never-ending quest to define that special concept, 'Scandinavian modern'. This book also has the advantage of a very good, well-selected bibliography.

845 **Design in Sweden.**
Åke Stavenow, Åke H. Huldt. Stockholm: Gothia, 1964. 268p.

This large-format book, intended to celebrate the Swedish pavilion in the New York World's Fair of 1964, is in two sections, the first showing how modern Swedish design and designers come into being and the second showing a wide range of examples of this design. It deals almost exclusively with the post-war period.

846 **New design in stitchery/wood/weaving/jewelry/ceramics.**
Donald J. Willcox. New York: Van Nostrand, Reinhold, 1970.
5 vols.

Each of the books in this series begins with a few words about the medium and then proceeds to a great many annotated photographs.

Performing arts

Theatre

847 **Das schwedische Theater: von den Gauklern bis zum Happening.**
(The Swedish theatre: from the travelling players to the happening.)
Verner Arpe. Stockholm: Svenska bokförlaget, 1969. 426p.
bibliog.

A fairly thorough illustrated history of the Swedish stage as a whole, with half the book dealing with the 20th century. The bibliography is especially good as a starting-point.

848 **Swedish theatre.**
Niklas Brunius, Göran O. Eriksson, Rolf Rembe, translated from the Swedish by Keith Bradfield. Stockholm: Swedish Institute, 1967. 109p.

This is a brief but useful look at the modern Swedish theatre. It also has a bibliography of Swedish plays in translation, not out of date. See *Swedish plays in English translation.*

849   **Swedish theatre today.**
      P. G. Engel, translated from the Swedish by Claude
      Stephenson.   Stockholm: Svensk teaterunion, 1977. 48p.

A brief summary of the state of all areas of the Swedish theatre in the mid-1970s,
from the union's point of view.

850   **The Sunday promenade.**
      Lars Forsell, translated from the Swedish by Harry Carlson.   In:
      The New Theatre of Europe – 3. Edited by Robert W. Corrigan.
      New York: Delta, 1968, pp. 119–210.

This is a fine translation of what is arguably the best post-war Swedish play yet
written.

851   **Modern Nordic plays: Sweden.**
      Edited by Helmer Lång.   Oslo: Universitetsforlaget, 1973. 419p.

This is an interesting anthology of plays by four writers, Lars Forsell, Folke
Fridell, Lars Görling and Björn-Erik Höijer, of whom only the first has achieved
his reputation chiefly as a playwright. As an alternative view of Swedish
literature, this anthology is useful and Lång's brief survey of 20th-century Swedish
theatre is a masterpiece of compression and clarity. Except for those of
Strindberg, plays have never been the great Swedish literary form, and these are
of interest, not least for that reason.

852   **Ingmar Bergman: four decades in the theatre.**
      Lise-Lone Marker, Frederik J. Marker.   Cambridge, England:
      Cambridge University Press, 1982. 262p.

It is easy to forget that Ingmar Bergman has always been associated with the
theatre, so long has his name been linked with films. This book, built in part on
interviews, is an attempt to look at his art from the perspective of the theatre, and
to see the relationship of theatre and film in the whole body of his work through
his productions of plays by Strindberg, Ibsen, Molière, and Büchner.

853   **The Scandinavian theatre: a short history.**
      Frederik J. Marker, Lise-Lone Marker.   Oxford: Blackwell, 1975.
      303p. bibliog.

A good regional survey, about half of which is devoted to the modern period from
Ibsen onward. There is also a useful working bibliography for those starting to
look at the various national theatres. In this context, 'Scandinavia' means only
Denmark, Norway and Sweden.

854 **Svensk teater och svenska skådespelare från Gustav III till våra dagar.** (Swedish theatre and Swedish actors from Gustav III to our day.)
Georg Nordensvan.   Stockholm: Albert Bonniers, 1917, 1918.
2 vols. bibliog.
The standard work of its time, closely linked to the actor's point of view. Nordensvan relied heavily on actors' memoirs to shape his narrative.

855 **Stage and society in Sweden: aspects of Swedish theatre since 1945.**
Henrik Sjögren, translated from the Swedish by Paul Britten Austin.   Stockholm: Swedish Institute, 1979. 181p.
A survey of the theatre of the period is coupled with consideration of the relations, especially financial, between state and stage. The author's view goes further, however, in also dealing with the function of theatre in a modern democratic society and thus asks not only *what* theatre is for, but *whom* is it for.

Opera

856 **Drottningholmsteatern förr och nu: the Drottningholm theatre – past and present.**
Gustaf Hilleström, translated from the Swedish by Joseph Stewart.   Stockholm: Natur & Kultur, 1980. 126p.
A fine book with many pictures about this remarkable and fully operational 18th-century theatre. Slightly shorter and in English, the text is by the theatre's curator for many years, who re-established opera there, it is intelligent and useful.

857 **The Royal Opera Stockholm.**
Gustaf Hilleström.   Stockholm: Kungliga teatern and Swedish Institute, 1960. 83p.
A brief history of this distinguished 200-year-old institution, accompanied by many pictures.

Cinema

858 **Ingmar Bergman and society.**
Maria Bergom-Larsson, translated from the Swedish by Barrie Selman.   London: Tantivy Press; New York: A. S. Barnes, 1978. 128p. (Film in Sweden.)
This discussion puts Ingmar Bergman into a socio-critical perspective and proceeds to divide his work thematically – violence, the artist in society, the patriarch, and so forth. Unfortunately, a film such as *The Magic Flute* (1975) does not fit into these categories and so is not discussed.

859   **The new directors.**
      Stig Björkman, translated from the Swedish by Barrie Selman.
      London: Tantivy Press; New York: A. S. Barnes, 1977. 128p.
      (Film in Sweden).

This too-brief book is nevertheless helpful in pointing to a number of younger film-makers who are trying to win fame outside Sweden without becoming caught in Ingmar Bergman's shadow. Probably only Jan Troell has made it, but the others are certainly worth reckoning with (Bo Widerberg, Mai Zetterling, Kjell Grede).

860   **Bergman on Bergman.**
      Stig Björkman, Torsten Manns, Jonas Süna, translated from the
      Swedish by Paul Britten Austin.   London: Secker & Warburg,
      1973; New York: Simon & Schuster, 1986. 288p.

A useful reference book incorporating some of Bergman's own views on his work.

861   **Swedish cinema: from *Ingeborg Holm* to *Fanny and Alexander*.**
      Peter Cowie.   Stockholm: Swedish Institute, 1985. 160p.

A good, general survey of the increasing riches of the Swedish film world, by an expert on Ingmar Bergman.

862   **Swedish film classics: a pictorial survey of 25 films from 1913 to
      1957.**
      Aleksander Kwiatkowski.   New York: Dover, 1983. 112p.

A quick tour of highlights from *Ingeborg Holm* to *Wild Strawberries*.

Music

863   **Svensk musik.**
      Arne Aulin, Herbert Connor.   Stockholm: Albert Bonniers, 1974,
      1977. 2 vols.

There is no good history of Swedish music in any language. This is the best so far, but it is patchy. It is organized around topics instead of providing a consistent narrative. Within those limits, however, some of the topics are quite well treated. (See also *Musiken i Sverige*.)

864   **ABBA by ABBA.**
      Edited by Christer Borg.   Cammeray, Australia: Horwitz, 1977.
      124p.

Unashamedly, a promotional book about this group.

865 **Contemporary Swedish music.**
Claes M. Cnattingius, translated from the Swedish by Claude
Stephenson. Stockholm: Swedish Institute, 1973. 84p.
A very rapid look at the major Swedish composers since 1940.

866 **Scandinavian music: a short history.**
John Horton. London: Faber & Faber, 1963. 180p.
The only reasonably successful attempt to write a coherent narrative history of
Scandinavian music. As is to be expected, it is thin on the 20th century.

867 **Musiken i Sverige.** (Music in Sweden.)
Stig Jacobsson. Västerås, Sweden: ICA–förlag, 1975. 286p.
bibliog., discog.
Intended in some magical way to accompany the active record listener, this book
provides a short but well-written narrative of the main lines in Swedish music.

868 **Franz Berwald.**
Robert Layton, foreword by Gerald Abraham. London: Anthony
Blond, 1959. 194p. bibliog.
The standard study of one of Sweden's most original 19th-century composers
(1796–1868), whose work has been rediscovered recently in England and the
United States. This biography also has a list of works and a discography to date.

869 **Tradition and progress in Swedish music.**
Edited by Bengt Pleijel, translated from the Swedish by Brian
Willson. (Special edition of *Musikrevy*, nd). Stockholm: np,
1973. 116p.
This mixed bag of short articles on the Swedish musical scene of the 1960s is still
useful, since many of the people and institutions are still very much alive.

870 **Folkmusikvågen. The folk music vogue.**
Edited by Lena Roth, translated by Michael Johns. Stockholm:
Rikskonserter, 1985. 227p. discography. (Accent number 10.)
Most of this text is in Swedish with an English abridgement at the end. The book
describes the enormous upswing in popularity of traditional music during the
1970s, especially among the young. This is almost a sociological study, and it is
accompanied by a cassette of musicians playing examples mentioned in the text
(Caprice CAP 11309).

871 **Twentieth century composers – 3: Britain, Scandinavia and the Netherlands.**
Humphrey Searle, Robert Layton.   London: Weidenfeld & Nicolson, 1972. 200p.

Not quite 50 pages of this book deal with Scandinavians, but, after a chapter on Nielsen and Sibelius, there are sympathetic treatments of William Stenhammar (1871–1927), Hugo Alfvén (1872–1960), Hilding Rosenberg (1892–), Gösta Nyström (1890–1966), Dag Wirén (1905–), L. E. Larsson (1908–1987), Gunnar de Frumerie (1908–), K. B. Blomdahl (1916–1968), Sven-Erik Bäck (1919–), Ingvar Lidholm (1921–), and a few words about Allan Pettersson (1911–1980), whose work was only just achieving general acceptance when this book appeared.

872 **The Nordic sound: explorations into the music of Denmark, Norway, Sweden.**
John H. Yoell.   Boston, Massachusetts: Crescendo Publishing Co., 1974. 264p. discog.

This quirky, personal view of contemporary Swedish music is uneven, but useful. After a brief historical survey, Yoell takes on individual composers in a few pages each. Nineteen of the forty-three so dealt with are Swedish, though it is stretching a point to call Carl Michael Bellman a composer.

Manor houses and royal castles in Sweden. . .
See item no. 40.

The Vikings.
See item no. 163.

The Vikings: an illustrated history of their voyages, battles, customs and decorative arts.
See item no. 169.

The Vikings.
See item no. 174.

The Viking achievement: a survey of the society and culture of early medieval Scandinavia.
See item no. 175.

The Viking world.
See item no. 176.

Queen Christina of Sweden: documents and studies.
See item no. 213.

Swedish emigrant ballads.
See item no. 367.

Children's theatre in Sweden.
See item no. 472.

Sju decennier: svensk teater under 1900-talet. (Seven decades: Swedish theatre in the twentieth century.)
See item no. 775.

Scandinavian plays of the twentieth century: first series.
See item no. 780.

Den dubbla scenen: muntlig diktning från eddan till ABBA. (The double stage: oral poetry from the Edda to ABBA.)
See item no. 790.

Strindberg and the poetry of myth.
See item no. 794.

Strindberg and the historical drama.
See item no. 796.

August Strindberg.
See item no. 799.

Strindberg: a biography.
See item no. 800.

Strindberg as a dramatist.
See item no. 803.

August Strindberg.
See item no. 804.

Strindbergian drama: themes and structures.
See item no. 806.

Strindberg on stage.
See item no. 807.

Carl Michael Bellman: genius of the Swedish rococo.
See item no. 809.

Carl Michael Bellmans skrifter. (Carl Michael Bellman's writings.)
See item no. 810.

Modern theatre: seven plays and an essay.
See item no. 815.

Sohlmans musiklexikon. (Sohlman's music encyclopaedia.)
See item no. 948.

Famous Swedes.
See item no. 949.

Svenska tonsättare: diskografi. (Swedish composers: discography.)
See item no. 952.

Art consulting: Scandinavia: book on art and architecture.
See item no. 963.

Swedish plays in English translation from Strindberg to the present.
See item no. 969.

A Jussi Björling phonography.
See item no. 976.

Great Swedish fairy tales: illustrated by John Bauer.
See item no. 1011.

Folklore, Folk-art and Customs

Folklore

873 **Scandinavian legends and folk-tales.**
Gwyn Jones. London: Oxford University Press, 1956. 223p.
This is probably the best one-volume sampler of the most famous Nordic tales and sagas. Jones is the great master of re-telling these stories – one might only be bothered by his preference for translating place-names literally. The collection has most of the favourite saga stories, including the ever-charming 'Authun and the Bear'.

874 **Swedish legends and folktales.**
John Lindow. Berkeley, California: University of California Press, 1978. 219p. bibliog.
A fairly recent collection of 100 stories from all parts of Sweden, this is useful to academic and layman alike. There is a large introduction about collecting folktales and the themes of these stories. Each tale has a bibliographical note and a commentary to put it into a wider context. The general bibliography at the end is a first-rate place to look for the latest information and for sources of other tales.

875 **Scandinavian stories.**
Margaret Sperry. London: Dent, 1971. 288p.
The Swedish stories in this collection are largely from the work of Ana Wahlenberg (1858–1933), with one contribution of a genuine folk character from those collected by Gunnar Hyltén-Cavallius (1818–1889). There are also three Lapp tales as told by the great Swedish–Finnish Romantic writer, Zacharius Topelius (1818–1898).

Folk-art

876 **Folk costumes of Sweden – a living tradition.**
Inga Arnö Berg, Gunnel Hazelius Berg. Västeras, Sweden: ICA
bokförlag, 1975. 239p. bibliog.

Sometimes known as the 'Great Folk Costume Book', this has become the
standard reference work on the subject. It has a brief history of the folk costume
movement and then shows each costume, in full colour, on models, parish by
parish. There are even a few useful tips on how to make such a costume, but one
will need more than these instructions to do so.

877 **Biblia dalecarlia: the life of Jesus in Dalecarlian paintings.**
La Leufvén, Svante Svärdström. Stockholm: Studiebokförlaget,
1965. 91p.

Excellent reproductions of one of the true Swedish folk-treasures, the 18th–19th
century home wall-paintings, chiefly from Dalarna (Dalecarlia), mostly on
religious themes. The introduction is in Swedish, English, German and French.

878 **Swedish handcraft.**
Anna-Maja Nylén, translated from the Swedish by A. C. Hanes-
Harvey. Lund, Sweden: Håkan Olssons förlag, 1968. 428p.
bibliog.

This is the standard survey in English of that large field the Swedes call *hemslöjd*,
those things made at home for home use. Most of this book deals with textiles in
various forms, but there are sections on wood- and metalwork as well.

Holidays, customs and festivities

879 **The year in Sweden.**
Lena Larsson, translated from the Swedish by Keith Bradfield.
Stockholm: Trevi, 1984. 64p.

Despite its organization by the months of the year, this is an impressionistic view
of Sweden and a few of its folk-customs.

880 **Traditional festivities in Sweden.**
Ingemar Liman, translated from the Swedish by Charly Hultén.
Stockholm: Swedish Institute, 1966. 31p.

Brief descriptions of the major traditional holidays accompanied by apt and
attractive illustrations.

881 **Holidays in Scandinavia.**
Lee Wyndham. Champaign, Illinois: Garrard, 1975. 95p.
(Around the World Holidays).
Describes both official and unofficial holidays in the Scandinavian countries, such as Sweden's *Vasaloppet* (cross-country ski race) and Walpurgis Night (April 30) as well as more common observances such as Christmas and the New Year.

Of Swedish ways.
See item no. 8.

Sweden.
See item no. 11.

Folkmusikvågen. The folk music vogue.
See item no. 870.

Cuisine

882 **The best of Swedish cooking.**
Edited by Stina Algotson, translated from the Swedish by Mona
Oksbro. Stockholm: LTs förlag, 1985. 176p.

Contains a standard collection of Swedish recipes. The conversions from metric
measurements are made to both British imperial and American measures. Also
includes a section of typical menus for some traditional holidays.

883 **The cooking of Scandinavia.**
Edited by Dale Brown. New York: Time-Life International,
1968. 2 vols.

Two works providing a cookery book (96p.) of classical Scandinavian recipes and
a more extensive (206p.) and well-illustrated study of the place of food in
Scandinavian culture, including a picture lesson by Max von Sydow of how to
skål.

884 **Swedish cooking.**
Görel Kristina Näslund. Västerås, Sweden: ICA bokförlag, 1983.
128p.

About one-third of the work is a presentation of how and when Swedish food is
used. Ingredients of recipes are given in both metric and American measures.

885 **The Swedish smörgåsbord.**
Tore Wretman, translated from the Swedish by Clare
James. Stockholm: Forum, 1983. 132p.

The definitive book on this uniquely Swedish institution by the best-known
Swedish cook and restaurateur of this century. Discusses the traditional five
courses and adds an extra section on the Christmas table. Measurements are given
in metric and American forms.

Numismatics, Philately and Flags

886 **The national flags of Sweden.**
Alf Åberg. *American Scandinavian Review*, vol. 62, no. 1 (1974), p. 13–23.

Discusses the origin of Swedish banners during the late Middle Ages and variations in the flags used until the Flag Act of 1906. An informative, concise survey.

887 **Catalogue of Scandinavian coins: gold, silver and minor coins since 1534 and their valuations.**
Burton Hobson. New York: Sterling; London: Oak Tree Press, 1970. 128p.

The section on Sweden (p. 71–121) provides illustrations of Swedish coins from 1534 to 1966, descriptions of their distinctive markings, and estimated worth in 1964. A valuable reference work.

888 **A stamp journey through Sweden.**
Stockholm: Swedish Post Office, Stamps and Philatelic Society, 1984. 23p. map.

A collection of recent Swedish stamps representing the different provinces of the country. For stamp collectors and those with a general interest in the country.

Studies in Northern coinages of the eleventh century.
See item no. 165.

Nobel Prizes

889 **Alfred Nobel: the man and his work.**
Erik Bergengren, translated from the Swedish by Alan Blair,
foreword by Dag Hammarskjöld, foreword by Winston Churchill,
preface by Arne Tiselius. Edinburgh: Thomas Nelson & Sons,
1962. 222p. bibliog.
Authorized by the Nobel Foundation, it is a chronological account of Nobel's
early life, discoveries, and business affairs. An excellent survey for all readers.
Nils Ståhle has appended a brief discussion of the Nobel Prizes and their
administration. Ståhle has since published a similar work, *Alfred Nobel and the
Nobel Prizes* (Stockholm: Nobel Foundation, Swedish Institute, 1968).

890 **Nobel: the man and his prizes.**
Henrik Schück, Ragnar Sohlman, A. Österling, G. Liljestrand,
A. Westgren, M. Siegbahn, A. Schou, Nils K. Ståhle, edited by
the Nobel Foundation. Amsterdam: Elsevier, 1962. 2nd rev. ed.
690p.
First published in 1950 (Norman, Oklahoma: University of Oklahoma Press;
Stockholm: Sohlmans Förlag), the contributors provide a brief sketch of Nobel's
life and more detailed studies of the Nobel Foundation itself and discussions of
the individual prize and past recipients. In need of revision but still the major
study of this topic. For other studies of the Nobel Prize and recipients, see *Nobel
Prize winners*, edited by L. J. Ludovici (Westport, Connecticut: Associated
Booksellers, 1957), and Olga S. Opfell's *The lady laureates: women who have won
the Nobel Prize* (Metuchen, New Jersey; London: Scarecrow Press, 1978).

891 **Nobel: dynamite and peace.**
Ragnar Sohlman, Henrik Schück, translated from the Swedish by
Brian Lynn, Beatrix Lynn. New York: Cosmopolitan Books,
1929. 353p.

A work authorized by the Nobel Foundation, it is still the most thorough study of
Nobel for all readers. First published in Sweden in 1926 as *Alfred Nobel och hans
släkt* (Alfred Nobel and his family), it was published in England as *The life of
Alfred Nobel* (London: Wm. Heinemann). For a discussion of Sohlman's role in
the implementation of Nobel's bequest, see Joseph B. Board, Jr.'s 'Spokesman
for the soul', *Scandinavian Review*, vol. 67, no. 4 (1979), p. 17–25.

892 **The Nobel Prize.**
Peter Wilhelm. London: Springwood Books, 1983. 111p.

A richly-illustrated sketch of Alfred Nobel, the creation of his awards, the Nobel
Foundation, the selection process, a photographic record of Professor Kenichi
Fukui's visit to Stockholm to receive the 1981 Nobel Prize for chemistry, and a list
of all prize-winners from 1901–1982. A basic introduction which readers may wish
to supplement with other works.

Sports and
Recreation

893 My life and game.
Björn Borg, Eugene L. Scott. New York: Simon & Schuster,
1981. 192p.

First published in 1980, it combines a commentary on Borg's life with his advice for tennis players. For another description of Borg's career, see Larry Audette's *Bjorn Borg* (New York: Quick Fox, 1979) and for a picture book, *Borg by Borg* (London: Octopus Books, 1980), first published in French as *Borg par Borg* (Paris: Fernand Nathan, 1979).

894 The Björn Borg story.
Björn Borg, translated from the Swedish by Joan Tate. London:
Pelham Books, 1975. 96p. (A Sporting Print).

The best discussion by Borg of his early tennis career.

**895 Nordic touring and cross country skiing: technique, equipment,
waxing, clothing.**
M. Michael Brady. Oslo: Dreyer Forlag, 1971. 80p.

The work is basically an instruction manual but also discusses Scandinavian training methods, and past stars of the sport.

896 New breed from the North.
Curry Kirkpatrick. *Sports Illustrated*, vol. 62, no. 25 (June 24,
1985), p. 74–88.

Discusses the national junior tennis programme created in Sweden to develop future tennis stars and the major tournament players who are the products of this system. An informative article for all readers.

Sports and Recreation

897 **Scandinavia.**
Anders Nordlund.   In: *The world today in health, physical education, and recreation*. Edited by C. Lynn Vendien, John E. Nixon. Englewood Cliffs, New Jersey: Prentice-Hall, 1968, p. 190–219. maps. bibliog.
Describes the nature of programmes in Sweden particularly those designed to promote athletics, physical education, and recreation. A very useful introduction for all readers on the subject.

898 **The Viking drivers: Ronnie Peterson and Gunnar Nilsson.**
Frederik af Petersens.   London: William Kimber, 1979. 208p.
Describes in journalistic fashion the racing exploits of the two Swedes during the 1970s and their deaths in 1978. For another work on Peterson, see Alan Henry's *Ronnie Peterson: Super Swede* (Sparkford, England: Haynes, 1978).

899 **The Swedish challenge: America's Cup 1977.**
Stellan Westerdahl, Lars Åhren, Peter Rhedin, Peter Adler. Gothenburg, Sweden: Wezäta Idé, 1977. 93p. maps.
A work commemorating *Sverige*'s participation in the 1977 America's Cup competition for twelve-metre sailboats. It is a richly-illustrated description of the race, Swedish sailing and shipping traditions, and the boat itself.

A journey in Lapland: the hard way to Haparanda.
See item no. 49.

Small boat through Sweden.
See item no. 52.

On foot through Europe, a trail guide to Scandinavia: includes Denmark, Finland, Greenland, Iceland, Norway and Sweden: walking, backpacking, ski touring, climbing – everything you can do on foot.
See item no. 105.

Libraries, Archives and Museums

900 **Library instruction in academic libraries in Sweden.**
Nancy Fjällbrant, Sven Westberg. Gothenburg, Sweden:
Elanders, 1974. 27p. (Chalmers Tekniska Högskolans
Handlingar/Transactions of Chalmers University of Technology,
the Library, no. 2).
Presents the results of a survey undertaken on the question.

901 **Libraries in Scandinavia.**
K. C. Harrison. London: André Deutsch, 1969. 2nd ed. 288p.
The section on Sweden (p. 85–156) surveys national and university libraries,
special libraries, library law, state aid, education of librarians, central library
services, public libraries, children's libraries, and other services. A very useful
summary now in need of revision.

902 **The publication policies and practices of the Nordic archives.**
Harald Jørgensen. *American Archivist*, vol. 46, no. 4 (1983),
p. 400–14.
An overview of the development of archives in Denmark, Finland, Norway, and
Sweden and some of the catalogues and collections published by both the central
and provincial archives of the countries.

Libraries, Archives and Museums

903 **Public libraries in the Nordic countries.**
Hilkka Kauppi. In: *Nordic democracy: ideas, issues, and institutions in politics, economy, education, social and cultural affairs of Denmark, Finland, Iceland, Norway, and Sweden.* Edited by Erik Allardt, Nils Andrén, Erik J. Friis, Gylfi T. Gislason, Sten Sparre Nilson, Henry Valen, Frantz Wendt, Folmer Wisti. Copenhagen: Det Danske Selskab, 1981, p. 495–503.

An introduction to the origins of public libraries in the Nordic countries, the means by which they are financed, and the training of librarians.

904 **Sweden.**
Raymond E. Lindgren. In: *The new guide to the diplomatic archives of Western Europe.* Edited by Daniel H. Thomas, Lynn M. Case. Philadelphia, Pennsylvania: University of Pennsylvania Press 1975, p. 314–27. bibliog.

A revision by Lindgren of the article on Sweden by Florence Janson Sheriff that appeared in the first edition of the work in 1959. Contains information on the origin and organization of the *Riksarkiv* (National Archives) in Stockholm and other major research libraries in Sweden. Essential and important information for scholars wishing to do diplomatic or historical research in Sweden. For a work now badly in need of revision, see Gösta Ottervik, Sigurd Möhlenbrock, Ingvar Andersson, *Libraries and archives in Sweden* (Stockholm: Swedish Institute, 1954).

905 **Museiboken: Sveriges länsmuseer.** (Museum book: Sweden's county museums.)
Edited by Gunnar Lindqvist, Lars Thor, Trygve Carlsson, translated from the Swedish by Angela Adegren. Stockholm: Carlssons, 1984. 248p.

A bilingual (Swedish–English) description of Sweden's county museums. Includes a sketch of each museum's history, a description of its collections and some photographs. An essential work for all serious scholars.

906 **Museiguiden: vägledning till svenska museer.** (Museum guide: an introduction to Swedish museums.)
Edited by Bengt Nyström. Stockholm: LTs Förlag, 1984. 136p.

A handy pocket-guide to every museum in Sweden, giving a concise summary of their holdings, addresses, phone numbers, and opening times. A summary of the museum's contents is also provided in English. As some of the smaller museums have less regular hours, the opening times given in the work are not absolutely reliable. Ruins and a number of palaces are not included.

907 **Stockholms museer.** (Stockholm's museums.)
Bo Wingren. Stockholm: Liber, 1978. 118p. bibliog.
A succinct guide to all of Stockholm's museums except for the Medieval Museum opened in 1986.

The Nordiska Museet and Skansen: an introduction to the history and activities of a famous Swedish museum.
See item no. 113.

Swedish cultural policy in the 20th century.
See item no. 823.

Drottningholmsteatern förr och nu: the Drottningholm theatre – past and present.
See item no. 856.

Kulturkatalogen. (The cultural catalogue.)
See item no. 959.

The world of learning.
See item no. 961.

Mass Media

General

908 **Media in transition: Swedish mass communication. Research on new information technology.**
Edited by Ulla Carlson, translated from the Swedish by Charly Hultén, Michael Johns, Roland Stanbridge. Gothenburg, Sweden: Nordicom-Sweden, 1986. 119p. bibliog.
A series of brief but informative essays on recent research in and on Swedish mass communication. The book includes a bibliography with abstracts of other recent work.

909 **Disorder in the orbit: the fate of NORDSAT, the Nordic television satellite.**
Hans Dahl. *Scandinavian Review*, vol. 72, no. 3 (1984), p. 25–30.
Discusses the problems that have delayed and possibly destroyed plans for a television satellite offering all Scandinavian viewers the television programmes broadcast from Finland, Sweden, Norway, and Denmark.

910 **Censorship and freedom of expression in Scandinavia.**
Paul O. Frisch. *Scandinavian Review*, vol. 56, no. 1 (1968), p. 13–19.
Compares censorship regulations in the Scandinavian countries as they pertain to films and television, and press laws regarding published material.

911 **Some reflections on newspaper concentration.**
Lars Furhoff. *Scandinavian Economic History Review*, vol. 21,
no. 1 (1973), p. 1–27.
Examines the difficulties faced by 'second newspapers' in a market already
dominated by another newspaper and popular misconceptions regarding newspaper concentration. On the same subject, see Karl-Erik Gustafsson, 'The
circulation spurt and the principle of household coverage', vol. 26, no. 1 (1978),
p. 1–14.

912 **Hundred years of Swedish press history from general surveys to
problem-oriented research.**
Elisabeth Sandlund Gäfvert, Jarl Torbacke. *Scandinavian Journal
of History*, vol. 7, no. 1 (1982), p. 31–48.
A rich historiographical discussion of research on Sweden's newspapers, and
suggestions for future research. Its notes provide an excellent bibliography. For
all interested readers. Part of an issue on 'Research on press history in
Scandinavia'.

913 **Swedish press policy.**
Karl-Erik Gustafsson, Stig Hadenius, translated from the Swedish
by Charly Hultén. Stockholm: Swedish Institute, 1976. 127p.
Written after the change in cultural policy in 1974, this book reflects the current
position of the government with respect to its new intervention to preserve a
diverse press.

914 **Nordic radio and television via satellite: final report.**
Translated from the Swedish by Charly Hultén. Stockholm:
Nordic Council of Ministers, Secretariat for Nordic Cultural
Cooperation, 1980. 210p.
This fascinating document (NU A 1979) chronicles the history of the troubled
negotiations about NORDSAT, the Nordic TV satellite, long-proposed but never
finally agreed upon. Much of the trouble stems from the unwillingness of Sweden,
Norway and Denmark to accept the commercials of Iceland and Finland.

915 **Mass media and state support in Sweden.**
Olof Hultén, translated from the Swedish by Charly
Hultén. Stockholm: Swedish Institute, 1984. 61p.
A concise but wide-ranging survey. Swedish newspapers and journals are
elaborately and heavily subsidized by the government.

916 **Invandrare i tystnadsspiralen.** (Immigrants in the spiral of silence.)
[No editor.] Stockholm: Arbetsmarknadsdepartementet, 1985.
239p.
This report is one of a series from the Commission on Discrimination
(*Diskrimineringsutredningen*) and is concerned with the relation of the immigrant

to the mass media. The first two of the three essays show how the media ignore immigrants until something negative occurs. The third is a polemical attack on this one-sided attitude.

917　**The art of the book in Sweden: five centuries of printing.**
　　　Sten G. Lindberg, translated from the Swedish by Roger G.
　　　Tanner. Stockholm: Swedish Institute, 1983. 31p.

A concise pamphlet on the art of book publishing in Sweden. Consideration begins with 15th-century works but primarily concerns books from the 18th century to the present. A well-written survey of a topic demanding greater attention.

918　**Advertising on Swedish T.V.**
　　　Sam Nilsson, translated from the Swedish by Mari Soutine.
　　　Scandinavian Review, vol. 73, no. 1 (1985), p. 43–45.

Discusses the options for future funding of Swedish television, including a system of advertising. A useful introduction to a subject demanding greater treatment. The author is the head of Sweden's public television company.

919　**Politics and the development of mass communications.**
　　　Niels Thomsen.　In: *Nordic democracy: ideas, issues, and
　　　institutions in politics, economy, education, social and cultural
　　　affairs in Denmark, Finland, Iceland, Norway, and Sweden.* Edited
　　　by Erik Allardt, Nils Andrén, Erik J. Friis, Gylfi T. Gislason, Sten
　　　Sparre Nilson, Henry Valen, Frantz Wendt, Folmer Wisti.
　　　Copenhagen: Det Danske Selskab, 1981, p. 517–51.

A wide-ranging discussion of the mass media, primarily in Norway, Sweden, and Denmark, and its relationship to politics and government. The author outlines the development of the press and its early difficulties with censorship. He also discusses the origins of radio and television, the administration of the latter by public agencies, the question of controls associated with it, and recent general changes experienced by newspapers. The most recent and clearest survey of the subject.

Newspapers

920　**Aftonbladet.** (The evening paper.)
　　　Stockholm: Aftonbladets AB, 1830– .

An evening tabloid associated with the Social Democratic Party and not generally known for the calmness of its reporting. Founded 1830 as a liberal newspaper.

921 **Dagens nyheter.** (The day's news.)
Stockholm: Dagens nyheters AB, 1864– .

A daily paper, now calling itself 'independent liberal', with good writing and responsible reportage, perhaps the most influential Swedish newspaper, and the one most often quoted abroad.

922 **Expressen.** (The express.)
Stockholm: AB Kvällstidningen Expressen, 1944– .

An independent evening tabloid of great popularity.

923 **Göteborgs–Posten.** (The Gothenburg post.)
Gothenburg: Göteborgs–Postens Nya AB, 1858– .

This is the chief Swedish west-coast daily paper, middle-of-the-road politically, but with decent cultural pages.

924 **Svenska dagbladet.** (The Swedish daily paper.)
Stockholm: Handelsbolaget Svenska dagbladets AB, 1884– .

A morning paper, previously closely allied with the Conservative Party, and still generally so. The writing, especially on the cultural pages, is of a high quality.

925 **Sydsvenska dagbladet.** (The south-Swedish daily news.)
Malmö, Sweden: Sydsvenska dagbladets AB, 1848– .

The principal south-Swedish daily paper is also a national newspaper of some standing, especially for its cultural reportage.

The debate on the foreign policy of Sweden 1918–1939.
See item no. 275.

Scandinavia at the polls: recent political trends in Denmark, Norway, and Sweden.
See item no. 544.

State–media relations in Sweden.
See item no. 743.

The Swedish writer and his rights.
See item no. 776.

Cultural policy in Sweden.
See item no. 822.

Mass media 1985: handbok för journalister, informatörer och andra som följer press, radio och tv. (Handbook for journalists, public relations and others who follow the press, radio and television.)
See item no. 950.

Mass Media. Newspapers

Kulturtidskriften: 1986 katolog över kulturtidskrifter i Sverige. (The cultural journal: 1986 catalogue of cultural journals in Sweden.) *See* item no. 955.

Litterära tidskrifter i Sverige 1900–1970: en kommenterad bibliografi. (Literary journals in Sweden 1900–70: an annotated bibliography.) *See* item no. 979.

Professional
Periodicals

926 **Acta Archaeologica.**
   Copenhagen: Munksgaard, 1930– . annual.
A scholarly journal containing articles in English and other major languages,
written mainly by Scandinavian archaeologists.

927 **Acta Sociologica: The Journal of the Scandinavian Sociological
   Association.**
   Oslo: Universitetsforlaget, 1955– . quarterly.
One of the organizations which founded this research journal was the Swedish
Sociological Society. Its articles are in English, and most deal with research
carried out in Scandinavia. In addition to the articles, the journal also contains
research notes, review essays and book reviews.

928 **Boreas: An International Journal of Quaternary Geology.**
   Oslo: Universitetsforlaget, 1972– . quarterly.
Sponsored by the National Councils for Scientific Research in Denmark, Finland,
Norway and Sweden, the journal considers all branches of Quaternary geology,
including conditions in periodically glaciated areas of the world and both
biological and non-biological aspects of Quaternary environment. Almost all of
the articles are in English and most deal with Scandinavian subjects.

929 **Cooperation and Conflict: Journal of International Politics.**
   Oslo: Universitetsforlaget, 1965– . quarterly.
The journal is published by the Nordic Cooperation Committee for International
Politics. The articles, which are in English, deal mainly with foreign policy,
disarmament, and international security. The journal also contains research notes

269

Professional Periodicals

and reviews. Many of the articles are by Scandinavian scholars and concern Scandinavian topics. The journal's contents up to 1976 are included in Janet Kvamme's *Index Nordicus* (q.v.).

930 **Documents on Swedish Foreign Policy.**
Stockholm: Ministry for Foreign Affairs, 1950– . annual.

Translations into English of official documents, speeches, and policy statements on subjects of importance to Swedish foreign relations including Nordic affairs, disarmament, space, environment and human rights.

931 **Geografiska Annaler.**
Stockholm: Almqvist & Wiksell, 1919– . semi-annually.

The journal is sponsored by the *Svenska Sällskapet för Antropologi och Geografi* (The Swedish Anthropology and Geography Society). In 1965 the journal was divided into Series A dealing with physical geography and glaciology and Series B for research in human economics, social, cultural and historical geography. The articles are usually in English with exceptional presentations in another scholarly language. Articles on any part of the world are published but most concern Scandinavian subjects.

932 **Invandrare & minoriteter: tidskrift för kultur, politik, forskning och debatt.** (Immigrants and minorities: journal for culture, politics, research and debate.)
Stockholm: Stiftelsen för invandrare och minoriteter, 1973– . 6 issues per year..

A journal devoted to immigrant issues, primarily in Sweden today, though occasionally extending to the rest of Scandinavia as well.

933 **The Nordic Bulletin: A Monthly Calendar of Nordic Events.**
Minneapolis: University of Minnesota Center for Northwest European Language and Area Studies, 1980– . 10 issues per year.

A newsletter describing cultural and academic events throughout the United States regarding Scandinavian studies, exchanges, fellowships, recently published books, and other information.

934 **Nordic Journal of Botany.**
Copenhagen: Council for Nordic Publications in Botany, 1981– . bi-monthly.

The journal has an editorial board of botanists from the universities of Denmark, Finland, Norway, and Sweden. Its sections comprise holarctic and general taxonomy, geobotany, structural botany, mycology, lichenology and phycology. Articles are devoted to Scandinavian botany and to relevant topics in other countries.

935 **Scandinavian Economic History Review.**
Oslo: Universitetsforlaget, 1953– . quarterly.
Published by the Scandinavian Society for Economic and Social History and
Historical Geography, it is a scholarly English-language journal dealing in a very
broad sense with Scandinavian economic and social history. Review articles and
book reviews are also included regularly. In 1980 it incorporated *Economy and
History*, a similar journal published in Lund, Sweden, by the Institute of
Economic History, University of Lund (vols 1–23, 1958–80). An index for
vols 1–20 (1953–72) was published in 1972 and the journal is catalogued in Janet
Kvamme's *Index Nordicus* (q.v.).

936 **Scandinavian Journal of Economics.**
Stockholm: Almqvist & Wiksell, 1899– . quarterly.
Originally called the *Swedish Journal of Economics* up until 1975 (vol. 77), it is an
international journal, publishing a wide variety of articles, notes, and book
reviews in English on many facets of economics. Scandinavian scholars, however,
are frequent contributors and Scandinavian topics are often published in it.

937 **Scandinavian Journal of History.**
Stockholm: Almqvist & Wiksell, 1976– . quarterly.
Contains articles in English by Scandinavian scholars, mostly on Scandinavian
subjects. Beginning in 1985 the journal included book reviews and assumed the
bibliographical functions previously exercised by *Excerpta Historica Nordica* from
1955 until 1985 as a bibliography of historical materials published in the
Scandinavian languages.

938 **Scandinavian Journal of Psychology.**
Stockholm: Almqvist & Wiksell, 1960– . quarterly.
This scholarly English-language journal published by the Psychological Associations of Denmark, Finland, Norway and Sweden, publishes empirical reports and
theoretical and methodological papers. It also reviews Scandinavian books and
dissertations.

939 **Scandinavian Political Studies.**
Oslo: Universitetsforlaget, 1966– . quarterly.
The journal of the Nordic Political Science Association containing articles in
English on Scandinavian law, government and politics. Volumes 1–12 were issued
from 1966 to 1977. The numbering system for the journal was revised in 1978 so
that the numbers issued that year began again as Volume 1 (New series). Notes
and book reviews are also included and a bibliography of Nordic political science
appears regularly. The journal was indexed up to 1976 in *Index Nordicus* (q.v.).

940 **Scandinavian Population Studies.**
Helsinki: Scandinavian Demographic Society, 1969– . irregular.
Proceedings of the symposia held by the Scandinavian Demographic Society. It
publishes the papers presented at symposium seminars, most of which are by
Scandinavian scholars and treat specific studies in Scandinavian demographics.

271

941 **Scandinavian Review.**
New York: American–Scandinavian Foundation, 1913– . quarterly.
The official publication of the American–Scandinavian Foundation, containing articles, short stories, poetry and photographic essays. Written in English, the journal often contains works that were originally published in a Scandinavian language. Many issues include notes on current events, book reviews, and notices of books, films, and records available on Scandinavia. Members also receive a newsletter, *Scan*, that provides information on the activities of the foundation's independent chapters throughout the United States, scholarship and exchange programmes with Scandinavia, and other information. The journal itself was entitled *American Scandinavian Review* until 1974. For a bibliography of the journal until 1976 see Janet Kvamme's *Index Nordicus* (q.v.).

942 **Scandinavian Studies.**
Urbana, Illinois: University of Illinois Press, 1911– . quarterly.
The journal of the Society for the Advancement of Scandinavian Study, the chief professional organization of Scandinavian scholars in the United States. It publishes articles in English on Scandinavian literature, linguistics, history and political science. It regularly contains book reviews and book notes. The newsletter of the society, *News and Notes*, provides information on conferences, grants, programmes and exchanges. Originally entitled *Publications of the Society for the Advancement of Scandinavian Study*, the journal became *Scandinavian News and Notes* with vol. 4 in 1917 and assumed its present title with vol. 16 in 1941. For several years the society sponsored an annual bibliography of works on Scandinavia compiled by Marianne Tiblin and Erwin Welsh that appeared in the final number of each volume or as a special supplement. It was issued as a separate publication by the Center for Northwestern European Studies, University of Minnesota in 1975 and discontinued thereafter. The journal was indexed until 1976 in *Index Nordicus* (q.v.).

943 **Scandinavian Studies in Criminology.**
Oslo: Universitetsforlaget, 1965– . annual.
Published by the Scandinavian Research Council for Criminology, its articles examine the sociological and legal aspects of criminology and law enforcement.

944 **Scandinavian Studies in Law.**
Stockholm: Almqvist & Wiksell, 1957– . annual.
The journal publishes articles in English on virtually all facets of law, including aspects of Swedish law, and Swedish scholars are frequent contributors.

945 **Scandinavica: An International Journal of Scandinavian Studies.**
Norwich, England: University of East Anglia, 1961– . quarterly.
Concentrates primarily on studies of Scandinavian literature and language by international specialists, although articles on other topics do appear. It also includes book reviews of scholarly works in all fields and a selective bibliography of Scandinavian literary journals and of books on Scandinavia in non-

Scandinavian languages. An index to the journal for vols 1–10 appeared in vol. 10 (1971) and for vols 11–20 in vol. 20 (1981). The journal is indexed in Janet Kvamme's *Index Nordicus* (q.v.).

946   **Skandinaviska Enskilda Banken Quarterly Review.**
Stockholm: Skandinaviska Enskilda Bank, 1920– . quarterly.
Publishes articles on economics, finance and banking. Published until 1971 as *Skandinaviska Banken Quarterly Review*.

947   **Swedish–American Historical Quarterly.**
Chicago, Illinois: Swedish–American Historical Society, 1950– . quarterly.
Published as the *Swedish Pioneer Historical Quarterly* until 1982 (vol. 33), both the organization and journal changed names at that time. It contains articles, book reviews and notes. The basic source for the continuing study of Swedish America.

Kulturtidskriften: 1986 katalog över kulturtidskrifter i Sverige. (The cultural journal: 1986 catalogue of cultural journals in Sweden.)
See item no. 955.

Index Nordicus: a cumulative index to English periodicals on Scandinavian studies.
See item no. 982.

Reference Works and Directories

948 **Sohlmans musiklexikon.** (Sohlman's music encyclopaedia.)
Edited by Hans Åstrand. Stockholm: Sohlmans förlag, 1975.
5 vols.
Nominally a general music encyclopaedia, Sohlman's is especially known for its
complete picture of Scandinavian music in general and Swedish music and
musicians (incl. ballet) in particular. This makes it an invaluable reference work
but, alas, only in Swedish.

949 **Famous Swedes.**
Paul Britten Austin. Stockholm: Bokförlaget Fabel, 1962. 98p.
Brief biographical sketches of the lives of a few well-known Swedes, including St.
Birgitta, Carl Linnaeus, Axel von Fersen, Jenny Lind, August Strindberg and
Greta Garbo. They are brief, anecdotal and amusing.

950 **Mass media 1985: handbok för journalister, informatörer och andra
som följer press, radio och tv.** (Handbook for journalists, public
relations people and others who follow the press, radio and
television.)
Edited by Tom Carlsson. Stockholm: Tidens förlag/Svenska
journalistförbundet, 1985. 419p.
An immensely informative handbook, listing every serial publisher in Sweden,
members of government and the *Riksdag* (Parliament), and a summary of laws
relating to the press and other journalistic media.

951 **Förteckning över lexikon och ordlistor.** (List of dictionaries and
glossaries.)
Siv Higelin.   Stockholm: Skolöverstyrelsen, 1982. 191p.
This is a list of all dictionaries and glossaries published in Sweden. Each work is
described but not evaluated.

952 **Svenska tonsättare: diskografi.** (Swedish composers: discography.)
Edited by Stig Jacobsson.   Stockholm: Rikskonserter, 1985. 266p.
About as complete a listing, by composer, as one is likely to find anywhere, with a
separate section by record company. Only classical music, no jazz, rock, or folk.
Brief summaries in English.

953 **Dictionary of Scandinavian biography: with a memoir on the work
of the Nordic Council by G. F. D. Dawson and with a full text of the
treaty of cooperation between Denmark, Finland, Iceland, Norway,
and Sweden.**
Edited by Ernest Kay.   Cambridge, England: International
Centre, 1976. 2nd ed. 497p.
Biographies in English of living Scandinavians. Eminent Swedes are well
represented in the work by short but useful sketches.

954 **Swedish men of science 1650–1950.**
Edited and introduction by Sten Lindroth, translated from the
Swedish by Burnett Anderson.   Stockholm: Swedish Institute;
Almqvist & Wiksell, 1952. 295p. bibliog.
Relatively detailed biographies of twenty-nine prominent Swedish scientists from
Olof Rudbeck in the 17th century to those active in the mid-20th century.

955 **Kulturtidskriften: 1986 katalog över kulturtidskrifter i Sverige.**
(The cultural journal: 1986 catalogue of cultural journals in
Sweden.)
Leif Nelson, Bertil R. Widerberg, Erik Östling.   Stockholm:
Statens Kulturråd, 1986. 124p.
A descriptive catalogue of all the cultural journals and magazines currently
published in Sweden, from *Abracadabra* (about children's culture) to *Östeuropa
solidaritet* (a magazine that chiefly follows civil rights events in the Eastern Bloc).
Subject index and detailed information about the editors, contents, and cost of
each magazine.

956 **Dictionary of Scandinavian history.**
Edited by Byron Nordstrom.   Westport, Connecticut: Greenwood
Press, 1986. 703p. bibliog.
Over 400 entries on the outstanding individuals and events in Scandinavian
history. Although some coverage is given to prehistoric and Viking times, most of

the entries are on topics from the Middle Ages to the present. Short bibliographies follow each entry and a larger one by the editor lists the major historical works on Scandinavia in English.

957 **Swedish scholars of the 20th century.**
Wilhelm Odelberg, translated from the Swedish by
Victor J. Kayfetz. Stockholm: Swedish Institute, 1972. 22p.

Very brief biographical sketches of eminent Swedish scholars of the 20th century in several fields of research.

958 **Scandinavia: a bibliographic survey of literature.**
United States Department of the Army. Washington, DC:
Government Printing Office, 1975. 121p. maps. bibliog.
(Bibliographic Surveys of other Areas of the World, DA PAM 550–18).

Contains a general section of works on all of Scandinavia, chapters on each of the five Nordic countries, a final section of general reference units, and appendixes of political and military information. Most of the references relate to politics, defence, and foreign relations and are often taken from military and popular periodicals.

959 **Kulturkatalogen.** (The cultural catalogue.)
Edited by Märta Urhagen. Stockholm: Statens Kulturråd, 1986.
107p.

The latest edition of *the* list of Sweden's national cultural organizations and administrative bodies. It covers the classical cultural associations dealing with music, theatre, art, and so on, as well as special ones dealing with minorities, regional museum groups, etc. Each entry has the expected address and phone number, as well as a description of what the particular group or museum does.

960 **Scandinavia: a chronology and fact book.**
Edited by Robert T. Vexler. Dobbs Ferry, New York: Oceana
Publications, 1977. 185p.

The work is divided into chronologies of key dates in Scandinavian history and those of the three countries, including Sweden. This is followed by a series of important public documents important to each of the countries covered in the work.

961 **The world of learning.**
London: Europa, 1947– . annual.

Entries for Sweden include membership of Swedish learned honorary organizations, the addresses and officers of learned societies, research institutes, libraries, archives, museums, art galleries, and the addresses, administrative officers and professors of Sweden's universities and advanced training institutions. A valuable reference work, particularly for anyone planning to do research in Sweden.

Scandinavia.
See item no. 20.

The Scandinavians in America 986–1970: a chronology and fact book.
See item no. 342.

Vem äger vad i svensk näringsliv/Who owns what in Swedish industry.
See item no. 715.

A bibliography of Scandinavian dictionaries.
See item no. 975.

Bibliographies

962   **The cultural heritage of the Swedish immigrant.**
O. Fritiof Ander.   Rock Island, Illinois: Augustana College
Library, 1956. 191p.

A good select bibliography of printed material, organized by subject (churches,
the arts, etc.). Each of the ten chapters includes introductory remarks by way of a
survey. This bibliography is now continued annually in the *Swedish–American
Historical Quarterly* (q.v.), whose pages constitute the best continuing record of
Swedish–American studies.

963   **Art consulting: Scandinavia: books on art and architecture.**
Malibu, California: Art Consultants: Scandinavia, 1986. 24p.

Nominally a catalogue of books for sale, the annotated entries form a select
bibliography of available books in English on Scandinavian art. Available from
Art Consultants: Scandinavia, 3507 Cross Creek Lane, Malibu, California 90265,
USA, for $2.00 (1986).

964   **Fourteen years of educational and psychological research in
Sweden: a bibliography of publications in English 1967–1980.**
Compiled by Åke Bjerstedt.   Lund, Sweden: C. W. K. Gleerup,
1982. 266p. bibliog. (Studia Psychologica et Paedagogica, Series
Altera, vol. 63).

An extensive, unannotated bibliography arranged alphabetically but without sub-
topics. An extension of the compiler's first bibliography, *Twelve years of
educational and psychological research in Sweden* (Lund: Gleerup, 1968).

Bibliographies

965 **Itineraria Svecana: bibliografisk förteckning över resor i Sverige fram till 1950.** (Itineraria Svecana: a bibliographical listing of travels in Sweden until 1950.)
Samuel E. Bring. Stockholm: Almqvist & Wiksell, 1954. 586p. bibliog. (Svenska Bibliotekariesamfundets Skriftserie, vol. 3).
In the main bibliography Bring has arranged the works by the year in which the travel in Sweden took place. Annotations to the entries are made in Swedish but the entries are in the language of the publication. Topographical and author indexes to the main bibliography are also included. An essential work on a fascinating subject.

966 **Föräldrar och barn: en kommenterad litteraturlista.** (Parents and children: an annotated bibliography.)
Edited by Karin Broman, Siv Björkman. Lund, Sweden: Bibliotekstjänst, 1973. 64p.
Though rather old, this list of about 300 titles is still useful as a guide to a Swedish view of children, a view which is often, at least officially, different from that of the rest of the world. The no-spanking law is one example.

967 **A selective bibliography of Scandinavian politics and policy.**
Compiled by Eric S. Einhorn, John Logue. Amherst, Massachusetts: International Area Studies Programs, University of Massachusetts at Amherst, 1984. 17p. (Program in West European Studies, Occasional Papers, no. 1).
A brief, unannotated bibliography containing entries relevant not only to politics and government but also to economics, industrial relations and sociology.

968 **Scandinavian political institutions and political behavior 1970–1980: an annotated bibliography.**
Compiled by Kjell A. Eliassen, Mogens N. Pedersen. Odense, Denmark: Odense University Press, 1985. 168p.
Contains entries that deal with political institutions and behaviour in Denmark, Norway, and Sweden. Both Scandinavian and non-Scandinavian works are considered with an English translation of all important entries and an English summary.

969 **Swedish plays in English translation from Strindberg to the present.**
Edited by Ann Mari Engel, Ann Sonnerman. Stockholm: Swedish Institute, 1985. 24p.
This brief bibliography is useful because, in addition to the expected information, it also tells where one should enquire for performance rights. More than half of the entries cover Strindberg, who has a whole section to himself. This part of the list is organized by the plays' Swedish title. The rest of the list is arranged by author and English title.

970 **Scandinavian education: a bibliography of English-language materials.**
Stewart E. Fraser, Barbara J. Fraser, foreword by Raymond E. Wanner. White Plains, New York: International Arts and Sciences Press, 1973. 271p. bibliog.

Contains an extensive, annotated section (p. 163–271) on Sweden. A major resource on the subject.

971 **Norse sagas translated into English: a bibliography.**
Compiled by Donald K. Fry. New York: AMS Press, 1980. 139p.

A bibliography of Old Norse sagas available in English translation up to 1979. Entries are arranged alphabetically by saga and subdivided by the various translations that have been made.

972 **Scandinavia in social science literature: an English-language bibliography.**
Compiled by Sven Groennings. Bloomington, Indiana: Indiana University Press, [1970]. 284p.

An excellent, detailed, unannotated bibliography covering economics, education, geography, history, international relations, law, political science and sociology. Entries are made for Scandinavia as a whole and for each of the five Nordic nations.

973 **Scandinavian social economics: 1850–1930: a bibliographic note.**
Richard D. Hacken. *Review of Social Economy*, vol. 41, no. 2 (1983), p. 137–51.

An unannotated bibliography divided into seven major topics. Supplemented ably by the compiler's 'Scandinavian social economics since 1930: a bibliographic note', vol. 44, no. 2 (1986), p. 159–77 which reflects the larger number of works in non-Scandinavian languages on this period.

974 **Swedish immigration research: introductory survey and annotated bibliography. Report 10.**
Tomas Hammar, Kerstin Lindby. Stockholm: Commission on Immigration Research, Department of Labour, 1979. 150p.

A good select survey of recent Swedish immigration (and some emigration) research. This bibliography has extensive annotations in the form of abstracts of the books listed. What makes it interesting is that much of this work has had a direct effect on modern Swedish immigration policy.

Bibliographies

975 **A bibliography of Scandinavian dictionaries.**
Compiled by Eva L. Haugen, introduction by Einar I. Haugen.
White Plains, New York: Kraus International Publications, 1984.
387p.

Covers dictionaries published in Scandinavia from 1510 to 1980. It is arranged topically and alphabetically with brief annotations on the publishing history and contents of each entry. The introduction provides a survey of the publishing of dictionaries during the period.

976 **A Jussi Björling phonography.**
Edited by Harald Henrysson, Jack W. Porter.
Stockholm: Svenskt musikhistoriskt arkiv, 1984. 269p.

Something over 6,000 titles, also listed by recording company, with all the information the Björling discophile will ever want. The essential discography.

977 **Svenska författninger översatta till främmande språk: en**
förteckning. (Swedish statutes translated into foreign languages: a catalogue.)
Ann Hökstrand. Stockholm: Statsrådsberedningen, 1984. 49p.

All Swedish laws available in translation, primarily into English.

978 **About Sweden 1900–1960: a bibliographic outline.**
Edited by Bure Holmbäck, Ulla-Märta Abrahamson, Marianne Tiblin. Stockholm: Swedish Institute, 1968. 94p.

A useful supplement to the present work, this collection of about 5,000 unannotated titles is organized according to the Swedish library cataloguing system. Continued as *Suecana extranea* (q.v.).

979 **Litterära tidskrifter i Sverige 1900–1970: en kommenterad**
bibliografi. (Literary journals in Sweden 1900–70: an annotated bibliography.)
Edited by Claes-Göran Holmberg. Lund, Sweden: Litteraturvetenskapliga institutionen, 1975. 188p. (*Press och Litteratur* 8).

A splendid little bibliography, extensively annotated, of the sixty-seven literary and cultural magazines and journals in Sweden during the period.

980 **Scandinavian legal bibliography.**
Compiled by Stig Iuul, Åke Malmström, Jens Søndergaard.
Stockholm: Almqvist & Wiksell, [1961]. 196p. (Acta Upsaliensis Iurisprudentiae Comparativae, vol. 4).

A short summary of the basic printed works on Swedish law by Åke Malmström (p. 25–35) is one of several such expositions on the Scandinavian states. The remainder of the book contains the bibliography, which is organized by topic. Almost all of the works are in the Scandinavian languages but translations of the titles into English are provided.

981 **Women and men in Swedish society: research projects supported by the Bank of Sweden Tercentenary Foundation.**
Edited by Ann-Sofie Kälvemark, translated from the Swedish by William P. Michael. Stockholm: Liber, 1983. 54p. (Riksbankens Jubileumsfond; R.J. 1983:1).

A brief presentation of research support given by the Bank of Sweden Tercentenary Foundation and a bibliography and abstracts of recent and present research projects being carried out on women and sex roles in Swedish society. A helpful guide.

982 **Index Nordicus: a cumulative index to English periodicals on Scandinavian studies.**
Compiled by Janet Kvamme. Boston: G. K. Hall, 1980. 601p.

An extensive bibliography of the contents of six major scholarly English journals on Scandinavia from their origins until 1976. The journals indexed are *Cooperation and Conflict, Scandinavian Economic History Review, Scandinavian Political Studies, Scandinavian Review, Scandinavian Studies,* and *Scandinavica.* Entries are made by subject, title, author's name, or book reviewer.

983 **Scandinavian government and politics: a bibliography of materials in English.**
Compiled by Robert B. Kvavik. Minneapolis, Minnesota: University of Minnesota, 1984. 21p. (Minnesota Papers in Political Science).

A listing of recent books and articles published on Scandinavian politics. The main categories covered include general resources, social democracy, political institutions, political behaviour, political organization and public policy.

984 **Läromedelsförteckning för lärare i svenska som främmande språk utomlands.** (List of materials for teachers of Swedish as a foreign language outside Sweden.)
Stockholm: Swedish Institute, 1985. 133p.

A comprehensive, annotated (in Swedish) bibliography of the subject.

985 **Swedish commentators on America 1638–1865.**
Esther Elizabeth Larson. New York: New York Public Library; Chicago: Swedish Pioneer Historical Society, 1963. 139p.

This is an annotated list of major manuscript and printed material on the subject in libraries of the United States and Sweden. There are 683 entries and, as is to be expected, a considerable number are devoted to Pehr Kalm and Fredrika Bremer. A major lacuna is the omission of the travel diary and letters of Rosalie Roos, who came in 1851. These have been published in English as *Travels in America*, translated and edited by Carl L. Anderson (Carbondale: Southern Illinois University Press, 1982).

986   **Books on Sweden in English.**
Edited by Susan Larson-Fleming, Lena Daun, Marna Feldt.
New York: Swedish Information Service, 1983. 61p.
Organized according to the Dewey Decimal system, this list of 505 titles has material only in English and chiefly available in the United States.

987   **Guide to Nordic bibliography.**
Edited by Erland Munch-Petersen.   Copenhagen: Nordisk
Ministerråd, 1984. 235p.
This bibliography of bibliographies is organized by subject, including a special section on bibliographies of specific authors, and has 836 well-annotated entries. This is the natural starting-place for most of what one wants to know about Scandinavia and together with its supplement, the guide can be ordered from the Nordic Council of Ministers, Snaregade 10, DK–1205 Copenhagen K, Denmark.

988   **Scandinavian literature in English translation 1928–1977.**
Compiled by Maria Ng, Michael S. Batts.   Vancouver, Canada:
Canadian Association of University Teachers of German, 1978.
95p.
The bibliography is divided into a general section on Scandinavia and separate units for each country. Publishing information for each work is given and entries in anthologies edited by others are cross-referenced.

989   **Scandinavian history 1520–1970: a list of books and articles in English.**
Compiled by Stewart P. Oakley.   London: Historical Association,
1984. 232p. (Helps for Students of History, no. 91).
A very useful, partially annotated bibliography of works printed from 1880 to 1980 on Scandinavian history. The work is divided into six chronological periods which are further subdivided into sections for works on Scandinavia and each of the five Nordic countries.

990   **Folk schools in social change: a partisan guide to the international literature.**
Edited by Rolland G. Paulston.   Pittsburgh, Pennsylvania:
University Center for International Studies, University of
Pittsburgh, 1974. 194p.
A partly annotated bibliography of 5,348 entries, designed to persuade people that the folk high school, so specific to Scandinavia, is a good idea for dealing with adult education and might be profitably imitated in other countries.

Bibliographies

991 **Publications on Sweden.**
Stockholm: Swedish Institute, 1986. 68p.

Since 1984, the Distribution Section of the Swedish Institute has published this list of materials available free to Swedish diplomatic missions. Most of this material is free on request, through the nearest consulate or the Swedish Information Service. Addresses are provided.

992 **Litteratur om etniska minoritetsgrupper i Sverige.** (Literature about ethnic minority groups in Sweden.)
Edited by Marianne Schmid, Chagan Lalloo. Lund, Sweden: Sociologiska institutionen, Lunds universitet, 1967. 73p.

A partly annotated bibliography on minority issues made just at the time that Sweden began to experience a large influx of non-European immigrants.

993 **Invandrar- och minoritetsforskning: en bibliografi.** (Immigrant- and minority-research: a bibliography.)
David Schwartz. Stockholm: Stockholms universitet, 1973. 77p.

An unannotated bibliography of 425 entries, intended for people who work with minorities in Sweden.

994 **Suecana extranea: books on Sweden and Swedish literature in foreign languages.**
Edited by the Bibliographical Department of the Royal Library. Stockholm: Kungliga biblioteket.

The first version of this bibliography covered the years 1963–66. After some irregular appearances in the 1970s, it has settled down to an annual volume issued by the Royal Library. This has also material in languages other than English and Swedish.

995 **Svensk historisk bibliografi.** (Swedish historical bibliography.)
Stockholm: Svenska Historiska Föreningen, 1880– . annual.

An annual bibliography published by the Swedish Historical association. Volumes 1–70 (1880–1949) were issued as a supplement to *Historisk Tidskrift* (Historical Journal), the association's journal. The annual volumes have also been irregularly collected in separate volumes covering 1771–1874 (a retrospective work by Kristian Setterwall in 1937); 1875–1900; 1901–20; 1921–35; 1936–50; 1951–60; and 1961–70. An essential source for the study of Swedish history.

996 **Sveriges statliga publikationer: bibliografi.** (Sweden's official publications: bibliography.)
Riksdagsbiblioteket. Stockholm: Riksdagsbiblioteket, 1930– .

This is the survey of everything official in print in Sweden. It appears yearly, but before volume 46 (1976) it was called *Årsbibliografi över Sveriges offentliga publikationer* (Yearly bibliography of Sweden's official publications). It is organized by department, and the newer versions are much easier to negotiate than the older ones. A useful guide to finding documents in this bibliography is *Hitta rätt i offentligt material (Find your way in official documents)* by Arne Gustafsson and Urban Swahn (Lund, Sweden: Bokförlaget Dialog, 1979), 61p.

997 **Guide to Swedish–American archival and manuscript sources in the United States.**
Edited by Wesley M. Westerberg, Lennart Setterdahl (et al.).
Chicago, Illinois: Swedish–American Historical Society, 1983.
600p.

An invaluable starting-point for manuscript research on Swedes in the United States, but it lists only the sources available to the public.

Historical geography in Scandinavia.
See item no. 64.

The Vikings.
See item no. 174.

The Swedish crime story: *svenska deckare.*
See item no. 778.

Children's Literature

998 **Vanishing Lapland.**
Arthur Catherall.   New York: Franklin Watts, 1972. 118p. map.
An introduction for the general reader to the customs and daily life among the Reindeer Lapps. Consideration is given to topics such as young children, marriage practices and reindeer herding.

999 **The land of the long night.**
Paul du Chaillu.   Detroit, Michigan: Tower Books, 1971. 266p.
Originally published in 1899, it is a book written especially for children describing his winter trip to Northern Scandinavia when he travelled extensively with the Reindeer Lapps throughout the region.

1000 **Culture for Swedish children.**
[No editor.]   Stockholm: Swedish Institute for Children's Books, 1982. 104p.
A useful starting-point for getting a sense of what is happening to children's books in Sweden, an area of considerable public and private concern and one that has engaged some of Sweden's leading writers. Some of the best children's books produced anywhere today come from Sweden.

1001 **The Vikings.**
Michael Gibson.   London: Macdonald Educational, 1976. 61p.
maps. (Peoples of the Past).
Concise explanation of life in Scandinavia and of Viking ships and culture in addition to a description of Viking expansion. Well illustrated with drawings, photographs, and maps. A very useful work for upper elementary and junior secondary school pupils.

1002   **The Swedes and their chieftains.**
Verner von Heidenstam, translated from the Swedish by Charles
Wharton Stork.   New York: American–Scandinavian
Foundation; London: Humphrey Milford, Oxford University
Press, 1925. 346p. (Scandinavian Classics, vol. 25).
An abridgement of the two-volume Swedish original published in 1909.
Heidenstam has recreated with poetic licence chapters in Swedish history from the
pre-Viking period until the early 19th century. Although not an entirely accurate
record of the past, it remains a vivid collection of essays on Sweden's heroes
appealing both to young adults and the general reader.

1003   **Sweden.**
Martin Hintz.   Chicago, Illinois: Children's Press, 1985. 126p.
maps. (Enchantment of the World).
An excellent introduction to Sweden for older children and young adults. It is an
informative, well-illustrated description of Sweden's history, culture, and
economy.

1004   **Sweden: focus on post-industrialism.**
Karen Hopkins.   Englewood Cliffs, New Jersey: Prentice-Hall,
1977. 122p. map. bibliog. (Inquiry into World Cultures).
Designed primarily for secondary school social studies classes, it briefly surveys
Swedish history and the country's present economic and political structures. It
emphasizes Sweden's social welfare programmes, social issues, and the ways in
which Sweden characterizes the post-industrial society. An excellent introduction
to contemporary developments and issues for young adults and the general
reader.

1005   **Pippi Longstocking.**
Astrid Lindgren, translated from the Swedish by Edna Hurup
(1954).   London: Puffin/Penguin, 1976. 176p.
The classic story by Sweden's post-war doyen of children's literature. There is a
long run of Pippi books after this one. For children 6–10.

1006   **Ronia, the robber's daughter.**
Astrid Lindgren, translated from the Swedish by Patricia
Compton.   London: Puffin/Penguin, 1983. 176p.
A quasi-medieval tale, a kind of children's *Romeo and Juliet* without the tears.
An unsentimental story of great charm, whose British translation changes the
names of many of the characters, including the girl in the title.

1007 **The brothers Lionheart.**
Astrid Lindgren, translated from the Swedish by Joan Tate
(1975). London: Knight/Hodder & Stoughton, 1975. 192p.
An astonishingly powerful story for older children (9–12), mostly a medieval fantasy, but one dealing openly with death, as well as courage. According to the author, this book has had some of its strongest supporters among terminally ill children.

1008 **The six Bullerby children.**
Astrid Lindgren, translated from the Swedish by Evelyn Ramsden.
London: Magnet/Methuen, 1963. 92p.
The first of a long series, several of which are now available in translation. Ages 5–8.

1009 **Travels.**
Carl Linnaeus, edited by David Black. New York: Charles
Scribner's Sons, 1979. 108p. maps. bibliog. (Nature Classics).
Extracts from Linnaeus' published travels to Lapland, Öland, and Gotland. It includes good illustrations by Stephen Lee of flora described by Linnaeus and scenery from his journeys. William T. Stearn has added a brief description of the Linnaean classification system. Suitable for both the young adult and general reader. For a very brief account for children, see 'Linnaeus and the Far North [Lapland]', in Wyatt Blassingame's *Naturalist explorers* (New York: Franklin Watts, 1964), p. 1–11.

1010 **Sweden.**
Helen Hynson Merrick. New York: Franklin Watts, 1971. 87p.
map. (The First Book Series).
An introduction to the country suitable for older children. Covers many topics, including the Vikings, Sweden's kings, the union with Norway, economic life, culture, and famous Swedes.

1011 **Great Swedish fairy tales: illustrated by John Bauer.**
Edited by Elsa Olenius, translated from the Swedish by
Holger Lundbergh. London: Chatto & Windus, 1966. 239p.
This collection of stories (fairy tales does not properly convey their nature) is really an excuse to collect together most of John Bauer's illustrations for Christmas books. These stories are fairly well known in Sweden, but the pictures are a part of every Swede's childhood. The shapes with which he endowed the trolls have established their classic form.

1012 **The Vikings.**
George L. Proctor. Harlow, England: Longman, 1959. 108p.
bibliog. (Then and There Series).

A survey of Scandinavian life during the Viking Age and of Viking expansion for children in the upper classes of primary schools and junior forms in secondary schools.

1013 **Ancient Scandinavia.**
George L. Proctor. London: Weidenfeld & Nicolson, 1965.
128p. maps. bibliog. (Young Historian Books).

An excellent, non-technical presentation of the early development of Man in Scandinavia during the pre-Viking period and the Viking Age. It is particularly appropriate for the young adult and the general reader.

1014 **Dag Hammarskjöld.**
Norman Richards. Chicago, Illinois: Children's Press, 1968.
95p. bibliog. (People of Destiny, A Humanities Series).

Discusses his early life and career in more detail than is often found elsewhere, as well as his work as Secretary-General of the United Nations. An excellent biography for young adults, or those requiring a relatively brief work on the subject.

1015 **The Vikings.**
Robert Wernick and the editors of Time-Life Books.
Alexandria, Virginia: Time-Life Books, 1979. 176p. maps.
bibliog.

A description of Viking ships and an account of Viking expansion and adventure based loosely on the sagas. Most appropriate for the general reader or young adult.

The wonderful adventures of Nils and the further adventures of Nils.
See item no. 46.

Viking ways: on the Viking Age in Sweden.
See item no. 182.

The land of the Lapps.
See item no. 325.

Scandinavian legends and folk-tales.
See item no. 873.

Swedish legends and folktales.
See item no. 874.

Scandinavian stories.
See item no. 875.

Children's Literature

Holidays in Scandinavia.
See item no. 881.

Index

The index is a single alphabetical sequence of authors (personal and corporate), titles of publications and subjects. Index entries refer both to the main items and to other works mentioned in the notes to each item. Title entries are in italics. Numeration refers to the items as numbered.

293

299

302

industrial 655, 660, 683, 696-698,
 700-703, 706
local government reform 567
multinational corporations' effects
 709
Scandinavian 14, 19
social 259, 498-499, 525, 536, 538,
 540, 983
*Democracy and elections: electoral
 systems and their political
 consequences* 543
*Democracy on the shop floor: an
 American look at employee
 influence in Scandinavia today* 697
*Democratic Socialism: the mass left in
 advanced industrial societies* 529
Democratization 266
Demographic factors
 abortion 300
 age differentiations 311
 birth control 300
 birth rate 309-311
 death rates 310-311
 external migration 311
 family planning 300, 312
 geographical differentiations 311
 immigration 300
 internal migration 302
 marriage 310
 population movement 68, 300, 302,
  311
 sex differentiations 311
 social mobility 306, 309
Demography
 abortion 477
 data base 307
 historiography 293
 history 298-299, 305-313
 methodology 307, 346
 periodical 940
 statistics 747
 studies 306-313, 344, 347, 349, 940
 symposia 940
Denitch, B. 529
Denmark 14-24, 31, 39, 262
 archives 902
 Augsburg Confession impact 426
 communism 533
 demography 310
 economic development 265
 economic interests 619
 education 438, 448-449, 452-453

ethnic minorities 316
foreign policy 600
geography 62-74
geology 98
government 518
health care 493
history 14, 18-19, 42, 57, 128, 156,
 161, 209, 211, 235, 244, 265
housing 485
legal system 571
Lutheran Church 415, 426
mass media 919
National Council for Scientific
 Research 928
national theatre 853
political institutions and behaviour
 968
political interests 619
political parties 518
political trends 544
prehistory 128, 131
Psychological Association 938
social democracy 498
Social Democratic Party 532
teenage drinking 461
television 909, 914
trade union movement 689
travel guides 105, 110, 112, 114
travellers' accounts 42-43, 57, 60
universities 934
US policy toward 613
*Dental health care in Scandinavia:
 achievements and future strategies*
 490
Department of Interior, Office of
 Geography 75
Deposing
 Gustav IV Adolf 232, 237
Depression 259, 269
Derry, T. K. 156
*Description of Swedland, Gotland, and
 Finland* 50
*Desertion and land colonization in the
 Nordic countries c.1300-1600:
 comparative report from the
 Scandinavian Research Project on
 Deserted Farms and Villages* 194
Design 843, 845
 bibliography 844
 'Scandinavian modern' 20, 842, 844
Design in Sweden 843, 845
Deskriptiv Svensk grammatik 391

primary 434, 438
reference work 961
reform 432-433, 439, 441, 444, 446-
447, 772
research 431
role in cultural cooperation 599,
609
Scandinavia 14, 159, 438, 448-449,
451-453
Scandinavian studies university
programmes 357, 609
secondary 434, 438
sex 479
social change 475
special 453-454
survey 434, 438, 445, 453
tradition 432
universities 193, 439-447
university programmes 107, 357
women 475, 484
Edwards, M. 471
EEC (European Economic
Community) 455, 618-619, 712
EFTA (European Free Trade
Association) 604, 607, 619
Ehlers, J. 97
Ehrensvärd, Carl August 43
Eichenberg, R. 747
EIFO (Expertgruppen för
invandrarforskning) 318
*Einar Billing: en studie i svensk teologi
före 1920* 429
Einhorn, E. S. 518, 697, 967
Ej till salu 474
Ekecrantz, J. 743
Ekelöf, Gunnar 779, 784
Ekman, E. 288
Elden, M. 696
Elder, N. C. M. 519, 530, 545, 557
Elder Edda 398
*Elderly and their environment: research
in Sweden* 466
Eldjárn, K. 162
Eldredge, H. W. 761
Elections 543-544
1946 537
1948 537
1976 599
1982 549
1985 549
party preference 542
Scandinavia 544

strategies 526
Electorate 548, 550
Electronics
dictionary 377
research 767
Elements of Nordic public law 575
Eliassen, K. A. 546, 968
Eliasson, G. 738
Élites
aristocracy 154, 195, 197, 200, 217,
230, 240, 306
economic 455
political 455, 555
power élite theory 455
Elizabeth I 50
Elliot, G. 141, 335
Elliot, J. H. 204
Elmen, P. 368
Elson, R. T. 675
Elstob, E. C. 143
Elting, J. R. 277
Elvander, N. 493, 520, 524, 531-532,
547
Elver, E. 676
Emanuel Swedenborg 417
*Emanuel Swedenborg: scientist and
mystic* 428
Emigrants
assimilation 351, 366
biography 358
colonies 368-373
Delaware Valley 370-373
education 364
in Chicago 349
Mormons in Utah 360, 416
press 351, 356
religious practice 359-360, 364
social life 359
Emigration
bibliography 346, 363, 962, 974
Bishop Hill colony 368-369
causes 355, 365, 368
correspondence 348
demographic aspects 356
historiography 293
history 342, 344-350, 356, 359-360,
365-373
literature 353, 363
mass 355, 365
New Sweden 370-373
reaction 355
research 315, 341, 974

312

315

Government policy 155, 249, 266, 268-269, 282, 509, 512, 599, 651
  adoption 556
  agriculture 720-721
  arts 822-823
  bibliography 983
  clean air 756
  development aid 622, 624
  employment 681
  energy 736-737
  environmental 752, 756, 758, 760
  formulation 556
  implementation 556
  land and water resources management 758
  mass media 743, 913, 919
  press 913
  referendum influence 562
  regional development 758
  research development 718
  role in economic growth 718
  Scandinavia 983
  science 770, 772-773
Grabosky, P. N. 584
Graburn, N. H. H. 322
Gradualism 705
Graham, J., Jr. 485
Graham-Campbell, J. 176, 188
Grammars 388-389, 391-393, 395-396
Granath, K-E. 831
Granath, O. 827
Grandeur et liberté de la Suède (1660-1792) 153
Gravier, M. 158
Gray, J. 442
Great cities of the world: their government, politics, and planning 567
Great Copper Mountain 732
Great Swedish fairy tales: illustrated by John Bauer 1011
Greatest fire: a study of August Strindberg 804
Grede, Kjell 859
Greek mythology 402
Greene, A. 278, 285-286
Greene, E. 278, 285-286
Greene, Graham 279
Greenhill, B. 177
Greenland
  travel guide 105
  Viking settlement 189

Griffith, W. E. 539
Grimes, W. F. 177
Groennings, S. 972
Gross domestic product of Sweden and its composition 1861-1955 649
Group of Lovaro gypsies settle down in Sweden: an analysis of their acculturation 331
Growth and fluctuations of Swedish industry 1869-1912: studies in the process of industrialisation 717
Growth and transformation of the modern city: the Stockholm conference September 1978 753
Growth of Scandinavian law 576
Gruber, L. J. 486
Guide to the industrial archaeology of Europe 108
Guide to Nordic bibliography 987
Guide to Swedish-American archival and manuscript sources in the United States 997
Gullberg, I. E. 379
Gullers, K. W. 27-30
Gullers, P. 29
Gunzburg, D. 700
Gurr, T. R. 584
Gustafson, A. 777, 780
Gustafsson, Agne 568
Gustafsson, Arne 996
Gustafsson, B. 412, 420, 646
Gustafsson, G. 569
Gustafsson, K-E. 911, 913
Gustafsson, Lars 784, 789
Gustafsson, Lennart 722
Gustav Vasa 50, 144, 158
  Reformation role 408
Gustav II Adolf 154, 203, 217
  biography 201, 215-216
  domestic reforms 211
Gustav III 58, 153-154, 160, 230, 234, 825, 854
  assassination 154, 237, 242
  biography 228
  Enlightenment influence 231
  reforms 231
Gustav IV Adolf 230
  deposing 232, 237
Gustav V 259, 272
Gustav Adolf the great 201
Gustavsen, B. 703
Gustavson, C. G. 716

317

319

History *contd.*
    Pomerania, Erik of 195
    postal service 744
    Precambrian Age 98
    pre-Christian 401
    prehistoric 97-102, 124-125, 127-129,
        131-133, 136, 139-141, 956
    press 351, 356, 912, 919
    pre-Viking 124, 138-140, 178-179,
        185, 192, 196, 398, 404, 1002,
        1013
    Price Revolution 205
    prices 650
    Prussia 211, 666
    Quaternary Age 97-98, 101
    radio 919
    railway system 745
    Reformation 158, 408, 426, 430
    regicide 154, 206, 221, 237, 242
    religion 134, 139, 158-159, 169, 175-
        176, 182, 196, 215, 220, 359-360,
        364, 368-373, 397-430
    research 289-292, 294, 904
    research projects 194, 247, 280, 285-
        286, 344, 726
    revolutions 144, 195, 205, 229-230,
        232, 234, 245, 248, 716
    Riksdag (Parliament) 201, 212, 218,
        233, 238, 241, 257, 272, 282, 550,
        557, 559, 565, 705
    rulers 144, 153-154, 158, 160, 171,
        195, 197, 201-204, 211-218, 221-
        222, 225-232, 234-235, 237, 242-
        245, 272, 406, 408, 1010
    runes 134, 176
    Russia 163-164, 166, 168, 170, 172-
        173, 187, 209, 211, 233, 238, 251,
        280
    Russian Primary Chronicle 170
    Saracens 181
    Scandinavia 14-15, 18-24, 31, 41-42,
        69, 71-74, 80, 86, 97-98, 100, 110,
        128-129, 131, 156-194, 198-199,
        209-211, 224, 230, 234-235, 253-
        254, 264, 267-268, 271, 277, 281,
        284, 289, 397-430, 509, 935, 942,
        956, 960, 989, 999, 1001, 1012-
        1013
    Scandinavian Airlines System 740
    science 766, 769, 771, 954
    ships 122, 126, 137, 149, 162, 176-
        177, 183, 186, 262, 1001, 1015

    slavery 188, 199
    social 144, 155, 158-159, 174-176,
        182-183, 186, 188, 190, 196, 200,
        215, 218-220, 224, 236, 259, 291,
        293, 935
    Social Democratic Party 528, 530,
        535, 537, 704
    social policy 247
    social welfare legislation 509
    social welfare policy 496, 498, 500,
        502, 504
    social welfare state 7, 503, 509
    Solander, Daniel Carl 122
    Stone Age 128-129, 133, 140
    succession crisis (1066) 188
    succession crisis (1809-1810) 235
    suffrage 255, 257
    surveys 141-147, 157, 161, 182, 215,
        218, 277, 326, 329, 361-362, 372,
        500, 573, 686, 745, 829, 862, 886,
        889, 975, 1004, 1012
    Sweden–Norway union 234, 250-252,
        258
    taxation 667
    technical developments 716
    technology 763
    telephone 739
    television 919
    theatre 775, 847, 854-856
    timber trade 723
    town planning 249
    trade 127, 159, 167, 175, 184, 188,
        196, 207, 261-262, 265, 278, 285
    trade union 689, 912
    Treaty of Kiel 244
    Uppsala University 442
    urban 63, 95, 124, 162, 174, 182,
        198, 292
    USA 168, 174, 189, 266, 271
    Varangians 165, 170, 187, 376
    Viking period 78, 95, 126, 134, 138-
        140, 144, 146, 158, 160, 162-192,
        196, 376, 398, 400, 956, 1001,
        1010, 1012-1013, 1015
    wages 643
    Wallenberg, Raoul 333, 637-641
    World War I 259-260, 262, 266, 269,
        272
    World War II 259, 270, 274, 276-
        286, 333, 630, 637, 639, 641, 664
    Yaroslav the Wise 171
    History of New Sweden 370

322

329

337

344

Religion *contd.*
  prehistoric 139, 403
  Swedish church in Delaware 370,
    373
  theology 368, 408-410, 413, 417, 419,
    425, 427-429
  Vikings 162, 169, 175-176, 182, 397-
    402, 404-405
  worship of the dead 400
*Reluctant Europeans: the attitudes of
  the Nordic countries towards
  European integration* 619
Rembe, R. 848
Report from a Swedish village 456
*Report of the eighteenth session of the
  International Geological Congress,
  Great Britain 1948* 730
Republic
  aristocratic 197
Research
  archaeology 127, 132, 173
  bibliographies 974, 981, 985, 993,
    997
  biotechnology 767
  building industry future 486
  care of the elderly 466
  demographic 301-302
  dictionary 379
  diplomatic 904
  economics 672
  education 431, 964
  electronics 767
  emigration 315, 341, 974
  facilities 445, 904
  foreign relations 588
  genealogical 314-315
  historiography 289-292, 294
  immigration 318, 974, 993
  institutions 672, 904, 961, 985, 997
  language 376
  law 431
  libraries 904
  limitations 295
  manuscript sources 985, 997
  mass media 908
  minorities 993
  newspapers 912
  Nordic cooperation 767
  police 585
  political science 524
  projects 194, 247, 280, 285-286, 301,
    341, 344, 542, 726, 981

  psychology 964
  reference work 961
  Scandinavian studies 357
  science 440, 765, 767-768, 772
  social sciences 431
  sociology 458, 981
  Swedish America 997
  technical 772
  technology 440
Research organizations
  alcohol and drug abuse 460
Resistance, Right of 237
*Retailing and the competitive challenge:
  a study of retail trends in the
  Common Market, Sweden and the
  USA* 712
Reunification
  Scandinavia 235
*Réveil national et culture populaire en
  Scandinavie: la genèse de la
  højskole nordique* 452
Revolution
  1809 232, 234
  Dacke, Nils 144
  Engelbrektsson, Engelbrekt 144, 195
  French 229-230, 245
  Industrial 248, 716
  Price 205
Reynolds, W. M. 370
Rhedin, P. 899
Rhenman, E. 491
Rice, A. L. 393, 396, 826
Richards, N. 1014
Richardson, J. J. 760
Riddarholmen 106
Ries, M. 473
*Righteous Gentile: the story of Raoul
  Wallenberg, missing hero of the
  Holocaust* 638
Rights of labor 704
Riksarkiv (National Archives) 904
Riksdag (Parliament) 218, 233, 238,
    257, 272, 282, 550, 552, 557, 705
  Act 552
  civil service relations 555
  Gustav II Adolf 201
  Karl XII 212
  members 950
  parliamentary development 241, 550
  Queen Christina 218
  recent role 558
  reform 257, 557, 559, 565

358

361

363

364

W

369

Map of Sweden

This map shows the more important towns and other features.

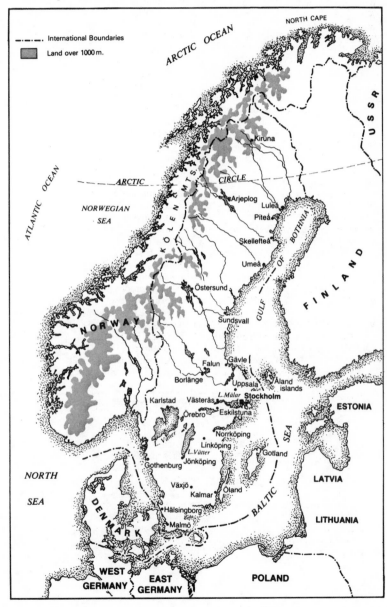

- - - . International Boundaries

Land over 1000 m.

ARCTIC OCEAN

NORTH CAPE

ATLANTIC OCEAN

NORWEGIAN SEA

ARCTIC CIRCLE

KÖLEN MTS.

Kiruna

Arjeplog

Luleå

Piteå

Skellefteå

GULF OF BOTHNIA

Umeå

Östersund

FINLAND

Sundsvall

NORWAY

Falun

Gävle

Borlänge

Uppsala

Åland islands

Karlstad

Västerås

L.Mälar

Stockholm

Örebro

Eskilstuna

ESTONIA

L. Väner

Norrköping

Linköping

L.Vätter

Gotland

Gothenburg

Jönköping

BALTIC SEA

NORTH SEA

Växjö

Kalmar

Öland

LATVIA

Hälsingborg

Malmö

DENMARK

LITHUANIA

WEST GERMANY

EAST GERMANY

POLAND

USSR